Praise For *The Predictive Enterprise*

Edmund lays out the issues that companies have when looking at AI as primarily an overlay to existing processes and playbooks. The adaptive enterprise correctly examines how to not only use AI, but re-engineer how work is done when people and AI work together to deliver the optimal outcomes. I have directly seen how procurement organizations have used these concepts to deliver outsized savings as well as risk reduction. This is not to say that making these changes is easy, but this book lays out the concepts that modern, high performing organizations will need to embrace to compete in the modern world.

—Micky Keck,
former Director Analyst for Procurement Applications, Gartner

The supply chain has always been a part of the business everyone talks about, but few actually reimagined. Edmund doesn't just talk about it—he shows what happens when AI stops assisting the supply chain and starts running it. From predictive logistics to autonomous negotiations, *The Predictive Enterprise* makes the case that the next competitive edge won't come from optimizing what already exists, but from building supply chains that predict, adapt, and act before a human ever has to. For anyone leading transformation in this space, this is less a forecast and more of a blueprint for transformation—and a genuinely fun read on top of it.

—Adrian Penka,
Vice President, Supply Chain Transformation and Advisory,
Capgemini Invent

Every business establishes processes that help guide the work of employees and set expectations for performance. But what happens when that work is now augmented by AI? And what happens when the work is being done not just by internal employees, but by suppliers augmented with AI, as well? *The Predictive Enterprise* shows how AI deployed at global scale is transforming our ways of working today, not just for internal teams but across the supply chain, and in the process rewriting the expectations and playbooks for global business.

—Russ Fradin,
serial entrepreneur and Co-Founder and CEO of Larridin.com

Executive teams often struggle to identify the area where new technologies can make the biggest differences. In *The Predictive Enterprise*, Edmund de-mystifies the power of AI for back office processes. Traditional processes are built for standardization, but what happens when the steps in a process can be instantly customized? Leaders from the industrial and manufacturing world should take note.

—Paul Wellener,
retired Vice Chair, Deloitte

The energy industry is complex and capital intensive, and due to volatility in commodity prices, managing risks and costs are the key to success. AI-driven predictive procurement, as brilliantly outlined in *The Predictive Enterprise*, is game changing technology that drives costs out of the system, expands margins, creates significant efficiency gains for employees, and drives bottom line financial results and value to the enterprise. Edmund's grasp of the challenges and solutions to this important segment of our business is invaluable.

—Robert Turnham,
Co-Founder and former President, Goodrich Petroleum Corporation

The Predictive Enterprise provides thoughtful insight into the future of work in this new AI-driven digital age we're now entering. Edmund's deep knowledge and perspective paint a clear picture of the power of predictive tools to make better decisions.

—Edwin Bennett,
former Chief Operating Officer, EY

The bigger the business, the more process matters. Traditionally, architects of large enterprises have focused on people, process, and technology as three co-equal branches of the operating model. But what happens when technology–specifically AI–allows the steps in any process to adapt in real time based on its predicted outcome? In *The Predictive Enterprise*, Edmund unpacks the implications of predictive AI for supply chain teams operating at global scale, where process architectures extend beyond one enterprise into tens of thousands of suppliers. The scale of this change is creating new ways of working. Not tomorrow, but today.

—Avanish Sahai,
technology executive, investor, and advisor;
formerly at Oracle, Salesforce, and ServiceNow

"Omne trium perfectum", the Latin adage meaning *everything that comes in threes is complete*, couldn't be more fitting for the evolution of procurement technology. Having experienced the first two major waves of procurement innovation firsthand, I do not doubt that the third, Artificial Intelligence, is the most transformative yet. *The Predictive Enterprise* is essential reading for procurement professionals at every stage of their careers, as well as C-suite executives looking to unlock procurement's strategic value. It provides a compelling roadmap for how AI is reshaping the function, moving it from a transactional cost center to a driver of competitive advantage.

—John P. "Jack" Miles,
former Chief Procurement Officer at CIBC, AIG, and Cigna;
former Secretary of The Florida Department of Management Services

The world needs more detailed, positive visions of the AI future. It's great to see a contribution to this genre from a domain expert, in one of the most important sectors of the economy.

—Jason Crawford,
Roots of Progress Institute

A must-read for procurement professionals to learn how to leverage predictive procurement to create breakthrough business results; it provides a practical playbook for leaders to:

- Transform sourcing speed and effectiveness—cover 2x addressable spend in 1/2 the time.
- Deliver double digit percentage price savings—smart item by item "defaults" help anchor pricing and process embeds best practices and negotiation/behavior theory (e.g. FOMO).
- Strengthen supply chain resilience, supplier management, and fact-based, transparent relationships.

Learn valuable insights to help you thrive and elevate procurement as a trusted advisor to your company!

—Drew Sheffield,
Principal Consultant, DS Group Advisors LLC. Former Purchasing Director,
Ford Motor Company; Global Purchasing Director, ZF Group;
and Executive Director, Purchasing, TI Automotive

THE PREDICTIVE ENTERPRISE

HOW SUPERHUMAN SUPPLY CHAINS TRANSFORM GLOBAL BUSINESS

EDMUND ZAGORIN

FOREWORD BY JEFFREY IMMELT

CONCLUSION BY LEN DECANDIA

WILEY

Published by John Wiley & Sons, Inc., Hoboken, New Jersey.

For general information on our other products and services or for technical support, please contact our Customer Care Department within the United States at (800) 762-2974, outside the United States at (317) 572-3993 or fax (317) 572-4002.

Wiley also publishes its books in a variety of electronic formats. Some content that appears in print may not be available in electronic formats. For more information about Wiley products, visit our website at www.wiley.com.

Library of Congress Cataloging-in-Publication Data:

ISBN: 9781394370511 (Cloth)
ISBN: 9781394370535 (ePub)
ISBN: 9781394370528 (ePDF)

Cover Design: Wiley
Cover Image: © Sabura/Shutterstock
Author Photo Credit: Charlene Hsiao
Printed and bound by CPI Group (UK) Ltd, Croydon, CR0 4YY

C9781394370511_130826

To Rob DeSantis.

For all the scary fun.

To Charlotte De Brabandt.

No time to waste.

Let's get it done.

Showtime!

Contents

Epigraph

Show me your cost sheets. It is more interesting to know how well and how cheaply you have done this thing than how much money you have made, because the one is a temporary result, due possibly to special conditions of trade, but the other means a permanency that will go on with the works as long as they last.

—Andrew Carnegie, as quoted by H.W. Brands

AI Disclosure

ChatGPT 5.1 was used to generate images in this book of a supply chain leader playing tennis. The author prompted the AI to create the image with several custom modifications and edits. Additionally, the author asked both ChatGPT 5.1 and Claude 4.5 one interview question about the impact of AI on the future of manufacturing and supply chain and included their responses verbatim alongside human futurists and experts in the back matter of this book. These are the only uses of Large Language Models in this book.

Foreword

The power of AI is becoming more impressive every day.

Five or ten years ago, even tech-focused people like me believed that there were certain aspects of business that would be too specific and niche for AI to handle well. I think that companies like Arkestro have proven this assumption wrong. The main obstacles we face today in ushering in transformation are social rather than technological.

In *The Predictive Enterprise*, Arkestro founder Edmund Zagorin helps us take a hard look at our legacy workflows and helps executives to better understand the opportunity created by AI at an enterprise-scale business. This is an exciting read for anyone thinking seriously about the future of work in large enterprises.

I came of age in the era of "professional management." Those days are over. I'm not advocating for "unprofessional management," but this is the era of technology. In this regard, AI might be the most transformative wave thus far. If you are a legacy manager waiting for permission from the CIO, you are lost.

In my time as CEO of GE (2001–2018), we viewed the CEO, CFO, and HR leaders as the three people who were actually running the company. Importantly, the CFO was trained to be copilot of the business. They had to know all the functions of finance, but they also had to understand manufacturing, sales, and technology. They had to be there to help grow the company, grow the business, and think strategically. While they knew their governance role and fiduciary role, they used these roles as a framework to reposition, grow, and drive competitiveness across the business.

A good CFO hungers for growth, productivity, and change. They don't get stuck on following a process. A good CFO is constantly searching for new tools. When it comes to procurement, it's no longer the case that the CFO just waits for the CIO to hand down digital tools to use. CFOs now need to be active players who are both interested in and knowledgeable about available technology, especially when it comes to AI.

Procurement is a natural place for CEOs and CFOs to search for value. AI will facilitate insight, speed, and decision-making; all essential for effective supply chain management. Leaders must thirst for productivity; they cannot let pride or politics get in the way.

This book explores how large global enterprises have laid the groundwork for this predictive future with measurable returns. It shows how their finance, procurement, and supply chain teams are using the Predictive Enterprise to expand margin and focus more of their best people's time where it matters most. It's not about people versus AI. It's about people using AI outperforming people who aren't using AI.

When a CFO begins at a new company or job, they usually ask themselves, "How can I make an impact quickly?"

Procurement should be the first stop.

Good CFOs tend to find good procurement leaders almost immediately because whereas it may take you five years to redesign a new jet engine to have fewer parts and things like that, you can buy the parts you're already using more efficiently right away. CFOs know how to find good procurement leaders because they can move the needle more quickly and in a profound way. But procurement leaders shouldn't wait for the CFO to knock on their door. They should lead the hunt for new technology. AI transformation will be accelerated by business leaders at all levels finding more productive ways to do their work.

One of the most important things that a leader does is what I call *instrumentation*. What are the operating processes—or instruments—that can improve your key metrics? This may sound easy, but it requires sustained focus. Instrumentation turns out to be a profound secret to success. Finance is, of course, the lever-puller for many important instruments at a business. The CFO must be effective at taking ideas, products, and technologies and figuring out how those interact with the income statement, the balance sheet, and with cash.

Lastly, I think a lot of CFOs have been through digital transformation already. If you think about the state of the world from the standpoint of a digital System of Record, CFOs have had a generation now to work with General Ledgers, ERPs, and even Procure-to-Pay systems. In that way, CFOs can be a digital partner to procurement, whereas historically supply chain has almost always been behind the curve from the standpoint of digital tools.

■ ■ ■

The word productivity gets thrown around by everyone these days.

The CFO must break that word into numbers for their own purposes. And there is also the cost of something taking too long versus the benefits of getting to a decision earlier. This could mean getting a product to market earlier, getting a production site stood up earlier, being able to recognize revenue earlier. That's why being specific about the value of productivity is key.

What does a word like *productivity* actually mean for your business? Once again, it's about understanding the instrumentation across your own portfolio of activities.

For instance, I would always ask our CEOs at GE, "What percentage of our BOM (Bill of Materials) for this product is dual-sourced or greater?" If that percentage goes up—i.e., we have multiple good sources to choose from for parts—then I would expect that the instrumentation will allow us to keep and even expand margin as we ramp up production to higher volumes to meet demand. You need to understand this like night follows day.

Don't just throw around the words. Give them the weight of your understanding. Track them with numbers. And make sure that the right people have ownership over the right numbers.

Once everyone agrees on what these shared terms really mean, I also think repetition is the secret to progress. I like to use similar presentation formats again and again so that the only thing changing is the numbers and the dates. The only thing that changes is the progress itself. Whether it's a daily meeting, a weekly meeting, a monthly meeting, or a quarterly meeting, repetition often goes hand in hand with progress.

If I had two meetings or business reviews in consecutive months and the metrics changed—I don't mean the numbers, but the actual types of metrics—I knew something was wrong. I would always look for that because it would either mean we were not making progress or that we didn't fully understand the instrumentation.

In the industrial world I would guesstimate that the majority of all the dollars invested in technology have been on Systems of Record. This means ERP systems, order management systems, CRM, and tech products like that. These Systems of Record usually tend to be large, costly, and slow. These technologies might improve compliance, and they may help the finance person close the books in a week instead of three weeks, but very few of them actually deliver a significant return to the business.

While it's true that all technology tools should build on what's been done before, leaders should aim to ensure a return on investment, so that putting in technology directly connects to the one or two numbers that actually drive the business. This is one reason why I am excited about the AI that's described in the Predictive Enterprise.

AI in procurement today can materially impact the top-line or bottom-line revenue of a company in a matter of weeks or months. And these solutions can be driven by the CEO and CFO, not just CIO-driven. Because when it's measured correctly, the value of AI is so easy to understand that it's almost a no-brainer. We are still in the beginning of this new mentality around what technology means for business leaders.

If you're a CEO or CFO of a big company, small company, industrial company, financial services, it doesn't matter—you've already been in the digital age for a generation.

Now you're in the AI age.

If you're sitting around waiting for the perfect solution to arrive, you're really not participating in the opportunity. You're just sitting there. That's not what boards expect from executive leadership anymore. Those days are over.

Additionally, instead of investing in the newest tech marketed to you by Salesforce or SAP, keep a few developers hanging around who actually understand your business, your needs, and the technology landscape and can advise and facilitate the adoption of new technology. The results will be obvious in days or weeks, not years.

■ ■ ■

Finally, let's consider the importance of supply chain leaders in the era of tariffs.

It surprises me how many companies are still running the old playbook when it comes to operations. Twenty-five years ago, if you were deciding whether to manufacture a refrigerator in Mexico or the United States, Mexico was a no-brainer because the labor cost 10 times less. However, most of that production can be moved back to the United States or Europe now because a lot of the wage arbitrage has been eaten up in productivity, in automation, and things like that. It's wild to see how many things are made in other places under the legacy justification of low-cost labor simply because companies don't take advantage of new technology.

Cost is always important and quality is always important, but where we make something becomes as important to marketing as it is for manufacturing. Being able to make things where you sell them is now quite material in terms of how people look at you. It brings credibility that is important and meaningful. People want to spend money with people they like, companies they trust, and that also extends to suppliers.

AI may be required in order to make this sort of pivot easier and more successful.

Make no mistake. AI will change the decision-making around where physical products get manufactured and assembled. It's not just the current tariffs and shifts in global trade. It's the fact that with AI we are dramatically changing the cost profile of making just about anything, which means we may soon be able to make most of our products just about anywhere, too.

There is a cultural aspect to the role of supply chain leaders in the AI era. You must know the technology, demand investment, and sign up for outcomes. These decisions shouldn't be spoon fed to you by the CIO like a child. Salespeople are often delightfully effective with technology, and that's probably why a lot of digital transformation starts with sales and the customer experience or the customer relationship and works backward. That's because it's easy to tie value and return on investment back to an attributable increase in top-line revenue.

However, it's time for that focus to shift.

We all know that costs are an important driver of business outcomes, not just top-line revenue. Historically, supply chain and procurement have been the receiver rather than the driver of new technology. Thankfully, this is also changing, and fast.

Today, transformation needs to be driven from the back office, and especially by the CFO, who has nothing to gain and everything to lose by waiting. Competitors can eat your lunch if you're not careful. This new approach around the Predictive Enterprise is a big part of what's making it happen. And it's already happening in large enterprises today on a global scale.

It's my belief that AI and the Predictive Enterprise are going to fundamentally shift the way leaders think about transformation in large enterprises, and especially with regards to the role of procurement and supply chain.

—Jeffrey R. Immelt, 2025

Introduction

The Power of Process in the Predictive Enterprise

LIKE MANY OF my colleagues, I began working in procurement largely by accident. When my job at a university required that I take procurement training, I was baffled by how boring and administrative the process felt to approve a simple expense. And getting a new contract with a supplier signed off? That required an extraordinary amount of time and effort. Having grown up with the iPhone, I knew that digital technology could be simple and labor-saving, even delightful. Why had procurement and supply chain at large organizations been left behind?

My academic background in social network analysis gave me the frameworks for mapping patterns in spend data. But I soon discovered a passion for executing supplier negotiations, often with multiple suppliers simultaneously. It was this passion that led me to become a procurement consultant specializing in strategic sourcing, with a focus on negotiating and awarding contracts using game theory.

For years I supported procurement teams through thousands of supplier negotiations. Together, we awarded contracts for everything from office supplies to water treatment chemicals, from professional services to software, from capital project construction to cafeteria serve ware. It was from this experience doing thousands of supplier negotiations that I saw firsthand the power of game theory and behavioral science, and especially the Fear of Missing Out (FOMO). I also experienced the leverage that comes from knowing the outcome of a negotiation before it begins. The procurement teams that I partnered with as a consultant could often predict which supplier would win the contract, as well as what a winning offer might realistically look like.

That's quite interesting, I thought.

If people with sufficient experience can predict the outcome of a supplier negotiation before it begins, then perhaps an AI model can do it, too.

This idea of predicting the outcome of a process before it begins and then reverse-engineering the required steps to improve or accelerate it is the core idea of the Predictive Enterprise.

In this short introduction, I will define the pillars of the Predictive Enterprise using both a clear framework and real-world examples. I'll also share my "aha" moment about why this approach specifically matters for procurement and supply chain teams. World-class procurement organizations often want to increase the number of data-driven decisions, influence more of their organizations' spend, shorten cycle times for every process, reduce the hours of human labor associated with completing each process, delight and dazzle their internal business stakeholders, and improve visibility and accountability across their supply base. The challenge is that none of this is possible without data. Most of the data that procurement teams need to make decisions must come from suppliers, and a lot of that data is created manually using webforms, surveys, and Excel spreadsheets attached to emails. Teams who are driving change in procurement using AI must reckon with the fact that their historical data is often messy, incomplete, siloed, or inaccessible. Because of my personal experience supporting procurement and supply chain teams at large enterprises, I have focused on AI transformations using the Predictive Enterprise that have been successful in spite of these obstacles and limitations.

This book is written for a general business audience of executives and employees who want to use AI to deliver measurable results on a global scale. At a time when "AI" has become a buzzword, I have made every effort to be specific, detail-oriented, and obsessively practical with examples so that anyone, regardless of technical background, can evaluate and act on the opportunity created by AI in the Predictive Enterprise.

The "Aha" Moment for the Predictive Enterprise

It was a hot summer night in San Francisco, and my friend Ben was having a party. Ben had risen through the ranks to become the youngest engineering manager at a startup called SurveyMonkey that was still a few years away from going public. We were celebrating Ben's birthday, and a few of his co-workers had shown up.

At the time, I was working on a few supplier negotiations in which my client wanted to qualify new suppliers. My team was doing this process by asking suppliers to answer survey questions. In fact, we were using surveys that we had created in spreadsheets using Excel and Google Sheets. That night I remember complaining to Ben about the fact that suppliers took forever to fill out our surveys, and they often gave us answers that were unhelpful or wrong. In several cases, these answers were obvious mistakes. One memorably lewd error was simply a typo.

Ben had just begun leading the enterprise mobile product at SurveyMonkey. He told me about a design concept they'd found helpful called "smart defaults." It turns out, Ben shared, that when you pre-fill the answer to a question with a preferred, qualified answer, you can increase the rate that a group of people complete a survey. And, the results of the survey are more usable.

Above my head, a lightbulb flicked on. What if pre-filling the answers to questions could increase the number of suppliers that qualified to participate in a contract bidding opportunity? What if that could widen the pool of qualified suppliers, increase competition, and drive savings?

This conversation with Ben would lead me on a journey to found an AI startup called Arkestro to scale a new approach to supplier negotiations called predictive procurement. In traditional procurement, suppliers make offers to buyers using quotes or proposals. In predictive procurement, the procurement team makes offers to suppliers using AI to generate suggested offers, by drafting and presenting the suppliers' salespeople with pre-filled quotes or proposals.

Consider that in traditional procurement, quotes are typically created by salespeople who often give a first offer that anchors the negotiation with a higher price. Salespeople do this to give themselves room to get negotiated down. In predictive procurement, quotes are created by procurement teams using AI, who anchor the negotiation with a competitive price that's closer to the supplier's best and final offer.

It's a simple process change enabled by AI that almost entirely eliminates the work associated with manual quote creation by salespeople and post-hoc quote analysis by procurement teams. It's also a powerful example of the Predictive Enterprise.

That conversation with Ben took place in 2016, when AI was still very nascent. In the decade since, I have had the unique opportunity to see what predictive procurement looks like on the scale of global business across different verticals of enterprise manufacturing, including chemical, automotive, pharma, oil and gas, food and beverage, construction, and logistics. Procurement and supply chain teams often find that this predictive approach cuts the calendar time by more than half per offer-to-agreement process. Predictive procurement also allows teams to increase the number of suppliers involved in a competitive negotiation without increasing the work associated with comparing additional offers. And time and time again, customers have found that predictive procurement can get them better cost savings results.

The reason for this dramatic impact is simple. It's exactly what Ben explained to me on that hot night in San Francisco. Most people hate making decisions. Most people hate typing text into form fields and spreadsheets. Most people hate trying to figure out what offer to make because most people hate losing. When you give most people a recommended next step that's already been vetted and checked by an AI model, you make it easy to say yes. You make it easy to get to a best and final offer faster.

In predictive procurement, the "smart default" of a suggested offer is more aligned with the interests of the buyer, rather than the seller. Predictive procurement illustrates a practical example of the Predictive Enterprise approach using AI, where AI is actually changing the steps and sequence of a process, rather than simply automating work in an existing workflow.

This example highlights an important aspect of the Predictive Enterprise: aligning the design and workflow of a process with the desired outcome, and then dynamically updating the user's experience of the process based on context.

The broader take-away for enterprise AI is clear. As Deloitte Tech Trends 2026 notes: "Gartner predicts that 40% of agentic projects will fail by 2027—not because the technology doesn't work, but because organizations are automating broken processes instead of redesigning operations. . . . Redesign, don't automate. That's the pattern separating success from failure.[1]"

Defining the Predictive Enterprise

Throughout this book, I'll refer to the Predictive Enterprise as a specific term of art. This term refers to a set of process changes in large enterprises that rest on the following three pillars:

Faster-Than-Human Decision-Making

The first pillar of the Predictive Enterprise involves decisions regarding the best next step in a process using AI that predicts the potential benefits and impact of the next step, rather than adhering to a single static and pre-defined workflow.

For example, when you receive a quote in traditional procurement, you might feel the need to get multiple additional quotes from other suppliers. However, if your predictive AI gives you a benchmark that tells you the quote you have is the best offer you are likely to get, then collecting additional quotes is not the best next step in the process. Collecting additional quotes that are less competitive and less desirable than the quote you already have is likely to add labor hours (clock time) and decision steps (calendar time) to the process without adding value. Therefore, the Predictive Enterprise enables Faster-Than-Human Decision-Making that results in a different best next step in the process of approving a quote from a supplier. The key here is that the AI is not automating pre-defined steps in an existing process. The AI is selecting the most desirable next step based on a prediction that compares the costs and benefits of taking this particular step versus all available alternatives.

Humanless Loops

The second pillar of the Predictive Enterprise removes human involvement from repetitive tasks to free up time for more high-impact and relationship-oriented work. Humanless loops can include porting data from one system to another, performing data validation, and generating transactional communication, such as invitations or updates.

For example, to measure cost savings in traditional procurement typically involves establishing a cost baseline using historical prices paid for the same item or service during an annual reporting period. When procurement teams execute a supplier negotiation, the price in the new offer is subtracted from the price in the cost baseline to calculate the value of identified cost savings. The performance of procurement teams is often measured by CFOs using cost savings as one significant metric, meaning that getting this cost baselining process right could impact people's job performance reviews, year-end bonuses, and so on. Creating a cost baseline often involves pulling data from Purchase Order records to determine the last price paid for an item or services during an annual reporting period. This task can now be done via Humanless Loops using AI instead of manually pulling down data, writing a query, or setting up a data integration. The key aspect of Humanless Loops is that it involves defining a desired outcome, and then letting AI figure out the activities needed to deliver the desired outcome at scale. Humanless Loops, in fact, can make the process of setting cost baselines in procurement for a set of items or services both dramatically scalable, and even continuous. This means that in the Predictive Enterprise, establishing the cost baseline for a single item and establishing the cost baseline for 100,000 items using the data analysis process steps described above should take nearly the same amount of clock time and calendar time, as well as the same amount of human effort: very close to zero.

Outcome-Based Process Re-Engineering

The third pillar of the Predictive Enterprise involves determining the most likely best case outcome of a process given the context, and then reverse engineering the required steps and sequence in order to deliver it.

For example, in traditional procurement it is common to refresh pricebooks with suppliers for existing catalogs of parts and materials. In contract manufacturing, procurement and sourcing teams will often set up a manual price refresh cycle with key suppliers that could run annually or quarterly. For large manufacturers, this price refresh cycle is done using a standard operating procedure in order to consolidate the process of receiving and updating ad hoc price changes from thousands of suppliers into a single, centralized workflow. This price refresh is done to create a common understanding on price between buyer and seller and therefore is not generally seen through the lens of negotiation.

However, if the most likely best case outcome of this process is to minimize the number of supplier price increases, then giving every supplier the opportunity to change every price during every price refresh cycle does not align with that desired outcome. By using AI to predict which suppliers are most likely to raise prices given the context of changing market conditions, and then re-sequencing the price refresh schedule to extend existing agreements earlier, procurement teams can deliver an outcome that avoids significant cost increases across thousands of parts and materials.

To be clear, this is what many procurement and sourcing teams already do. Running a price refresh cycle for a subset of suppliers has material cost advantages compared to running a one-size-fits-all process for all suppliers. The key is limiting or widening the scope of a given price refresh cycle so that it targets only the suppliers and spend categories where refreshing prices aligns with desired outcomes.

The Predictive Process Stack

The reason that the Predictive Enterprise approach is particularly exciting for large, global enterprises is that the bigger the organization, the more common it is to use a defined process or standard operating procedure to facilitate group decisions and workflows. Just like a set of technologies is sometimes called a "technology stack," I like to think of a set of processes that underlie organizational behavior as a "process stack." A process is simply a list of ordered steps that tells users what to do to achieve a desired outcome. A good process stack lists out both inputs and steps in a defined sequence that accounts for dependencies and context. A good process stack is widely adopted, broadly accessible, and extremely repeatable. A good process stack has a lot of advantages for large enterprises, including:

- Creating clarity and predictability for how decisions get made and how work gets done
- Enabling everyone involved to have confidence and place trust in the outcome of the process
- Defining roles and goals of participants in the process, thereby creating accountability

Unfortunately, over time the process stack of larger organizations may experience bloat, which tends to multiply the administrative burden of the process across more people. You may have heard the phrase "too many cooks in the kitchen." Steps are added to a process with the intention of increasing participation, transparency, and accountability for different stakeholders, but without necessarily adding value. This can lead to frustration and circumvention by the very individuals who the process was created to include and support.

The result is that over time, processes tend to get longer and more labor-intensive. The number of long meetings begin to multiply. In certain cases, the process gets so long and convoluted that the architecture of the process itself makes delivering a desired outcome all but impossible. A process that takes an unpredictable or extremely long amount of cycle time will give stakeholders a powerful reason to circumvent or avoid running the process altogether. As we'll discuss in the following chapters, process bloat and circumvention is the exact opposite of what procurement and supply chain leaders want to see. It also creates financial value leakage, and at scale, process circumvention can even erode operating margin and competitive advantage.

Moving from a Traditional to a Predictive Process Stack

To understand the difference between a traditional process stack and a predictive process stack, consider the difference between an analog paper map and a predictive map like Waze or Google Maps. Analog paper maps are a lot like traditional processes at large enterprises today.

For thousands of years, analog paper maps worked great. Having an analog paper map is certainly better than having no map at all. But analog paper maps do not know where you are right now. They do not know where you are going or where you want to go. They don't know the traffic patterns or the weather conditions that may exist along all the different possible routes. And they cannot compare all the different routes to show you the fastest way to get from where you are now to arrive at your destination.

Now let's think about a predictive map, like Waze or Google Maps. The map knows where you are because of the geo-locator on your phone. When you move, the map can see you move. When you select a destination, the map scale zooms in to frame your local area based on the distance that you're traveling and the route you might take. The map isolates and highlights both the route and the destination. The map compares all the possible routes to your destination and shows you the fastest way to get there. The map modifies and updates that route based on real-time context like traffic patterns and weather conditions. Predictive maps powered by AI have changed the way many of us move through the physical world, from driving to walking to taking public transit. Could a predictive process stack similarly change the way that teams at large enterprises move through the world of group decision-making and process workflows?

Let's think for a moment about what that would mean. What if your process knew where you were and where you wanted to go? What if your process changed based on the target outcome? What if the steps in your process updated based on real-time context like market conditions, supplier relationships, and a dynamic ranking of potential alternatives?

How to Use the Predictive Enterprise to Advance Your Career and Win Your Market

This book is filled with stories and real-world examples you can take with you into meetings at your own company, whether you are an executive or an employee. You can share them to spark discussion and inspire projects that will help you build your own understanding of AI, design your own use cases, move your business forward, and advance your career. This book is written to allow you to approach the topic of AI in procurement and supply chain with hard facts and proven strategies rather than untempered exuberance or negativity.

My grandfather used to say that he would rather be lucky than right. He also defined luck as the moment where opportunity meets the prepared mind. I think that's a good way to reckon with the evolving landscape created by AI today. Rather than trying to be exactly right about what AI can or cannot do, it's probably more helpful to figure out which AI bets are the likeliest to pay off for your career and for your business. This book is written in that spirit, to help guide your areas of focus, to help you select proven use cases linked to measurable value, and to help increase your win rate on bets involving AI across your procurement and supply chain functions.

One of the perils of writing a book like this is that the news about AI changes every week. New models are released, new investments are announced, and new companies unveil new product offerings at dizzying speed. Humans have been inventing new technologies for thousands of years, but no technology in world history has ever evolved as quickly or been adopted by more people as quickly as AI. Therefore, being right about specific AI timelines, inflection points, and capabilities is not a reasonable expectation to have for this book. But that doesn't mean you can't create dramatic value using AI in your business as it exists today.

In other words, I wrote this book to help you be lucky, rather than to help you be right.

1

Why AI Is Transforming Procurement and Supply Chain at Large Enterprises

"We tend to overestimate the effect of a technology in the short run and underestimate the effect in the long run."

—Amara's Law, from the futurist Roy Amara

ALL ACROSS THE world, AI is arriving in our supply chains.

As I write these words, AI is feeding data into our dashboards, updating our demand forecasts, emailing our suppliers, checking our pricing, reviewing our contracts, and answering our questions about tariffs.

Like the day that AI first appeared in Google Search, as a blurb of bulleted text, AI's arrival in our supply chains has been humble, and even a bit basic—less like a dramatic wave crashing over us and more like the gradual beginnings of a new season.

Executive leadership teams at large enterprises are now in the early days of this new season, which promises a vast AI paradigm shift in how supply chains work and how supplier deals get done. This book will help you understand what this AI paradigm shift in our supply chains means for your organization, your career, and your relationship with your customers, your suppliers, and your team.

The numbers are quite compelling. Gartner estimates that in large enterprise supply chains: "... 95% of data-driven decisions are expected to be at least partially automated." Gartner also expects that by 2030, at least half of all existing supply chain management solutions will contain ". . . intelligent agents to autonomously execute decisions in the ecosystem." Capgemini's 2025 annual study on enterprise AI adoption that surveys over 1,000 director-level or above executives at enterprises with annual revenues greater than $1 billion called AI . . . "one of the fastest-emerging technology adoption curves in recent times."

Over half of Capgemini's respondents (58%) called AI "a paradigm shift for their organization's productivity," with 76% believing that AI will ". . . handle one or more complete business processes . . ." in supply chain and procurement within the next 3–5 years. The report summarizes the state of enterprise adoption: "AI is in transition. The technology is moving from isolated pilots to sweeping, mainstream adoption at an unprecedented pace." Like the arrival of spring after a long winter, AI is popping up like dandelions in clumps across our economy.

Soon we may find that the AI spring is upon us, and the dandelions are everywhere.

Digital transformation in the supply chain is unique because it involves multiple organizations making changes in how they do business, rather than a single organization trying to change only the behavior of its own employees. Unlike previous waves of digital transformation that gave a lot more users access to a lot more systems, AI is actually removing the need for human users to take part in specific tasks, processes, and decisions. This is at the heart of the AI paradigm shift: removing human action as a dependency for process completion.

But that doesn't necessarily imply that the aggregate demand for human labor in our supply chains will decrease. In fact, it's quite possible for the exact opposite to happen.

Economist James Bessen was interviewed about the role of automation in taking or displacing jobs on the podcast *EconTalk*, and remarked: "So, what happened with textiles? During the nineteenth century, if you look at the tasks of weavers, 98% of the work was automated; yet the number of weavers continued to grow. The reason was the greater degree of automation meant that the price of cotton cloth went down, and people started using more cloth. This is sometimes called Jevons Paradox, which states that when consuming a resource becomes more efficient, demand for that resource increases. In other words, what if the demand for AI-enabled human labor is actually much higher than the demand for human labor without AI is today?"

The effects of induced demand for labor resulting from labor-saving technology also appear to have impacted the number of bank tellers in the decade following the introduction of Automated Teller Machines (ATMs). As Bessen explains: ". . . the average bank branch in an urban area required about 21 tellers. That was cut because of the ATM machine to about 13 tellers. But that meant it was cheaper to operate a branch. Well, banks wanted . . . to increase the number of branch offices. And when it became cheaper to do so, demand for branch offices increased. And as a result, demand for bank tellers increased. And it increased enough to offset the labor-saving losses of jobs that would have otherwise occurred. So, again, it was one of these more dynamic things where the labor-saving technology actually created more jobs."

It is also important to understand that automation generally has a different function in job roles where the core responsibilities include managing a human-to-human relationship, like a relationship with a customer or a supplier. In this book, I am going to share several cases where AI removes the need for a human to take part in a task, process, or decision, but that does not mean that human involvement won't add critical value to performing the job, or delivering an outcome. It also doesn't mean that a hybrid approach where human workers and AI are collaborating won't dramatically outperform AI deployed without human collaboration, supervision, or oversight. As famed AI luminary and investor Andrew Ng puts it: "For many jobs, AI will only automate or augment 20–30% of tasks. So, there's a huge productivity boost, but people are still required for the remaining 70% of the role."

The truth is that automation is only one aspect of the AI paradigm shift in our supply chains.

To understand the true opportunity that AI creates, we need to look at an example of two technology businesses in the area of fast food: the automat and the drive-thru.

What We Can Learn about AI from Automats Versus Drive-thrus

Think about how the business performance of automats—essentially restaurant-scale vending machines—compared to drive-thru fast-food franchises like McDonald's over the past 100 years.

McDonald's is famous for using technology, operations research, and process engineering to systematically optimize the steps involved in food preparation to the point that each customer's meal can be prepared made-to-order in mere minutes.

Customer after customer pulls their vehicle up to the kiosk, places their order, and then gets served a piping hot meal in a paper bag via a drive-thru window.

Now let's contrast that customer experience with automats.

The first automat opened in 1902 on Chestnut Street in Philadelphia, the brainchild of Joseph Horn and Frank Hardart. Horn and Hardart envisioned a fully automated self-service restaurant with a 400+ item menu, welcoming diners with a satisfying cup of coffee dispensed from a coin-operated spigot. No hosts, no waitstaff, no servers. Put in a coin, open a door, take out your meal. Fill up your cup and take a sip.

At its peak, Horn and Hardart had 171 locations that served more than 750,000 daily customers. But the automat wasn't designed for the world of American car ownership, suburban commutes, and interstate highways. As a result, automats struggled to compete with the drive-thru craze and the rapid rise of the fast-food hamburger beginning in the 1950s.

While the automat was far more automated than drive-thrus, the automation prevented customers from customizing their orders. For postwar American diners, getting a burger cooked and served right off the griddle was the key to a satisfying fast food experience.

Customers voted with their wallets for drive-thrus over automats, despite the latter being much faster, and much more automated. Why? Because customers vastly preferred the fast food product that was enabled by the drive-thru experience. For most of the second half of the twentieth century, the automat was on the decline. The last Horn and Hardart automat closed in 1991.

Today, McDonald's serves more than 63 million daily customers at more than 44,000 locations worldwide.

The experience of going to a McDonald's is extremely optimized, and increasingly self-service, but at its core is the human service experience: cashiers, cooks, managers, and franchisees.

This contrast illustrates a key nuance of the current AI paradigm shift in our supply chains. Just because AI makes it theoretically possible to fully automate the ways that most people take part in our supply chains does not in any way mean that it is advisable or beneficial to do so.

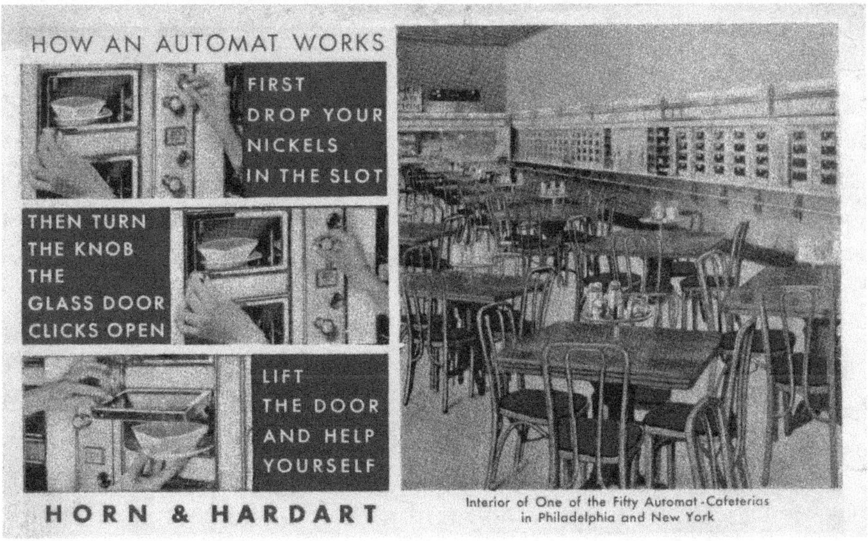

People establish and maintain interpersonal relationships through trust and communicate contexts and nuances that are increasingly important in a world defined by volatility and complexity.

Person-to-person trust is especially relevant in a world awash with misinformation, social deception, phishing, and advertising. People also bind commitments and create accountability by being embedded in a web of complex social roles and responsibilities in ways that AI is not.

Consider that despite all the digital automation at our fingertips, most large organizations' preferred way to bind an agreement is still for a specific individual employed by the organization to place an incomprehensible scribble, representing their first and last name, on a document. Whether that document is paper or electronic often no longer matters. That scribble of a person's signature carries greater force and meaning than a million AI-generated emails.

What Person-to-Person Accountability Means as a Constraint for AI in Supply Chains

After interviewing hundreds of executives working in large enterprises while researching this book, I can say that no one I spoke with truly believes that AI is going to put us all out of a job. That is at least in part because global supply chains and supplier dealmaking depend upon supplier performance, which in turn depends upon agreements between individual people deciding to trust each other. Agreements are driven by trust and relationships, and trust and relationships require being embedded in social roles and responsibilities in ways that are uniquely human.

However, the flip side is that nearly every executive I spoke with for this book also believes that AI will dramatically change our ways of working, our value propositions, our organizational designs, and the talent profile that procurement, supply chain, and operations teams hire for over the next one to five years. And many of the executives interviewed are both proud and enthusiastic to be leading that dramatic organizational change within their enterprises.

The fact is, at many large enterprises, AI is not replacing people so much as making up for an acute shortage of skilled workers available to participate in a business decision or execute steps in a traditional process stack. And because of this fact, the alternative to using AI often isn't hiring more people, since skilled workers with relevant domain experience are often unavailable to hire. The alternative to implementing AI is either overworking the existing team during peak times to the point of chronic burnout or experiencing painful delays and expensive operational failures.

Due to the path dependency of many of our supply chains on the single-threaded workflows of traditional process stacks, any delay in any single step can have the net effect of slowing down the end-to-end process. Delays create more delays. For this reason, there is a range of decisions at large enterprises that are getting slower and slower due to compounding labor shortages. At the same time, most global markets and customers are moving faster and faster. In other words, the default trend of a traditional process stack without AI is tilted toward less predictable, less repeatable outcomes with higher administrative burdens.

This is not what anyone wants.

In fact, while this trend toward leaner teams, greater complexity, and slower cycles is continuing, customers' expectations are trending toward greater and greater speed.

The center cannot hold.

The so-called Amazon Effect, where customers across industries often assume that product can be delivered next day or within two days because they can access these types of delivery speeds via Amazon, illustrates this quandary. There is never enough time to keep operational tempos moving faster and faster. That reality is only compounded by the administrative burden created by manual data form-fill System of Record technology or Excel spreadsheets attached to long email chains.

It is against this relentless backdrop that all conversations about AI in procurement and supply chain are now taking place: the truly unforgiving need for speed.

2

Between a Rock and a Hard Place

The Unforgiving Need for Speed

Faster operational tempos put every traditional process stack through the pressure cooker year after year. This state of affairs is clearly unsustainable without a material change in our ways of working.

But there is another part of the story here.

Faster operational tempos have measurable trade-offs when it comes to cost. When procurement teams working in a traditional process stack have less time to negotiate, less time to develop alternative scenarios, less time to analyze and evaluate the market, the suppliers' salesperson has greater leverage in setting a final negotiated price. Salespeople know this. This is one of many reasons why the unforgiving need for speed is having a measurable effect on the Cost of Goods Sold (COGS), operating margins, and Earnings Per Share of large enterprises. Speed may be required by customers, but at what price?

Here's what one Vice President of Global Supply Chain had to say during an October 2025 presentation:

"Let's talk about the problem. Who here is under pressure to lower their costs, use [fewer] resources, speed up delivery time, and oh, by the way, not sacrifice a bit of quality? Anyone? Yeah, I see all hands going up on that one. That is hard. Especially in an environment with reduced resources.

"We are all under pressure to do more with less. And that can be difficult when we don't have the time to spend on strategic sourcing, thinking about how we go to market, and quite frankly, not even being able to competitively bid much of our portfolio.

"Now, as an example, 60% of our buyers' time was spent on what I would call clerical activities. You know, administrative activities. Getting a PO, putting master data into a system, responding to emails, things that were absolutely necessary based on the processes that we had in place but weren't necessarily creating value. We needed them instead to focus on understanding the markets, on asking, 'How do we think about engaging with our vendors differently going forward?'"

The High Cost of "Do More with Less" in a Traditional Procurement Process Stack

This same Vice President of Global Supply Chain also highlighted how the "do more with less" pressure impacts the way that domain expertise gets used among employees in supply chain teams, stating: "Now also, because of this, our RFQ time was really short. We didn't have a lot of time to include a large number of vendors. And even if we could include a large number of vendors, our timelines were so condensed that we struggled to negotiate at the end of those RFQ processes. We sometimes accepted bids as they came in and that was good enough; we weren't negotiating. And even when we could negotiate, those skills were limited by the tacit knowledge of the employees that we had. You have a first-year buyer versus a 10-year buyer and their skill levels to negotiate are different, and that's going to lead to different results. And so we had non-repeatable results for our business units on a regular basis."

Let's break this down. "Do more with less" in procurement generally means fewer people. Fewer people doing procurement faster generally means less time to negotiate. Less time to negotiate generally means fewer competitive offers, less leverage, less spend influenced, and higher costs. Higher costs erode the enterprise's operating margins, as well obliterating any savings from the payroll reduction achieved from shrinking headcount.

That's a high price to pay for "do more with less." In the traditional process stack, it is safe to expect that this will be the predictable result of reducing headcount for the procurement and supply chain team without upgrading the traditional process stack. This scenario is hardly unique.

At Arkestro, our teams of AI scientists, engineers, and researchers work with a massive dataset of more than $400B+ in large enterprise spend transactions that contains identified product names, part numbers, quantities, units of measure, and prices. From this dataset, we have generally found that price dispersion, measured as the cost difference between the highest and lowest price that a large enterprise pays for the exact same item, lane, or service rate, tends to increase with enterprise size, scale, and geographical complexity. In other words, for a given sample of $1 billion in spend, we can correlate higher SKU count and higher number of geographies with higher variance in cost per unit. This variance tends to increase over time, both because of macroeconomic inflation on the one hand, and because economies of scale in certain categories and geographies tend to improve as businesses' demand grows. In other words, the absolute costs of items are growing higher in aggregate, but the power of large enterprises to secure lower relative costs by sourcing and procuring at massive scale is also growing larger.

High purchase price variance is another way of saying that across the thousands of items, raw materials, components, parts, freight lanes, and services agreements, large enterprises are systematically leaving money on the table. A lot of money.

Our dataset shows that large enterprises with a traditional process stack are leaving double-digit percentages of their total spend on the table. This equates to overpaying suppliers by billions of dollars every year due to not having enough bandwidth to effectively negotiate costs.

To be clear, the Arkestro dataset also shows that large enterprises do achieve economies of scale in aggregate through purchasing power in certain categories. They just also tend to pay a higher price for cost variance in absolute terms. Even a small number of cost exceptions can add up quickly at a large enterprise. One percent of $1 billion is $10 million. That's a lot of money.

High variance in costs for standard items and services that are purchased at scale is the exact opposite of what large enterprises want to see from their procurement function. Procurement is all about delivering predictable costs, which equate with predictable profit margins. Unpredictable costs in supplier deals can, over time, erode operating margins and profitability, creating systemic risks to business continuity.

That's exactly why the unforgiving need for speed plus "do more with less" puts procurement teams between a rock and a hard place when it comes to achieving cost savings targets at scale.

Most procurement and supply chain teams genuinely want to move faster. But the cost of leaving a supplier's offer un-negotiated is often extremely high, even if that cost goes unmeasured at the time the deal is approved. Less headcount means less bandwidth, and less procurement bandwidth makes trade-offs and double binds between speed and cost inevitable.

Moving from Cost Center to Strategic Business Partner Means Increasing Procurement Bandwidth Without Increasing Headcount

Over the years, the definition of "value" for procurement and supply chain functions has broadened beyond reducing per-unit costs to align with a range of strategic business goals. However, procurement's mechanism for creating this expanded scope of value largely remains the same as reducing normal per-unit costs: making better deals with suppliers. Procurement teams use the leverage of awarding a contract to a supplier to create a better deal for the enterprise at scale. Procurement's ability to get internal stakeholders, like budget owners, to then exclusively buy off the contracts they negotiate also plays a significant role in how excited the suppliers are to compete for their business opportunities. Without utilization by internal stakeholders, even the best contracts are worthless in terms of tangible business impact.

Traditionally, this leverage was called "purchasing power." By aggregating demand, enticing suppliers to make offers, and then negotiating contracts, procurement teams could use a large enterprise's purchasing power to achieve strategic business outcomes. Cost reduction may be one of these business outcomes, but many procurement teams use better deals with suppliers to advance other goals, such as launching new products, opening new markets, or accelerating delivery of product to customers. That is why this aspect of the procurement function is often called "strategic sourcing." Strategic sourcing differentiates the high-stakes work of managing supplier relationships and supplier dealmaking from more tactical purchasing tasks associated with placing orders and stocking inventory.

If "better deals" means awarding demand to the supplier with greater strategic alignments, greater value, and lower costs, rather than just lower per-unit prices, then that is what procurement will deliver. Sharon Moar, a procurement excellence leader at BMI, a global roofing manufacturer, explains this transition from cost center to strategic business partner:

> "Just as we provide our customers with integrated systems rather than mere components, our procurement team is evolving from a traditional cost center to a strategic business partner bringing additional value. It's about people moving from a 'support' mindset to a 'growth' mindset by embodying key cultural shifts. We believe a value-led approach is limitless. While fiscal discipline remains our foundation, we recognize that chasing the lowest "price per unit" is a short-term tactic, not a long-term strategy.
>
> "We don't just manage spend. We want to empower our team to be proactive partners to the business by identifying opportunities to improve business outcomes and drive the competitive advantage that our customers expect from us. . . . We don't want to be seen as just negotiators who manage price, but as business influencers, collaborators, and value-creators."[1]

And it is exactly this value creation lever that gets eroded over time in a traditional process stack as SKU count and complexity increase and as operational tempos continue to speed up.

When you squeeze a procurement team between a rock and a hard place, there is less bandwidth to deliver predictable cost savings, or to align those cost savings with other strategic business objectives.

This erosion in no way represents a fundamental decrease of the enterprise's purchasing power. Rather, it represents constraints on procurement's ability to gain leverage with suppliers within the amount of time they are given. The center cannot hold.

Measuring the Success of a Predictive Process Stack: Increasing Bandwidth and Throughput While Reducing Ramp Time and Barriers to Excellence for Junior Employees

Returning the leverage of purchasing power back to procurement teams may require redesigning the process to unlock greater bandwidth and faster throughput. But it also means re-defining the talent profile of what a successful procurement practitioner looks like to enable junior employees to ramp faster and overcome barriers to excellence. Rebuilding junior buyers' leverage in supplier negotiations means equipping more procurement professionals with the enablement, tools, and know-how to do better deals faster across the supply base.

It also means investing in a predictive process stack, where just like Waze or Google Maps, every process knows where you are going and can tell you the fastest route to get there.

Today, in a traditional process stack, if you want to negotiate a great deal with suppliers, you often need market-relevant domain expertise gained from decades of industry experience. But decades of industry experience are increasingly in short supply for many procurement teams. Armed with a predictive procurement process, junior buyers and newer category managers should be able to navigate as well or better than team members with decades of prior experience.

In fact, that is the example shared by the Vice President of Global Supply Chain speaking about their Predictive Enterprise journey: "First, we could elevate our team members through the application of game theory and behavioral science. So, think back to what I just said—it's difficult for a first-year buyer to have the same knowledge as a 10-year buyer. Well, game theory and behavioral science can take some of that out of the picture. And now we have elevated the capabilities of the junior buyers in our organization."

The impact of the Predictive Enterprise on talent profiles and workforce development in supply chain teams is validated by large-scale survey research, such as that conducted in a 2024 Economic Impact study. This study found that "Most enterprises are already seeing value creation from AI for procurement, but this is particularly the case at larger firms, where AI is being used not just to automate tasks but also to enhance decision-making processes. Sixty-nine percent of organizations with $500 million or more in annual revenue say that AI tools help procurement professionals do their jobs better. . . . AI's ongoing integration into procurement teams is changing the function at its core, enabling new kinds of work to take place."

This finding mirrors what James Bessen found with nineteenth-century weavers: inexperienced junior employees could become more productive fairly quickly by using automation, but only by acquiring specialized, firm-specific skills associated with their mills' machine configurations and production processes. As we look to bottlenecks, trade-offs, and double binds associated with skyrocketing complexity and the unforgiving need for speed, we should understand the opportunity of the Predictive Enterprise as enabling, unlocking, and super humanizing the procurement and supply chain workforce's productivity.

Overcoming Perceived Trade-Offs between Personas in the Enterprise Transformation Trio: Finance, Operations, and Budget Owners

Have you ever heard the expression that if you want something Good, Fast, and Cheap you will need to pick two? That means pick *only* two. When talking about AI in procurement and supply chain, it's useful to ask every persona involved in the transformation of supplier dealmaking a simple question: Which two are your preferred two?

Instead of Good, Fast, and Cheap, let's use Cost, Quality, and Speed. When I have done the Pick Two Exercise with executives at large enterprises, I have found that you can reveal a natural divergence in priorities between functional teams and leaders within the same business:

- **Finance:** Cost and Quality are need-to-haves, Speed is nice-to-have. That's because procurement teams are often focused on driving cost savings.
- **Operations:** Speed and Cost are the need-to-haves, Quality is nice-to-have. That's because supply chain teams are often focused on on-time delivery: the right part or material in the right place at the right time at the right cost.
- **Budget Owners:** Speed and Quality are the need-to-haves, Cost is the nice-to-have. That's because budget owners are often laser focused on the end customer of the business. They want to get their customer the best product in the fastest time, and are willing to pay higher costs to deliver Speed and Quality.

This meaningful difference in priorities is not misalignment. It is productive tension. This is how large enterprises are *supposed* to work. However, it also poses certain challenges for implementing AI in supply chains, which include all of the above personas as key stakeholders, alongside tens of thousands of suppliers. What outcome should you optimize for? How should you measure the success of an AI-driven process within this conflicting set of trilateral constraints? What is the quantifiable definition of benefits for the desired outcome?

The Predictive Enterprise offers a simple but compelling answer: re-design the process of supplier dealmaking so that the "smart default" outcome of the least-effort version of the process aligns measurable improvements in Speed, Cost, *and* Quality.

The lowest cost agreement with the most preferred supplier can be the outcome that has the fewest steps in the process, takes the least time, and requires the fewest number of decisions.. This may sound like a radical idea, but the truth about AI in large enterprise supply chains is that technology is not the real challenge. Culture and change management are the real challenges. In the Predictive Enterprise, we are not just designing and implementing new technology, throwing it over the fence, and hoping for the best. We are designing and implementing new patterns of organizational behavior that operate across multiple different personas at a global scale. It's just like Ben told me on that hot night in San Francisco: most people are actually pretty simple. We hate making decisions. We hate filling out forms. And we really hate waiting for an unknown or extremely long amount of time to get to the next step. The only thing worse than delaying gratification is delaying gratification for an unknown or extremely long amount of time.

Like Waze or Google Maps, we want turn-by-turn directions. We want a predictive map that sees us, a predictive map that knows where we are right now, a predictive map that knows where we want to go, and a predictive map that knows how to get us there.

That's the power of the Predictive Enterprise.

Going from Either/or Double Binds to an AI Transformation Based on Win-Wins

The Predictive Enterprise approach offers a differentiated playbook for implementing AI in enterprise supply chains to achieve tangible and meaningful value creation. The key to success is about transforming apparent trade-offs and double binds between conflicting personas into win-wins. Over the next three chapters, we'll look at three common trade-offs that take place for procurement and supply chain during digital transformations in a traditional process stack.

In Better Deals, Faster, we'll examine how to overcome the double bind between doing faster deals and doing more competitive deals. In Better Deals, Safer we'll look at overcoming the double bind between deals that reduce the total number of suppliers versus deals that create additional supply chain resiliency. And In Better Deals, Easier we'll look at the double bind between wanting to do deals that influence all spend across the enterprise, while flat headcount makes it challenging to increase the team's bandwidth.

For enterprises that are under intense pressure to do more with less, to take cost out of their supply chains, and to heed their customers' unforgiving need for speed, the Predictive Enterprise offers a compelling game plan to deliver a big win against daunting odds.

It is both a big challenge and an even bigger opportunity.

3

Better Deals, Faster

Overcoming the Speed and Cost Double Bind

"Show me the incentive and I'll show you the outcome."

—Charlie Munger

At a lot of large enterprises, the job of a Chief Procurement Officer (CPO) or Chief Supply Chain Officer (CSCO) is, on the one hand, infinitely complex, and on the other hand, brutally simple.

It's infinitely complex because at any given time multiple conflicting priorities effectively operate as decision constraints when it comes to selecting a supplier, getting a deal done, holding suppliers accountable for their ongoing performance, and managing a portfolio of activities and relationships across numerous categories of spend. In a lot of ways, being a CPO or CSCO is like managing a vast, globally distributed organization of employees—employees who just happen to work at other companies (e.g. for your suppliers), rather than for your business directly.

It's also brutally simple because the core mission is clear: keep your budget owner and stakeholders happy with A+ supplier quality and performance, while at the same time over-achieving the cost savings target number that's often given by the CFO, CEO, or Board of Directors.

That's it. Sounds easy, right?

There are usually other initiatives on top of this core mission, initiatives associated with Corporate Social Responsibility and linked to targets around Environmental, Social, and Governance metrics. Delivering on these initiatives aren't always considered wins unless the core mission has been satisfied first: enable the business to buy better.

Measure what "better" means using a combination of cost and value. "Better" may have a different definition if you are talking to Finance, Operations, or a budget owner and their employees. As much as possible, try to incorporate quantitative, indisputable definitions of "better" into your goals. That's because every decision made by your team involves trade-offs, and trade-offs invite all the blamers and complainers to give voice to their discontent.

The destination is clear, even if the route to get there is fraught with challenges, trade-offs, and double binds. And delivering on this core mission becomes exponentially more difficult with a leaner team operating against the unforgiving need for speed at global scale.

Go to any conference where procurement and supply chain executives congregate and you will hear the same mantra: Procurement now has a seat at the table. We are no longer a cost center. We are a strategic partner to enable high-priority business outcomes. Supply chain is no longer a back-office function. Operations are becoming a competitive advantage for large enterprises. Now is our time to receive the respect and appreciation we have so long deserved.

This all sounds nice. But what does the playbook look like to deliver this outcome to the business at the scale of large enterprises using a set of predictable, repeatable processes? What is the framework for measuring value and communicating impact to the CEO, CFO, and others?

Winning the Hearts and Minds of Budget Owners: Redesigning for Better Deals, Faster

As a procurement or supply chain leader, you have probably been told many times that you must first be a service provider to enable your budget owners. Whatever you do, don't try to outflank or overrule or chastise your budget owners or their direct reports. Because if you become their enemy, they will circumvent you and stop inviting you to important meetings. More significantly, they will stop bringing you into deals, which means you will have less spend to influence and less leverage with suppliers. You will go back to being a rubber stamp at the end of your budget owners' dealmaking process: negotiating without leverage, which is no fun. In other words: keep everything running smoothly and don't be a buzzkill.

As one Chief Procurement Officer wryly remarked to an audience of procurement practitioners at the 2025 Sourcing Industry Group Summit: "Do you know how many people at my company have ever been fired for not following our corporate procurement policy?"

The audience chuckled as he held up his fingers forming a big fat zero.

The fact is, procurement executives must often lead through influence, rather than through direct authority. Making enemies with budget owners or their direct reports is a losing proposition. This is a fight that many procurement leaders have fought, and few have won. That's because mandates associated with internal compliance cut against the grain for how large enterprise management cultures tend to operate today: cultures of de-centralized empowerment and functional ownership, rather than cultures of hierarchical mandates and punitive authority.

Enterprise CEOs generally seek to give budget owners maximum ownership and expect maximum accountability for top-line business outcomes. Budget owners are often institutionally powerful enough to circumvent the procurement process, which means as a CPO or CSCO you will then have less spend to influence and less demand to leverage, and your span of control will shrink along with your real and perceived effectiveness as an executive leader. This will in turn make it more difficult for you to hit your cost savings target for the CFO, and thus it will make it more difficult for you to earn your bonus or justify your team's budget requests for headcount.

That's why procurement executives are often maximally effective when they lead by offering budget owners a compelling value proposition, rather than demanding compliance with their process.

As my co-author, former Chief Procurement Officer of Johnson & Johnson Len DeCandia, often says about his tenure managing $40 billion in global spend: "Procurement must be understood as an enabler to the business. The key term is 'trusted advisor.' It's not about being a hall monitor. It's not about being a compliance jockey. It's not about being an administrative adversary to budget owners' teams. Procurement is about giving your budget owners a great customer service experience, getting them great deals with suppliers, and doing it fast and with the absolute minimum of hassle."

Let's be blunt: the traditional process stack in large enterprises does not make it particularly easy for procurement teams to be trusted advisors to their budget owners. That's because the traditional process stack is built to control spend, not to enable business outcomes. That's why it is mechanically difficult for a procurement team to perform all of the necessary steps involved in executing a supplier negotiation—especially a negotiation that entails collecting and comparing multiple complex offers using multiple different criteria—in a very short period of time when working in a traditional process stack. For numerous reasons, a very short period of time is what the procurement team often has to work with.

Budget owners today have never been more impatient. Procurement processes, in some cases, were specifically designed to add friction and clock time to every decision to spend the business's money. If a procurement process is perceived to add friction or delays, the CPO or CSCO will find budget owners trying to circumvent the procurement process entirely. This adversarial dynamic erodes the procurement team's negotiating leverage and makes it nearly impossible to harness the enterprise's full purchasing power at scale.

It is reasonable to assume that for every supplier offer that isn't negotiated, the enterprise is leaving money on the table. Offers that are approved without adequate negotiation are what drive variability in costs. Circumvention, even under the best intentions, has the unintended consequence of worse cost predictability and lower margins. That's the opposite of what every stakeholder involved in the Predictive Enterprise wants.

Building Empathy: Understanding the Fractal Complexity of Negotiating Multiple Complex Offers Simultaneously

This dynamic of budget owners and employees circumventing a traditional procurement process that they perceive to be frustratingly slow and administratively burdensome gets much worse due to the unforgiving need for speed.

Budget owners who grew up as digital natives with iPhone-level consumer technology expect a procurement process that's designed around ease of use and instant gratification. I relate to this desire for simplicity and speed on a personal level. Why does getting a supplier contract approved at a large enterprise take so much longer than almost any purchase I can make using my iPhone?

Procurement at many large enterprises is the exact opposite of instant gratification, especially when it involves a supplier contract negotiation. Yet the reason for this difference between expectations and reality may be due to a lack of appreciation for the fractal complexity associated with negotiating multiple complex offers simultaneously. If we are going to embark upon the ambitious task of re-designing the traditional process stack for procurement as part of delivering on the promise of the Predictive Enterprise, then we may need to employ some design thinking.

Design thinking is often comprised of the following steps:

Empathize	Define	Ideate	Prototype	Test

Let us, therefore, empathize with the plight of the procurement professional laboring under the yoke of a traditional process stack. Have you ever personally had to collect a quote from a supplier salesperson and then make a decision about what to do next? This task may sound easy, but it is deceptively difficult depending on what the quote is for. It may also be more difficult depending on your familiarity with the domain, the market, and the suppliers offering the quotes.

To understand why this can be difficult, let's use an analogy.

Picture a man playing tennis.

This man represents a category manager within an enterprise procurement team. The ball represents a quote given by a supplier for a set of items, sent as a PDF or Excel spreadsheet attached to an email. The email is sent by the supplier's sales team to the procurement team's category manager. To hit the ball back over the net, the category manager has to inspect the elements of the quote to determine whether they are being offered a good deal.

The quote's elements contain line items. Line items in a table form a market basket composed of distinct lots and often contain attributes that are relevant to evaluating the offer.

These attributes include the unit of measure, the quantity of units desired, and the lead time required, as well as the shipping and payment terms. As a category manager, you cannot say if it's a good deal or not without inspecting these elements alongside the line item's quoted price.

As you can see, even hitting one tennis ball back over the net is hardly a simple matter for the category manager. Hitting one tennis ball back requires that the category manager must first identify and then execute the correct next step across every line item for the quote's market basket, which may include giving the supplier's sales team feedback and asking for a revised quote.

It may also require that the category manager contact other suppliers to solicit additional quotes. The cognitive task facing the category manager upon receiving the quote is indeed far more complex than the one facing the tennis player with the tennis ball.

And yet, category managers, procurement directors, and buyers at large enterprises around the world receive and act on quotes every day, negotiate better deals, form Master Service Agreements, cut purchase orders, and perform a litany of other tasks that effectively match their organization's internal demand with available offers from across their base of qualified suppliers. Indeed, despite having millions of forehands, backhands, and volleys available at any given time in response to any given tennis ball, tennis players around the world somehow manage to see a ball, make contact with their racket, and hit the ball back over the net.

As I mentioned earlier, one of the ways that category managers working in enterprise procurement teams "hit the ball back over the net" is by obtaining multiple competitive quotes from other suppliers for the same set of line items. This process is often described as generating an "apples-to-apples" comparison based on total value rather than lowest price. Having more than one option also gives these procurement teams additional leverage for negotiating a better deal.

In fact, this practice for generating competitive leverage through optionality by requesting and comparing multiple quotes is often explicitly required by the corporate procurement policy of many large enterprises. The prevalence of this guidance in corporate procurement policies is sometimes called "three bids and a buy" as competition among suppliers has the well-documented power to improve the "best and final" offer that is ultimately approved by the customer.

The practice of requiring buyers at large enterprises to solicit multiple competitive quotes is extremely common as a matter of corporate procurement policy. In the United States, the Better Business Bureau identifies three benefits associated with getting at least three quotes: (1) Save on cost, (2) Find the right fit, and (3) Vet trustworthiness.

The purpose of collecting multiple offers is not just to reduce cost—it is to secure a better deal holistically with a preferred supplier. While collecting multiple quotes can result in measurable costs savings, its primary purpose is to secure the right supplier at a best value price and terms while also ensuring clear and auditable communication of the requirements associated with whatever is being procured. The process itself helps form a common understanding between buyer and seller regarding what value is being procured and on what terms.

Thus, regardless of cost savings, the process of evaluating multiple offers from suppliers is widely considered to be a best practice. The logic is similar to interviewing multiple candidates during a hiring process. Interviewing more candidates often increases the odds of hiring the best person for the job.

However, what then happens to the quantity of required labor hours (clock time) and the length of the process (calendar time) associated with our category manager when you go from one quote to three? What happens to a game of tennis when your rallying partner decides to hit three balls over the net at once?

Indeed, it is hard to argue that the game of tennis does not get fractally more difficult with three balls at once. For all the documented and well-understood advantages of requesting and comparing three or more quotes, it clearly makes the game of enterprise procurement and supply chain much more difficult as well, especially at scale.

Yet, the reality of most enterprise procurement teams is that they are performing these quote requests, quote analyses, supplier negotiations, and supplier best value selections at massive simultaneous scale across numerous simultaneous workstreams and across multiple simultaneous geographies. And the underlying markets that influence the costs of the goods and services being offered by suppliers are continuously changing at an ever-accelerating rate.

If it were only three quotes at a time, that would make a happy time at work for most large enterprise procurement teams. The harsh reality is that category managers are often responsible for groups of budget owners who are acting on hundreds of processes every week, and a single quote could contain thousands of uniquely identified items, each one with numerous individually associated attributes and features. Thus, the enterprise procurement team's cognitive game of tennis really looks a bit more like countless balls coming toward you at once, an overwhelming number of balls that makes it functionally impossible to return them all.

While this span of responsibilities may seem completely overwhelming, let's also remember that negotiating and acting on quotes is only one part of a category manager's job. Increasingly, enterprise procurement and supply chain teams must manage numerous supplier relationships, sell the value of their agreements internally to budget owners, and perform a whole host of activities related to launching new products, reconciling supplier agreements during mergers and acquisitions, and managing audit trails and compliance across a complex portfolio of third-party spend.

Historically, the procurement profession's approach to this overwhelming portfolio of responsibilities was twofold: 1) use the Pareto Principle to only focus on the ~20% of suppliers that represent ~80% of enterprise spend, and 2) hire very loyal employees with extraordinarily long tenures as category managers. During the early 2000s and 2010s it was common to meet procurement and supply chain professionals who had been in the same role for 20+, 30+, and even 40+ years. These extraordinarily long tenures enabled category managers to develop deep expertise in specific markets, geographies, and supply categories. Procurement category managers would have decades of domain expertise in procuring categories like Raw Materials, Capital Equipment, Packaging, Logistics, and Maintenance, Repair, and Operation (MRO), which often includes the negotiated procurement of spare parts and General Stores inventory.

Long tenures also allowed category managers in procurement teams to develop deep and trusting relationships with suppliers, which greatly simplifies the cognitive task associated with both negotiation and supplier selection during a quote analysis process. However, many of these tenured professionals retired or semi-retired following the onset of the 2020 pandemic when a lot of supply chains experienced significant disruptions. The buyers and category managers who replaced them often lacked the same long-tenured domain expertise, detailed knowledge of their respective category's markets, or trusted relationships with their suppliers.

Today the average tenure of a category manager in an enterprise procurement team is less than five years, and job-hopping even at the two-year mark has become increasingly common for procurement professionals. The result is that the domain knowledge needed by a category manager to even identify the line items within the market basket table of a quote is often less than adequate for the task at hand, representing a tremendous loss of institutional knowledge and category know-how.

This table is a small sample of a market basket from an actual quote in the procurement category of Maintenance, Repair, and Operations (MRO). Looking at these line-item identifiers, can you identify and estimate a reasonable cost for every item and get this request to a best next step so that you can hit the ball back over the net and put it in the supplier's court?

1045939	BEARING,DOUBLE ROW,80MMIDX140MMOD
1045940	KEY,FEATHER,28X16X180
1045941	RING,RETAINING,FRM215/14
1045943	BEARING,PILLOW BLOCK,110MM
1045944	FUSE,CLASS J,TIME DELAY,250A
1045945	LUBRICANT,OIL,COMPRESSOR 1 LITER

There's an even more powerful reason why better deals take longer. The traditional process stack for supplier dealmaking creates incentives for both sides to delay. Research by economist

Paul Oyer[1] found that these incentives concentrate sales activity near fiscal year-end, as sellers work to close deals before reporting periods end. Salespeople are often trained to hold back their best and final offer in order to close their deals prior to year-end, allowing them to earn individual bonus compensation. This also means that there's an incentive for procurement negotiators to withhold their sign-off on a deal as a negotiation tactic to extract additional concessions from salespeople. What we have here is a process where both sides have an incentive to delay required steps. Delays in supplier deal-making create costs. The spike year-end activity also magnifies the dynamic we described earlier: oversubscribed procurement teams with limited bandwidth who are forced to triage their best people's attention to handle the fractal complexity of negotiating multiple offers.

Harnessing Impatience: Using the Predictive Enterprise to Win with Budget Owners

Budget owners often want procurement teams to approve their deals faster. And yet, if they could get the same value from the preferred supplier at a lower cost, it is hard to dispute this outcome is more desirable than overpaying. How can procurement and supply chain teams harness the impatience of budget owners to drive toward a predictive process stack across the enterprise?

The key is to connect the value of predictive procurement with the underlying double bind that pits procurement and budget owners on different sides in a world where better deals take longer.

This simple chart illustrates how procurement teams at large enterprises have successfully used the impatience of budget owners to ignite their Predictive Enterprise journeys:

Traditional Process Stack	Predictive Process Stack
Offers are created by suppliers	Offers are created by procurement
Offers are created manually by salespeople	Offers are created using AI, then reviewed by salespeople
Better deals take longer to negotiate	Better deals are faster and take fewer steps

Budget owners are often initially skeptical of AI. Perhaps they have been told in the past that "digital transformations" would make their lives easier, only to spend months and years on systems' integrations. But that's why it is important to show that the Predictive Enterprise isn't just about technology. It's about using technology to enable new ways of working. Specifically, the Predictive Enterprise approach is designed to enable processes that have fewer steps and far less manual clerical support by procurement teams to maintain forward momentum.

In predictive procurement, AI simulates the entire multi-offer process before it begins in order to generate a target outcome. AI then gives your suppliers suggested offers that you can approve instantly once the suppliers have reviewed and approved. That's fewer steps. In a traditional process stack, better deals often take longer to settle because they require collecting more quotes and negotiating more times back-and-forth with more suppliers.

What if a predictive process stack offered better deals with fewer steps, less clock time, and less calendar time than less desirable deals with higher costs?

What if you could get multiple competitive quotes and approve your deal *faster* in the predictive process stack than you could get a single non-competitive quote approved today?

What if the better deals at your enterprise actually got done *faster* than the average deals?

Use Cases in Manufacturing: The Power of Removing Steps

Often, the challenge associated with measuring success in a supplier negotiation comes with apparent conflicts around comparing the perceived value of different suppliers.

For these three use cases, I am sharing outcomes associated with different large enterprises that used the Predictive Enterprise approach to redesign the process stack for their offer-to-agreement negotiations with suppliers and achieved a very specific outcome:

- The resulting deal continued the relationship with the existing preferred suppliers
- Same item specification, lead time, and requirements
- The resulting deal significantly lowered costs relative to the validated baseline costs

By normalizing for all other factors associated with the outcome of this negotiation, I think it's safe to assume that for all stakeholders involved, from Finance to Operations to the budget owner, the outcome delivered by the predictive process stack is unanimously considered to be a win.

Predictive Procurement for Electrical Components

Problem Statement:

> Multi-round negotiations at this manufacturer were rare due to the effort they demanded, resulting in limited cost savings and minimal supplier engagement. As a result, procurement lacked the agility to respond to shifting market dynamics or drive meaningful value across sourcing events. During times of peak demand, procurement was often backlogged, meaning that they would in certain cases revert to being price-takers and order-placers rather than leveraging their purchasing power for better deals.

Results Statement:

> Supplier negotiations using the Predictive Enterprise were completed in half the time, suppliers lowered costs round-over-round, and the company achieved greater savings with less manual effort. The new process drove efficiency and improved sourcing outcomes. Before implementing a predictive process stack, this manufacturer collected quotes through legacy software solutions, which they described as an overly manual and tedious process. Using a predictive procurement approach, the procurement team executed a multi-round negotiation with 20 supplier organizations in half the time compared to their existing process. Not only was the budget owner delighted by the speed, but the preferred supplier's offer saved 10%.

Predictive Sourcing for Raw Materials in a Chemical Formula

Problem Statement:

This chemical manufacturer's sourcing process was manual, repetitive, and time-consuming—limiting the number of events procurement teams could run simultaneously and reducing their ability to manage complex spend efficiently. This limitation was especially noticeable for large market baskets, which needed to be broken up into smaller negotiations even when the same suppliers were offering quotes on each project. This resulted in a backlog of projects and led to missed savings opportunities and resource strain across the team. Procurement buyers were often bogged down by administrative tasks, leaving little time for strategic sourcing or supplier development.

Results Statement:

The procurement teams ran 20x the sourcing projects in less than half the prior cycle time, achieving 13% savings through competitive, multi-round negotiations. Efficiency and productivity improved, freeing up time for strategic initiatives and higher-value work. Individual contributor productivity for each member of the procurement team increased by 6x across their spend portfolio. The suppliers were excited by the faster deal velocity, since the predictive process shortened the time between submitting an offer (which was provided to them as a suggested offer by the procurement team's AI model), and receiving a contract. The suggested offer also gave the suppliers insight into which line items of the business opportunity they were most likely to win, which improved the transparency and predictability of the process.

Strategic Procurement of over $100M in Steel for Engineered-to-Order Equipment

Problem Statement:

A global engineering company had traditionally taken a project-by-project approach to negotiating procurement spend for stainless steel. This strategy lacked the leverage and efficiency of long-term, bundled agreements, leading to higher costs, missed savings, additional manual effort, and increased organizational risk. A lot of time was spent cleaning data in supplier quotes rather than benchmarking the grades of steel against the market to set data-driven cost targets and create measurable leverage.

Results Statement:

Suppliers submitted competitive quotes, with the lowest offering 35% savings. The global engineering company ultimately chose to remain with its incumbent supplier, successfully renegotiating rates at a 32% reduction from historical pricing. This both secured substantial savings and preserved a trusted supplier relationship. It also helped to establish the total cost of ownership for this supplier compared to available competitive alternatives, which strengthened the long-term supplier relationship.

The Vice President of Global Supply Chain Perspective

The Vice President of Global Supply Chain shared the following perspective on this sourcing event for steel:

"Now I'll give you a real tangible example. In the last year we went to market for our global steel bid for the first time ever. Historically, we bought steel as individual sites, not aggregating our demand together, not leveraging our buying power. And we buy a decent amount of steel, not as much as automotive, but about $100 million in steel each year across a wide

> variety of different types of products. And in one particular case, we had two manufacturing sites that are about two hours away from each other that have never coordinated their steel buying. Ever. Just hadn't done it. So when we went to market and put this through Arkestro, we found that in that one example, with the two sites, we saved 32% versus what we had previously paid.
>
> "And I'll add: with our incumbent. Not with a new supplier. With our incumbent. So we were able to go to market, bring that market data back, through competition, through game theory, and end up in a position where we were much better off with our current supplier. So we didn't have to go through the change management of vetting a new supplier, bringing them on, doing trials, things like that. We were able to execute that quickly."

These results are particularly striking for an enterprise AI project, given the data that shows the vast majority of AI projects do not generate meaningful Return on Investment. In 2025, MIT's Project NANDA came out with a report titled "State of AI in Business, 2025." This report found that 95% of all AI projects in large enterprises are getting zero return on investment.

The MIT NANDA report found: "Just 5% of integrated AI pilots are extracting millions in value, while the vast majority remain stuck with no measurable P&L impact. This divide does not seem to be driven by model quality or regulation, but seems to be determined by approach."

That is a shocking finding.

It also suggests the extraordinary opportunity for those seeking to be among the 5% ". . . extracting millions in value . . ." versus the 95% getting ". . . no measurable P&L impact."

Measurably Better Outcomes, Faster Time-to-Value, Less Clock time Per Negotiated Offer

In these examples, the procurement teams used the Predictive Enterprise's three pillars to eliminate steps from the traditional process of going from offers to agreements.

Faster-Than-Human Decisions: Suggested offers allowed for a Faster-Than-Human decision around what offer was most desirable for each line item being sourced from suppliers.

Humanless Loops: AI-generated baselines enabled Humanless Loops that set cost baselines for each item while considering every relevant constraint and attribute. AI was also able to filter for outliers and anomalies, preventing messy data from introducing errors.

Outcome-Based Process Re-engineering: By understanding what the range of potential offers might look like before the negotiation even began, the procurement team was able to quickly get to next steps with every supplier simultaneously, rather than serially.

Eliminating steps in a traditional process stack is the primary characteristic of predictive procurement, a model where procurement makes offers to the suppliers instead of vice versa.

In doing so, predictive procurement eliminates the two steps of the traditional procurement process that often take the longest:

(1) the step where the supplier must create a quote by understanding the enterprise's demand and requirements, and
(2) the step where the category manager or the sourcing analyst must benchmark and evaluate the quote, compare it with other potential competitive quotes, and decide what to do next.

By eliminating steps from the traditional process stack associated with procurement, predictive AI enables a fundamentally redesigned process capable of delivering measurable benefits.

Empathizing with the Skeptics When Advancing the Predictive Enterprise

At this point, you may be asking yourself the question: If predictive procurement is truly so powerful and the results are so measurable and impactful, then why doesn't everyone do it?

Isn't the value proposition of "better deals, faster" obvious?

The reasons that people in large enterprise procurement teams resist transitioning to a predictive process stack may surprise you. Below we'll unpack some of the reasons that predictive procurement generates social discomfort. We'll also look at why addressing concerns associated with people's pre-existing beliefs about negotiations candidly and empathically is an important part of creating sustainable change and building organizational momentum in the Predictive Enterprise.

Reactive Procurement	Predictive Procurement
Measure outcome vs **backward-**looking baseline	Measure outcome vs **forward-**looking target
Quote is created by supplier, then analyzed and cleaned by procurement analyst	Quote is drafted by predictive AI and offered to the supplier who revises, receives feedback, and submits
Quotes from approved suppliers are compared apples-to-apples primarily based on lowest price	Quotes from approved suppliers are instantly ranked on all relevant dimensions, including capacity and lead time
Quotes from sole source or single source suppliers are often approved by default due to lack of leverage	Quotes from sole source or single source suppliers are instantly compared versus the predicted outcome and AI suggests fixes
Quoting can introduce errors in Item IDs and descriptions that complicate procurement's "data foundation" with noise	Quoting can validate and match multiple Item IDs, thereby continuously improving the quality of procurement's "data foundation"

The Contrarian Hypothesis of Predictive Procurement: Game Theory and Behavioral Science Win Out Over Social Discomfort

Believe it or not, when we started designing, building, and testing prototypes for the technology to enable predictive procurement back in 2017, there were not very many enterprise executives who were enthusiastic about the value proposition. In fact, I distinctly remember quite a few Chief Procurement Officers telling me that I must be an idiot. This idea for predictive procurement must be unworkable, even in a single supplier negotiation, let alone at enterprise scale. For years, experienced procurement practitioners would try to persuade me of the error of my ways. To this day, I still encounter individuals who believe that the idea of preempting a tendering process with a suggested offer indicates a kind of fundamental insanity, or at least a profound foolishness.

Why was there such a strong negative reaction to the idea of predictive procurement?

Because, despite its benefits, predictive procurement contains a core contrarian hypothesis about how negotiations work. Many people have been taught that making the first offer in a negotiation places you at a disadvantage. Because of this pervasive belief, the concept of predictive procurement may create social discomfort.

Part of what gave our early team at Arkestro conviction around predictive procurement was lessons learned about social discomfort from disruptive startups like Uber and Airbnb. When Uber started, it wasn't immediately obvious that people would be willing to overcome the fear, awkwardness, or hesitation associated with getting into the back seat of a stranger's car. Same with Airbnb. Inexpensive lodging in a vibey apartment may sound like a no-brainer now, but early on it wasn't clear that large numbers of travelers would be comfortable renting rooms from random people. To an extent, the contrarian hypotheses of both Uber and Airbnb involved betting that consumers would indeed overcome their social discomfort about stranger danger in order to enjoy the benefits of a superior product experience and a better value cost structure.

In hindsight, both bets turned out to be correct. Uber and Airbnb created wildly successful businesses. Both companies went public and created tens of billions of dollars in shareholder value.

At the beginning, however, success was far from certain.

The leading indicator of this disruptive opportunity for Uber and Airbnb, however, was not the technology itself but the pain, hassle, and inconvenience associated with traditional options. Hailing a ride without an app can be an unpleasant experience even when it's not cold and rainy or late at night. And with Uber you no longer had to experience the hassle of walking to a busy street corner, sticking out your hand and waving it around. You could hail a ride right on the app from your phone and a car would magically appear.

Critically, Uber also represents an early example of the Predictive Enterprise. Uber fundamentally transforms the experience of getting a ride by making one crucial change in the consumer's decision-making process. Uber provides riders with an agreed-upon price upfront, before a purchasing decision gets made. In contrast, most taxis and private cars at the time Uber launched charged riders using a meter. Riders would only find out at the end of a ride how much money they owed.

This seemingly minor change, enabled by the same type of predictive pricing models and AI that power predictive procurement in Arkestro, was transformative in terms of creating demand. Predictive pricing in Uber dramatically expanded the market of people willing to hail a ride in the first place. It turns out that one of the main reasons that people avoided metered taxis or private cars prior to Uber was uncertainty regarding the cost of the ride, a phenomenon known as "meter anxiety."

Who truly wants to consume a product or service without knowing how much it will cost beforehand? Yet that is exactly how metered taxis and private cars in the traditional process stack worked.

Uber's use of predictive pricing and the ability to commit to an agreed-upon price upfront using a suggested offer alleviated this anxiety and enabled consumers to make an informed buying decision. This was significant. The result was that the pool of people willing to get into an Uber is significantly larger than the pool of people willing to get into a metered taxi. In fact, authorities in a number of cities such as San Francisco have even allowed taxis to join Uber's ride-hailing network in a program named the Taxi Upfront Fare Program, effectively allowing consumers to substitute algorithmic pricing for metered pricing. Research suggests that this allows taxi drivers to book more rides due to the consumer preference for agreed-upon pricing:

"Survey results indicate that consumers are highly price-sensitive, with 60% of respondents selecting 'price of trip' as the most important factor when choosing whether to book taxi trips based on the upfront or metered fare (either through different options offered via an app or across apps). In addition, riders exhibit a stronger preference for upfront fares during peak hours, with 63% selecting it as their preferred fare type, compared to 16% who prefer metered fares . . . 58% of respondents agree that upfront fares are fairer and more beneficial overall for taxi riders, while others have cited the fact that upfront fares completely eliminate meter anxiety during taxi trips . . ."[2]

However, Uber's use of the Predictive Enterprise also did something else. It transformed the incentives between the rider and the driver. This is because when the price of a ride is metered, the taxi driver actually makes more money by taking a less efficient route.

Detouring by taxis is a practice that is regarded as both unscrupulous and extremely common. Behavioral economists refer to this misalignment of incentives using the term "moral hazard." Moral hazard crops up in many places across the economy, from bathroom remodel contractors who get paid more if they make costly mistakes, all the way to health insurance companies that make more money by denying your claim regardless of your legitimate need for medical treatment. The profit motive is a strong incentive guiding behavior, and when this incentive is not aligned with creating customer value, that's when bad things start to happen.

In 2018 researchers sought to quantify the operational and economic value of moral hazard associated with taxis detouring relative to Ubers. They found that controlling for all other variables and looking at a sample of only airport trips to/from New York City, taxis detoured an average of 7.4% more than Ubers. Writing for the Centre for Economic Policy Research, researchers noted: "Detouring on average leads to longer trip durations. . . . These time-wasting detours are more likely to be taken by taxi drivers with more experience on the specific route, suggesting that experienced drivers knowingly take the inefficient route. This is strong evidence for moral hazard. This is a large efficiency loss. Taxi driver detours result in 150 lost passenger hours per day in NYC, plus additional costs to the taxi driver in terms of time, gasoline, and mileage on the car. The lost passenger time from Uber detours is 10 times smaller."

Frankly, 10x is a pretty astonishing delta between taxi drivers and Uber drivers from what initially appears as a small, incremental difference between driving behaviors.

Uber made a bet that riders would prefer a system that leveraged AI to reduce moral hazard through transparent routing and an upfront offer-to-agreement flow that governs a ride's price.

Large enterprises that have implemented predictive procurement made a similar bet about the benefits of much faster procurement cycles, much lower costs, and a transformative reduction in the complexity associated with requesting, analyzing, comparing, and negotiating hundreds of thousands of quoted offers every year.

Overcoming the Speed and Cost Double Bind Means Reckoning with Fear of the Winner's Curse

Over the past decade, I have seen procurement and supply chain teams on the Predictive Enterprise journey encounter skepticism and hesitations and then overcome them by delivering better deals faster at scale. However, the social discomfort associated with not making a first offer in a negotiation is so widespread that it even has a name: Fear of the Winner's Curse.

The Winner's Curse is a phenomenon observed by game theorists and behavioral economists where motivated buyers involved in a transaction that involves price-setting (e.g. where no pre-determined price is listed) tend to make offers that are higher than economically rational.

Richard Thaler, who famously wrote a book on the topic, offered the following experiment. Imagine that you have a jar full of coins that you are auctioning off. The optimal winning bid is therefore less than the value of the coins in the jar (unless the winning bidder perhaps valued the jar itself separately and in excess of the value of the coins). However, Thaler shows that the following two outcomes tend to result from such an auction: (1) the average bid price is less than the value of coins in the jar, and (2) the winning bid price tends to exceed the value of coins in the jar. Therefore, the winner has won, but at the cost of offering a higher price than is economically rational.

Fear of the Winner's Curse is embodied in the folk assumption that to make the first offer in a negotiation is to put oneself at a disadvantage and is effectively to negotiate against oneself. However, except in rare cases where the buyer has next to zero information, making the first offer in negotiations results in measurable economic gains due to the so-called "anchoring effect." The "anchoring effect" indicates that the first price offered in a negotiation creates a psychological anchor that frames the participants' perceptions around what constitutes a "good deal."

Thirty years of research on interpersonal, business-to-business, and even online negotiations show that making the first offer in a price negotiation positively influences the outcome in favor of the offeror. One 2001 study by Galinsky and Mussweiler even went as far as to show that over half of the variance in negotiation outcomes could simply be attributed to who went first in the negotiation.

However, this research has had negligible impact on popular conceptions about business-to-business negotiations like the kind of dealmaking that takes place in enterprise supply chains. It has not effectively dispelled the Fear of the Winner's Curse when it comes to procurement teams.

In fact, there have even been studies that suggest that negotiation participants find the experience of this discomfort overpowering despite the economic benefits of going first in a negotiation. A 2014 study by Rosette, Kopelman, and Abbott reported: "Two studies tested whether making first offers influences negotiators' feelings of anxiety and their sense of satisfaction. The results of Study 1 show that the strategy of making the first offer led to decreased levels of satisfaction with the negotiation process and outcomes. This effect was mediated by perceived feelings of anxiety. Study 2 discerned that anxiety about making the first offer derived from self-perception concerns, represented as anxiety about being taken advantage of by the opposing party. In both studies, anxiety led negotiators who made the first offer to be relatively less satisfied with the negotiation, than negotiators who did not make the first offer, despite the increased economic gains associated with making the first offer."

This social discomfort and Fear of the Winner's Curse is part of why quite a few Chief Procurement Officers thought I was an idiot back in 2017 when we first started working on the AI models that power predictive procurement at Arkestro. Our hypothesis ran contrary to their fundamental belief structure about how negotiations with suppliers ought to work, a belief structure that was built up around generations of folk wisdom.

This folk wisdom reflects a general bias in negotiations: most people hate losing more than they love winning, even if the economic value of winning at scale is measurably greater. Nobel Prize-winning behavioral economist Daniel Kahneman estimated that most people hate losing twice as much as they love winning: "People put a lot more weight on negative events than on positive events, and on losses than on gains . . . if people are to gamble money on the toss of a coin and they stand to lose $100 they will demand more than $200 to accept the gamble which is in some ways ridiculously risk averse."[3] Loss aversion is especially true in supply chain, where losing is often more measurable and meaningful than winning, and failure is often punished more harshly than success is rewarded.

Learning to Love Winning vs. Fear Losing: Outcome-based Process Re-engineering

On its surface, the concept of getting a better deal faster than a worse deal is a no-brainer.

However, once you peel back the onion, you can see that the real work in moving from a traditional process stack to a predictive process stack involves empathizing with the social discomfort associated with the change and then staying focused on the business outcome.

Over the past decade, I have seen people get wrapped around the axle by trying to define the perfect process step-by-step for every archetype of spend and every category of supplier relationship.

You can spend a lot of time trying to define a process for strategic spend versus long-tail spend, for commodities versus services, and for new product introduction versus existing product lines. Process mapping is often helpful and necessary, but it is by no means sufficient to move the needle when it comes to changing behaviors at the scale of large enterprises. Instead, it's better to empathize with why the traditional process works the way it works today and look at the trade-offs it creates between the different personas.

In this case, the double bind is between process speed and the value in the form of cost savings, between budget owners on one hand, and procurement on the other.

This trade-off will exist in any traditional process stack where better deals take longer because they consume more back-and-forth rounds of negotiation, more calendar days, and more clock-time from the procurement team. At scale, this trade-off leads budget owners and their employees to circumvent the procurement process entirely for urgent, fast-moving deals.

As an advocate for the Predictive Enterprise at your own company, you can simply ask: What if there were a better way? What if the budget owner's desired outcome aligned perfectly with procurement's desired outcome? What would it take to align the outcome of better deals with the fewest and fastest number of steps?

Rather than spending a tremendous amount of time mapping or defining the current process as it exists today, it's probably more helpful to illustrate what trade-offs a process architecture creates between competing outcomes that are prioritized differently for different personas, such as cost above speed for procurement, or speed above cost for the budget owner.

As Wharton professor Ethan Mollick notes on his Substack:

> "One thing you learn studying (or working in) organizations is that they are all actually a bit of a mess. In fact, one classic

> organizational theory is actually called the Garbage Can Model. This views organizations as chaotic 'garbage cans' where problems, solutions, and decision-makers are dumped in together, and decisions often happen when these elements collide randomly, rather than through a fully rational process. Of course, it is easy to take this view too far—organizations do have structures, decision makers, and processes that actually matter. It is just that these structures often evolved and were negotiated among people, rather than being carefully designed and well-recorded. The Garbage Can represents a world where unwritten rules, bespoke knowledge, and complex and undocumented processes are critical. It is this situation that makes AI adoption in organizations difficult, because even though 43% of American workers have used AI at work, they are mostly doing it in informal ways, solving their own work problems. Scaling AI across the enterprise is hard because traditional automation requires clear rules and defined processes, the very things Garbage Can organizations lack."

That's why defining or mapping an existing process is important, but not enough to advance the Predictive Enterprise to create a process stack with more bandwidth and faster throughput. What are some signposts for measuring success in the Predictive Enterprise?

You can begin to see more frequent, measurable convergence of business outcomes that are gratifying to multiple personas' priorities simultaneously, rather than trading finance's priorities against operations, or procurement's priorities against the budget owner. Below is a framework that any enterprise with a process that runs on people filling out fields in a form can use to understand what the Predictive Enterprise opportunity might look like for a given process. In the next chapter, I'll share what this type of thinking looks like at enterprise scale across a global supply base where the historic conflict is between procurement on one hand, and operations on the other, over the optimal number of suppliers for an enterprise to manage.

Predictive Process Framework: Measuring the Predictability and Transparency of a Process's Path and Speed Under Variable Conditions Across Different Personas

Undefined	The predictability, standardized steps, and current state of a given process are unknown, unmeasured, and undefined. Nor is it known how the process path, speed, or output is affected by variable conditions.
Defined	The predictability and standardized steps of a given process are measured in quantified units of time and activity that enable a critical path (or "happy path") to be mapped and its target speed estimated. Additionally, the current state of the process is transparent and accessible, enabling the process' status to be measured, monitored, and managed continuously. However, the full range of the process's response to variable conditions, anomalous or exceptional cases, and associated trigger thresholds or path-switching decisions are left to ad hoc case-by-case process execution.
Reactive	The predictability and standardized steps of a given process are measured in quantified units of time and activity and the full range of responses has been defined according to threshold-based exception triggers using conditional logic that enables clear path-switching decisions to match the desired best next step with a range of possible variable circumstance scenarios. Additionally, the current state of the process and events within and adjacent to the process are transparent and accessible, as well as consumable by a monitoring and decisioning agent capable of intervening in the process as it runs. This level may also be described as Prescriptive.

(*continued*)

Predictive	The predictability and standardized steps of a given process are measured in quantified units of time and activity. The full range of responses to variable circumstances has been defined according to threshold-based exception triggers using conditional logic such that the steps in the process can be re-sequenced, re-ordered, and conditionally eliminated or repeated based on the observation of the current state of the process or events within or adjacent to the process by a monitoring and decisioning agent. The predictability and standardized steps of a given process may also be re-sequenced, re-ordered, and conditionally eliminated or repeated based on the agent's inference of a prediction for the process's most likely current outcome compared with a hypothetical outcome based on a change made to the standardized steps in the process. Critically, any change to the standardized steps, recommendations, or observability of process is made based on the predicted impact of these changes on the outcome of the specific process currently in-flight.

4

Better Deals, Safer

Overcoming the Supplier Rationalization and Resiliency Double Bind

THE CORE CHALLENGE procurement and supply chain teams face today can best be understood as a balancing act—balancing conflicting priorities and ever-changing constraints.

Measuring success in supply chain is not always easy. Yet one thing is clear. If the supply doesn't show up when and where it's supposed to, then something has gone horribly wrong.

Thus, optimizing for any one target objective without constraints on supplier performance can potentially prove disastrous. That's why procurement and supply chain strategy must be holistic, contextual, and balanced, including the introduction of AI into enterprise supply chains.

In his 1984 book *The Goal*, Dr. Eliyahu M. Goldratt observed this pattern in the case of manufacturing and codified it into a management framework called the Theory of Constraints. Rather than fight constraints, Dr. Goldratt argues that constraints are inherent to the process of managing the flow of materials and products through a manufacturing supply chain.

In the previous chapter, I focused on informal constraints dictated by the growing impatience of budget owners associated with the length and labor of a procurement process. However, that's very different from a formal operational constraint on lead time, which is often dictated by a manufacturing site's commitment to a detailed production schedule.

For manufacturing enterprises, the costs associated with failures or delays of the supply chain when it comes to running production are significant. These costs are measured in millions or tens of millions of dollars in wasted production capacity per hour. Supply chain failures negatively impact every operational metric of the enterprise in measurable and meaningful ways. And it fundamentally reduces the predictability of operating a large business at scale.

However, the recommended best practice for supply chain resiliency (to have multiple suppliers on contract for each material, good, or service) often runs in apparent contradiction to the best practice for leveraging purchasing power in dealmaking (to consolidate spend with as few suppliers as possible, thereby unlocking volume-based discounts and economies of scale).

In this chapter, I'll share how supply chain teams are using the Predictive Enterprise to overcome this apparent double bind between finance on one hand and operations on the other by aligning better cost outcomes with more resilient supply chain configurations.

If better deals can be re-designed to happen faster, why can't they be made safer, too?

Supplier Rationalization for Third-Party Risk Reduction and Economies of Scale

Large enterprises with global footprints are moving to actively reduce their total number of suppliers. This is a best practice initiative commonly referred to as "supplier rationalization."

The goal of these projects is straightforward: to reduce third-party risk, to consolidate spend with preferred suppliers, thereby unlocking volume-based discounts, and to reward trusted suppliers with higher rates of contract utilization. Len DeCandia shared this perspective as a four-time Chief Procurement Officer at several major publicly traded life sciences and pharmaceutical enterprises: "When I started at Johnson & Johnson, we had around 95,000 suppliers operating in about 130 countries for $40 billion in annual spend. That's a high cost to manage, and at the scale we're talking about supply management costs can impact operating margins. When I retired a decade later, we had around 42,000 suppliers in around 100 countries, with roughly the same amount of spend. Because as a Chief Procurement Officer, I regard every unique supplier as another source of business risk."

That makes sense from a compliance perspective. Every supplier creates costs associated with regulatory compliance that's magnified and multiplied by the number of countries. Compliance costs include everything from conducting due diligence associated with anti-money laundering legislation to ensuring alignment with trade sanctions. But doesn't shrinking the supply base also introduce risks, too? What about the risks of single points of failure?

Today, procurement and supply chain teams are often being told to mitigate risk and handle volatility from catastrophic events. That means having more suppliers, not fewer, right? Every time there's a war, an extreme weather event, or a geopolitical conflict that reduces the speed, throughput, or economics of cross-border trade, the message we hear is: Don't have all your eggs in one basket. Supply bases should be understood as diversified portfolios—a single-stock portfolio is a very risky portfolio.

Well, which is it? Should we have more suppliers or fewer suppliers?

On the surface, these goals are in direct conflict.

The Case for Supplier Rationalization

Supplier rationalization simplifies procurement by reducing scale to a manageable level. Instead of "boiling the ocean," teams often use the Pareto Approach (the 80/20 rule) to focus on the 20% of suppliers that account for 80% of total spend.

While the Pareto Approach prioritizes the most impactful relationships, it leaves the "long tail"—the remaining 80% of suppliers—unaddressed. Teams handle this tail by consolidating orders with redundant suppliers into agreements with preferred suppliers to achieve rationalization. Many procurement and supply chain teams wish they could simply eliminate the "long tail" of suppliers altogether, or hand them off to be managed by a third party.

The Case for Supply Chain Resiliency

The argument for supply chain resiliency is comparatively simple, especially for enterprises with global supply chains. Being dependent upon a small number of suppliers—and especially single sources—creates systemic risk, not just to cost or profitability, but to business continuity.

The pandemic showed everyone what happens to supply chains when borders close suddenly. Tariffs and wars have reinforced this painful and expensive lesson.

Thus, procurement and supply chain teams are also being told to diversify their supply base, even as they are also being told to reduce the total number of suppliers through rationalization. Hence, the apparent double bind within the traditional process stack.

Better Deals, Safer: Using the Predictive Enterprise Approach to Reduce Single-Source Risk While Still Decreasing the Total Number of Suppliers

Traditional procurement builds resilience by adding suppliers. Using the Predictive Enterprise flips this: you can reduce total suppliers while simultaneously increasing the alternative sources for every part, material, component, service agreement, and shipping lane.

By grouping suppliers into cohorts based on substitutability and stress-testing against risk scenarios, existing suppliers can serve as backup sources across multiple items. This reduces both supplier count and single-source risk. AI makes it easier than ever to create these cohorts of contextual substitutes for every uniquely identified part, material, component, service agreement, and shipping lane that you source and procure across your portfolio of third-party spend. This also has the side benefit of creating an effective supplier directory, indexed at the item level, and sorted based on the geographical context of the incoming demand signal.

By simulating the process of a multi-offer supplier negotiation before it begins, the Predictive Enterprise can generate and continuously refresh these cohorts of contextual substitutes at a global scale for every relevant business need in every local geography.

Contextual Substitutes vs. Multi-Sourcing: The Power of Incumbent Alternatives

The definition of an Incumbent Alternative supplier is a supplier who:

(1) has already completed a transaction with your organization (e.g. is already qualified to do business with your enterprise, is already set up and onboarded into your System of Record), and
(2) can provide an alternative offer to an existing single source supplier.

An Incumbent Alternative may be able to provide a contextual substitute for a demand signal if the current single source supplier is disrupted due to an unexpected catastrophic risk event.

By definition, an Incumbent Alternative supplier must provide multiple product lines or services. If the Incumbent Alternative were already providing the same product or service as the single source supplier, then that supplier would not be a single source supplier to begin with.

Rather than eroding the purchasing power of volume-based discounts by fragmenting demand even further, the Predictive Enterprise approach enables supply chain and procurement teams to identify potential Incumbent Alternatives and then solicits offers from them to validate their potential as a hypothetical contextual substitute.

The Predictive Enterprise approach is thus able to acknowledge the revealed preferences of supply managers that the single source contract decision reflects: a desire for fewer suppliers, lower compliance costs, deeper relationships, and being the Customer of Choice with strategic suppliers.

In the following examples, we'll explore how the use of the Predictive Enterprise approach created cohorts of Incumbent Alternatives suppliers to provide contextual substitutes in a way that not only generated cost leverage but improved supply resiliency by identifying a clear Plan B, Plan C, Plan D, and so on in the case of a catastrophic disruption event.

Predictive Logistics Management for North American Trucking

Problem Statement:

Before beginning their Predictive Enterprise journey, this construction materials manufacturer had a transportation team who was spread very thin across disconnected systems and processes. The team was buried in manual data work, and their legacy tools were too clunky to support real progress. As a result, a lot of freight capacity was ordered ad hoc and last minute by the production sites from the spot market with limited contract utilization and minimal leverage of purchasing power. Cost savings were a priority, but the existing process for sourcing rates from smaller carriers across the large portfolio of shipping lanes was simply too slow and inconsistent to scale effectively.

Results Statement:

By redesigning their carrier communication and rate management using the Predictive Enterprise approach, the transportation team had received offers from more than 400+ carriers on a logistics portfolio comprised of hundreds of to/from shipping lanes across North America. In addition to delivering meaningful cost reductions, the transportation team was able to help every production site to identify substitute freight capacity on every single lane using Incumbent Alternatives, creating visibility into their shipping capacity across multiple carriers. This visibility into carriers' capacity allowed them to both utilize their contracts more consistently and predictably, as well as reduce the time associated with sourcing spot rates.

Predictive Facilities Management for Site-Level Inspection Services

Problem Statement:

Before embarking on the Predictive Enterprise approach, this large oil and gas enterprise relied on a Time and Materials (T&M) model for inspection services at its refineries. Because the team couldn't effectively quote or negotiate with service providers at scale across all the service rates, costs were unpredictable and frequently over budget. The T&M model also made it difficult to control spend or compare performance across suppliers. As a result, different facilities were reliant on single source service providers to offer this critical site service to comply with applicable regulatory requirements.

Results Statement:

With the Predictive Enterprise approach, the facilities supplier management team transitioned from T&M to a fixed-price contract model that improved cost control and drove supplier competition. Simulating the offer-to-agreement process before it began enabled the team to clearly identify which single source suppliers offered contextual substitutes for each service rate at the refinery site level, since not all suppliers offer comparable services in all geographies. By creating cohorts of Incumbent Alternatives, the facilities supplier management team now has backups in case the preferred provider lacks capacity to provide an inspection within the required time period.

Predictive Landscaping, Snow Removal, and Site Services for Multi-Campus Retail

Problem Statement:

Before the Predictive Enterprise approach, each retail location managed its own supplier relationships across multiple categories of site services. With every location negotiating independently, pricing varied widely—even among stores in the same market. The decentralized approach limited visibility, especially into which suppliers could service which specific retail locations. This paradoxically meant that despite the enterprise having to manage hundreds of suppliers, resiliency at the retail location level was still low and most retail locations relied upon a single source for site services. This created challenges for both cost management and reliability.

Results Statement:

The multi-campus retail brand used the Predictive Enterprise approach to negotiate $21.3 million in spend across their retail network of 1,000+ distinct store locations and achieved more than $3 million in hard cost savings. The process of identifying Incumbent Alternatives at the site level now means that there are cohorts of contextual substitutes in the event that the supplier on contract for a specific site is unable to perform site services within the required time window. This availability of contextual substitutes enhances the resiliency of the supplier network for performing site service.

Incumbent Alternatives: A Strategy for AI to Boost Optionality During Supply Disruptions

Rather than requiring the fragmenting of demand across multiple suppliers upfront through multi-sourcing every demand signal, the use of Incumbent Alternatives builds supply chain resiliency through contingency options and contextual substitutes. This allows demand to cascade to alternative suppliers in the event that a primary or preferred supplier is knocked out or their capacity is unexpectedly depleted due to a catastrophic disruption event. In certain cases, this cascading of demand is simply a more directed, predictable form of spot buying, where the buying process sets price using a quote rather than a pre-negotiated contract.

However, this approach to developing systemic resiliency in the supply base by establishing cohorts of Incumbent Alternatives offers an exemplary use case of AI to create meaningful safeguards for supply continuity. As Arash Azadegan, professor of supply chain management at Rutgers Business School, notes in referring to the 2023 supply chain disruption in cancer drugs:

> "As of late, I am also intrigued to discover the applicability of novel Artificial Intelligence (AI) models and agents to supply management challenges, especially related to the phenomenon of 'Type 2 chaos' in supply chains, where predictions about a shortage can spread quickly, sparking a run on the market and further deepening the shortage.
>
> "Certainly, the US supply chain woes are related to this dynamic: our communication networks are able to spread sentiment virally, much faster than actors in a supply chain are able to communicate or revise demand signals. Therefore, the underlying dynamic behind most shortages, known as the 'Bullwhip Effect,' will become a sharper and sharper snap, with potentially devastating consequences, as we see in the cancer drug shortage.
>
> "Based on conversations with numerous stakeholders in the supply chain community, I have serious concerns that the introduction of AI into supply chain decision systems has the ability to rapidly accelerate and exacerbate these consequences. However, AI clearly also has the potential to help us increase the fundamental bulwark against harm: by building resilience and redundancy into our supply networks, by making sure that when it comes to supply management that efficiency and resiliency aren't zero-sum and enabling us to quickly respond by easily identifying spot capacity."

Writing in a 2023 *Harvard Business Review* article titled "How Global Companies Use AI to Prevent Supply Chain Disruptions," University of Arkansas professors of supply chain Remko van Hoek and Mary Lacity analyzed the technology and business impact associated with the Predictive Enterprise approach. Indeed, van Hoek and Lacity noted how AI can analyze patterns in historic transactions to not only generate Incumbent Alternatives but then can layer in predictive procurement capabilities to fetch additional offers from suppliers without adding cycle time.

Van Hoek and Lacity found that the predictive process is a measurable reduction in clock-time and calendar days from the process cycle time associated with pivoting demand:

> "Unlike traditional procurement methods that rely on managing suppliers based on high-level purchasing categories and aggregate spend, this AI tool delves into granular data, right down to the stock keeping unit (SKU). It generates supply options, often among existing suppliers, thereby reducing the need for drawn-out requests for quotes. The AI algorithm uses this historical data to automatically populate new requests for quotes (RFQs) with essential parameters like lead times, geographic locations, quantities, service-level agreements, and material costs. It then emails the RFQ to the respective supplier for review. A one-click submission is all it takes if the supplier agrees with the AI-generated quote. Should the supplier choose to modify the quote, the algorithm learns from these changes, continually refining its predictive capabilities. This mutually beneficial approach saves suppliers between 60% and 90% of the time typically spent on completing an RFQ."

Never Waste a Good Crisis: Investing in Speed and Supply Chain Agility as a Bulwark Against Systemic Risk From Future Catastrophic Supply Chain Disruption Events

Talking about supply chain risk in the context of large enterprise AI transformations is surprisingly difficult. This is in part because when risk is managed correctly, the successful outcome that gets measured is often: nothing. Nothing happens.

No one dies or gets injured, no orders get delayed, no customers complain or get frustrated, there are no cyberattacks, no negative media stories, no public backlash, and no one gets fired. It's just another day. A quiet day. Everything keeps running smoothly.

But often, "just another day" is the result of tremendous efforts undertaken by professionals across a range of functions working diligently to reduce systemic risk in operations, in compliance, in supply chain, in IT, and in finance. Professionals focused on managing third-party risk among suppliers will implement and execute processes and procedures that devote considerable resources toward constantly scanning for risks and stopping those risks from becoming actual harms.

Though often unsung heroes within their organization, it is the diligent stewardship of these third-party risk professionals that creates a workplace culture of vigilance and safety. These invisible costs associated with "just another day" can create a bias toward risk aversion among supply chain and procurement professionals that is often a well-earned bias based on experience.

It is also a bias that can make supply chain professionals resistant to change.

That's one reason why the concept of "never waste a good crisis" is so important. Historically, major companies neglected supply chain transformation and digital investments until catastrophic global disruptions, such as the pandemic, forced a change to happen.

Recent crises—from the pandemic to geopolitical upheavals like tariffs, the Suez Canal blockage, and the Ukraine and Iran conflicts—have exposed the fragility of supply chains built on Just In Time (JIT) principles. These catastrophic disruptions have highlighted the need for supply chain resiliency.

Amid these challenges, there lies an opportunity: supply chain crises can catalyze buy-in and funding for much-needed transformation initiatives associated with the Predictive Enterprise, such as creating cohorts of Incumbent Alternatives for critical materials and parts vulnerable to disruption.

Humans tend to address familiar issues before unfamiliar ones, making digital transformation in supply chains feel daunting. While the slow pace of change can frustrate leaders, understanding this bias to solve well-understood problems is crucial. Crises like shortages from wars or natural disasters clearly show that caution and consensus are often riskier than decisive actions taken quickly, especially if those actions are preventative rather than reactive.

It is also why the opportunities that we discussed in the prior chapters must be taken within the overall portfolio supply management, which include driving cost impact but never by adding unmanaged risk or decreasing supplier performance.

5

Better Deals, Easier

Overcoming the Scale and Bandwidth Double Bind

In the previous chapters, we looked at how procurement and supply chain teams are using the Predictive Enterprise to deliver better deals that are both faster and safer. But what about easier?

From the discussion of supplier rationalization and resiliency, it's evident that the core motion of decision-making in supply chain is a balancing act between different competing outcomes.

Balancing competing outcomes is hardly an easy feat. Let's imagine a literal balancing act—an acrobat at a circus who is spinning several plates at once. Let's say that each plate is a procurement project involving supplier selection, and each plate has three tiny plates balanced on it that are Cost, Quality, and Speed.

Now, let's imagine that the acrobat's ringmaster comes into the circus tent. "Times are tough," says the ringmaster. "And circus audiences have become more demanding. For our next performance, we're going to need to ask you to balance twice the number of plates."

The acrobat is stunned. Multiple plates, each of which is itself balancing three tiny plates, is already an extremely difficult challenge.

"Twice the number of plates is quite a tall order! Will there be additional acrobats able to assist me with the additional workload?"

The ringmaster shakes his head. "No. And in fact, we all think it might be even better if you did twice the plates while also balancing on one leg. To show that you are up for a challenge. And that you are a team player."

This is what introducing AI into enterprise procurement and supply chains often feels like. More plates to spin. More work to do. No additional acrobats. Just more plates. Standing on one leg, instead of two. A recent study by McKinsey found that over the past several years procurement teams have been asked to manage nearly 50% more spend. Almost none of these same teams have been given 50% more headcount to scale bandwidth proportional to workload. Asking the same number of people to do more work? This is how enterprises measure efficiency.

As we discussed in *Better Deals, Faster*, procurement is actually getting fractally harder due to skyrocketing complexity associated with the number of SKUs combined with much shorter professional tenures. But adding the dynamic of smaller, leaner teams, and the escalating workload makes projects like figuring out how AI can fit into existing tools and processes feel even more daunting and overwhelming.

The truth is, large enterprises will not be able to automate their way out of the bandwidth gap associated with leaner teams and heavier workloads. That's because full automation using AI requires both strong process definition and documentation alongside accessible, complete, and accurate data. Highly defined and well-documented process plus great data just isn't the reality that many procurement and supply chain teams are living in today, especially within a traditional process stack. That's why the Predictive Enterprise is not focused on automation, but rather is more about finding opportunities to re-design entire end-to-end workflows that can help teams remove manual steps and work backward from desired outcomes. But in order to enable this approach, it's critically important to understand why so many people who think about AI do so from the perspective of the Automation Enterprise. It's also important to understand how the Predictive Enterprise builds on this legacy foundation without requiring any rip-and-replace, but also without being limited by the traditional frameworks associated with Systems of Record.

Automation Enterprise	Predictive Enterprise
Automates Repetitive Task Completion Automation is focused on completing repetitive tasks that occur within a predictable sequence and observable flow.	**Faster-Than-Human Decisions** Predictive is focused on prompting faster-than-human decisions before a person would normally be aware of the need to act.
Human Must Configure & Initiate Automation Automation typically requires human to configure and initiate, then supervise until completion has been achieved.	**Humanless Loops** Predictive enables continuous monitoring of systems in motion to enable humanless loops focused on visibility and analysis.
Process Efficiency via Work Replacement Value is measured in units of human work replaced with machine work without making meaningful changes to the underlying process.	**Outcome-Based Process Re-Engineering** Value is measured by amplifying and accelerating human impact by allowing the steps in the process to dynamically change based on a predicted outcome.

Transforming Transformation Beyond Automation: Using Technology to Create Process

In the Automation Enterprise, which characterizes the development of technology in manufacturing and industrial enterprises since the beginning of the Industrial Revolution, the primary purpose of new technology advancement in an enterprise context is what Buckminster Fuller once stated: "Technology lets you do more and more with less and less until eventually you can do everything with nothing."

The Automation Enterprise gives us a theory of value, from implementing new technology that effectively maps all the required inputs for any enterprise business process to defined units of human activity, which are understood as both costs and dependencies to a given process running to completion and generating an output.

For example, in many digital supply chains, the work of approving suppliers' quotes is a dependency to generating a purchase order. This approval decision is a defined unit of work, and it's a dependency to the process running to completion. In a manufacturing line, loading materials or parts into a machine is often a dependency to running production. These loading tasks are defined units of work. If performing these units of work with machines instead of human workers produces the same output at lower cost, then the transformation delivers an improvement in efficiency.

In the Automation Enterprise, managers create and measure the value of automation by replacing defined units of human labor with identical units of machine activity, generating equivalent output without the labor costs. This replacement of human labor by machine activity is what enables the outcome of "do more with less" at scale. This labor substitution is also how large enterprises, especially those involved in manufacturing, have traditionally measured the relationship between investments in automation and the return on those investments associated with efficiency and productivity.

But when it comes to the AI paradigm shift, this is not the full story. Far from it.

Fuller's Ephemeralization and Outcome-Based Re-engineering of Physical Objects

Fuller persuasively made the case that this type of "do more with less" innovation also produces a second-order scale of efficiency through the progressive abstraction and dematerialization of the physical components of the work itself.

Take, as Fuller suggests, the door key as an example. Picture a physical key made of metal that is used to open a locked door. The key goes in the lock. The door opens. You can see that there must be all sorts of costs linked to the materials and labor required in order to mine and melt the metal, produce enough metal at a grade that is fit for making keys, and then you must also cut the metal into the precise shape of the specific key that will fit the door's lock.

But if you abstract away the function of the key from its specific physical embodiment, it quickly becomes clear that you could use a string of numbers or letters as a key (e.g. a password), or designate other existing objects to function as keys, such as fingerprints or irises (e.g. biometric authentication). Indeed, many new locks that you can buy today and install on your doors will allow you to use a string of numbers or your fingerprint as the key.

Fuller saw this trend toward dematerialization and abstraction as a lever for automation and efficiency as a core element of technological advancement, which he termed "ephemeralization" ("doing more with less" by effectively eliminating steps in a process through a progressive abstraction of their physical components). Ephemeralization is a foundational principle underlying Paul Graham's 2010 pronouncement that, "The advantages of doing things in software on a single device are so great that everything that can get turned into software will," and Marc Andreessen now-famous 2011 essay whose title summarized Graham's hypothesis by simply declaring that "Software is Eating the World."

What's different about what's happening today in the AI paradigm shift in comparison to previous waves of innovation is that what's being ephemeralized isn't an object like a door key that can be a fingerprint or a videotape that can now be a streaming file, or a camera or a wristwatch that can now be a widget on a smartphone.

Instead, it's our thought patterns, our decisions, our generative processes, our creativity, and our communication and coordination with each other. That's what AI can now often serve on-demand.

This is ephemeralization on a grand scale; it is a further abstraction of a process that is already quite abstract: decision-making itself. Disembodying and de-personalizing the process of decision-making from a human decision-maker may sound strange, because we often assume that decisions are grounded in personal and professional experience, tacit knowledge, and our embedded social roles that create trust and accountability. Yet to the extent that we can provide all the relevant inputs and context to an AI reasoning model, we may discover that it reaches decisions that are consistent with our own. In certain cases, AI may even make a better decision than we'd have made on our own.

Why AI in Systems of Action Differ from Automation in Systems of Record

AI is a big topic, and in this book, I have tried to avoid tech jargon rabbit holes as much as possible. If you want a primer on "what is AI" or "what is a Large Language Model" or "how is AI different from machine learning," you would likely be best served by asking ChatGPT (or your preferred Large Language Model) or watching a very short YouTube explainer video.

The truth is that a lot of these technical distinctions are just not that important for how and why AI creates dramatic business impact for large global enterprises. Talking about the inner workings of AI models also tends to make people's eyes glaze over. However, when executives at large enterprises ask me, "What's the one thing that I need to know about AI as a technology that's different than say, traditional digital automation?" there is always one important difference that comes to mind.

Whereas previous waves of digital technology have been driven by rules-based automation and programmable machines, AI is probabilistic and stochastic rather than deterministic.

Confused?

Let's break this statement down into its component parts.

Being probabilistic or stochastic means that AI will generate different outputs for the same input. For those familiar with digital technology, this can create confusion because it is the exact opposite of how we have been taught to understand computers, databases, and business applications in the System of Record world. Traditional automation operates on programming that applies a set of detailed and specific instructions to an input and thus always gives the same output.

But AI today is different.

This fact also means that we often do not and cannot know what the output of an AI will be prior to it being generated in response to a given prompt. This statement remains true even if we are able to produce a reasonable and valid post hoc explanation for why the output is the way it is. It also means that if you enter the same prompt into an AI system multiple times, you're very likely to get different outputs for each iteration.

If you think about a System of Record, where data that was once stored on paper in a filing cabinet is now stored in a digital database, you are thinking about pre-AI traditional digital technology. You are also thinking about technology that can store a record electronically but cannot make a decision or take an action without being instructed exactly what steps to follow. In other words, you are thinking of digital technology that is deterministic and rules-based, not probabilistic or stochastic.

That's why AI can be confusing to enterprise business leaders familiar with System of Record technology. In System of Record technology, the records live in a database. Records can be searched by users, so an application might have a search bar in the user interface into which you can type a keyword.

A Vice President of Sales, for example, might search in their System of Record to answer questions about how many customer orders have come in this month compared to the same month last year. A CFO might search a System of Record to discover how much budget was spent by a particular department or division. When a lot of enterprise business leaders talk about "digital transformation" they are often talking about Systems of Record.

Systems of Record were a meaningful improvement over paper filing cabinets, but they also created a lot of digital administrative and recordkeeping work, as well as work associated with moving data from one system to another.

When the quantity of this work became overwhelming and costly from an administrative perspective, a lot of large enterprises embarked upon an automation journey called Robotic Process Automation (RPA), which entailed buying and installing virtual robots within Systems of Record that can be programmed to perform highly defined tasks. For example, these tasks might involve comparing unique identifiers between two records, such as a Purchase Order and an invoice, and approving the invoice if and only if the two unique identifiers match.

The benefits and applications of having this type of digital automation sit on top of a System of Record have been obvious for some time, and there is a lot to be excited about when it comes to traditional rules-based digital automation.

But make no mistake: This is only a small part of the value proposition of the AI paradigm shift we are discussing.

The AI paradigm shift is not taking place because the cost or effort associated with System of Record automation has decreased. It is happening because AI today is now capable of generating entirely novel outputs from the same inputs. This is a big difference from Systems of Record. AI can now create detailed decision briefs and show its reasoning step-by-step. AI can craft detailed, exquisite, and horrifying images that have never existed before in the world.

AI is not pulling these images from a database or a System of Record. It is generating them full-cloth using a layered set of probabilistic models working in concert to compose entirely new outputs, token by token, pixel by pixel, word by word.

We are all probably now familiar with the idea that AI can generate text, images, sounds, and videos. What we are less aware of in the world of supply chain, procurement, and operations, is that AI can also generate business decisions.

Same Decision Quality, Less Effort: Simplicity as a Value Proposition

AI's business decisions are frequently framed as recommendations, and they can be served up to us with explanations, alternative scenarios, and contextual data. AI decisions can instantly be compared to all previous similar decisions made by all human decision-makers at a large enterprise. In the Predictive Enterprise, if we can anticipate the type of decision that a group of humans will likely make, then we can recommend that decision be made by the right person earlier in the process.

That's incredibly powerful.

AI can also score and rank the quality of all business decisions made by both humans and AI on a very large number of criteria, and it can even generate additional relevant criteria.

What happens when executives at large enterprises realize that specific decisions generated by AI result in better output than the equivalent decision made by humans?

In an interview about leading a Predictive Enterprise journey at BMI, a global roofing manufacturer, procurement excellence executive Sharon Moar noted that process simplicity often correlates with adoption, and that without consistent adoption of new process and technology, there can be no other value propositions:

> "It all comes down to unification and streamlining, which dovetails nicely with those cultural and organisational elements. By implementing a centralised spend cube, for example, we have established a single source of truth and enabled more seamless data extraction. We are also developing an integrated supplier platform in order to further drive simplification, mitigate risk and transform our data.
>
> "None of this was easy, however. It never is with digital intervention. The market is a 'minefield' of competing technologies, making the selection of the right-fit tools challenging. Given current market conditions, we cannot implement everything at once. Instead, we have formed a staged, multi-year roadmap that continues to prioritise high-impact interventions. This ensures we remain financially responsible while systematically replacing legacy systems with modern, scalable efficiency.
>
> "I must emphasise though, that a tool is only as good as its adoption. You can have all the best tools and processes in the world, but they are useless if you don't invest in the people. True value isn't found in the go-live date, it's created by training our teams on how to use these systems and making sure they know exactly where to find the resources they need. Most importantly, it's about fostering an environment where people feel empowered and confident to use these tools in their daily sourcing. Only then can we transform complex data into a clear competitive advantage."

This highlights one reason why procurement and supply chain organizations often aspire to achieve better deals in only a small percentage of their total addressable spend: it takes work. Spinning more plates at the same time may require that the acrobat learn to grow new fingers, perhaps even grow new arms.

Procurement teams that have backlogs of projects waiting to be negotiated are not likely to sign up for additional work, especially if they are being told to shrink headcount. And yet the lift associated with inventing and defining new processes that fit with the opportunity of AI in the Predictive Enterprise can itself be time-consuming. Changing behavior across a dispersed group of people's deeply ingrained patterns isn't exactly easy, either. Perhaps that is why the concept of an autonomous agent capable of doing most things that a human can do may feel seductive. However, this prospect is much less exciting if the task at hand is still very challenging, and where defining what success looks like is itself a step in the process. AI will be able to parallelize many streams of completing the same task simultaneously. Yet it will likely still require the intervention of a person to validate and complete the process. But how does this change when instead of completing a task, AI is given the opportunity to make a decision? How does the impact of a decision change when it can be made much earlier?

Machine Autonomy and the Opportunity of Process Transformation

Machine autonomy is all about fully delegating or outsourcing the decision to perform a human-like task to the AI itself. This may include cognitive tasks such as summarization, reasoning, and demand forecasting or planning in the digital supply chain, as well as physical navigation, manipulation, and dexterity tasks in the physical supply chain.

The key characteristic of autonomy is that the AI does not have to be told to perform a task, what steps to take, or what tools to use. AI makes and executes those decisions all by itself. This is what separates the new wave of autonomy driven by AI from traditional automation, which is highly dependent upon a stable, repeatable, defined process. This also illustrates how applying the probabilistic characteristics of

AI to the task of making business decisions can become quite a radical departure from previous waves of digital technology and rules-based automation.

The first time all this talk about autonomous AI felt viscerally real to me was the first time I got into the back seat of a Waymo car that had no driver behind the wheel. I was on a street near my home in San Francisco. The Waymo car took me across town exactly where I wanted to go, flawlessly, and without any human driver. In doing so, the Waymo provided an identical service experience to Uber or Lyft, just without the cost of human time and labor.

This is an example of pure autonomy: a system that replaces a step or action in a process that would otherwise have to be performed by a human (in this case: driving). What makes an autonomous system feel magical is that the user's experience is nearly identical to what would happen if the labor was, in fact, being performed by a human worker, driver, or decision-maker.

And while there are certainly predictive models, including machine learning models, which underlie the development of Waymo's autonomous system, for our purposes in this book, the Waymo car is *not* an example of the Predictive Enterprise. That's because the Waymo car has not altered the underlying process associated with app-based ride-hailing nearly at all: I still have to open the app, hail the car, pay for the ride, visually locate and get into the car, go to my destination, and disembark.

The Waymo does not anticipate my need for a ride, nor does it in any way predict or preempt my decision to hail one. And the framework for measuring or valuing the impact of this technology across a larger footprint of enterprise operations can be expressed as a total reduction in the costs of the human labor and time of the drivers: human labor substituted by machine activity.

Again, this is all squarely within the traditional value paradigm of the Automation Enterprise, just with much more sophisticated technology in the form of a driverless vehicle.

Doing more with less. A lot more, and with a lot less.

So, what is the paradigm shift toward the Predictive Enterprise? If it's not the substitution of human activity by machine activity, then what is the alternative framework for understanding and measuring the value of enterprise transformation through a predictive lens?

To be truly predictive, a technology must alter the underlying process by predicting and preempting the need for a human decision, thereby giving rise to the conditions for a fundamentally novel and re-designed process to take place. This is the part of the AI paradigm shift that supports Outcome-based Process Reengineering. Below are case studies that show how removing the need for a human decision much earlier in a process aligns the outcome of better deals with steps that are easier to execute.

Predictive Cost Estimating for Materials Management in Trade Contracting

Problem Statement

A trade contractor has to create proposals to bid on jobs from a general contractor. This trade contractor specializes in sub-contracting electrical work for new construction, including projects like sports arenas and college dormitories. The challenge is that the cost estimation that goes into the proposal takes place months or even years before the contractor has to perform the work. Over the time between the bid and the project itself starting, the price of materials may have increased significantly. For fixed-price projects, this puts the trade contractor in an uncomfortable position of having to potentially take a loss or put in a significant change order that could damage the relationship with the general contractor. As a result, the supply chain team decides that as soon as sales wins a new project, they want to procure the materials and hold the inventory. The only challenge is that doing so significantly adds to the upfront workload associated with materials management during the estimation process, since cost estimates associated with winning contracts are then followed by requests for quotes. It achieves a better outcome, but imposes a much higher workload.

Results Statement

Using the Predictive Enterprise, this trade contractor redesigned their process in order to simplify and reduce unnecessary work. Using a simulation of the offer-to-agreement process before it begins, the trade contractor is able to propose suggested offers to suppliers who can agree or revise, thereby generating data useful during the cost estimating process across multiple projects. This offer submission process then secures the quoted price for months after the initial offer period, allowing the supply chain team to convert any of these binding offers to purchase orders and then place those orders with the relevant qualified suppliers. The outcome of this process change using the Predictive Enterprise not only results in higher-fidelity and more accurate cost estimates (since they have been validated by the suppliers themselves) but also dramatically reduces the administrative burden associated both with generating estimates and procuring materials. In certain cases, it reduces the need for contractor to hold inventory themselves, as suppliers can hold the procured materials on the firm's behalf.

Predictive Payment Terms and Service Level Management For Auto Parts Suppliers

Problem Statement

An automotive manufacturer needed to capture savings across MRO and parts categories while also strengthening supply chain resilience in a challenging market. For B parts especially, stakeholders often preselected a preferred supplier, leaving little room to negotiate competitively. The procurement team also faced heavy administrative workloads and compliance risks when negotiating with suppliers. As a result, procurement team members did not feel that they had sufficient bandwidth to negotiate payment terms and service level agreements with suppliers in addition to validating operational and technical requirements for every part, as well as delivering per-unit cost savings. This created friction with other personas in finance, who viewed payment terms as important conditions of the deal that are relevant to managing cash.

Results Statement

By using the Predictive Enterprise, the procurement team was able to generate suggested offers that dramatically reduced the process of reviewing and negotiating payment terms and service levels with suppliers. The result was that in less than 60 days, more than 97% of suppliers had updated their payment terms and service levels to comply with the manufacturer's desired outcome. Because this did not add any additional workload, the procurement team was excited that they were able to score a measurable win with their finance partners without adding significant workload to their plates.

Predictive Maintenance and Technology Adoption in the Predictive Enterprise

Let's consider predictive maintenance as an example of the Predictive Enterprise approach to implementing AI. Maintaining equipment and machinery in manufacturing traditionally requires mechanics to check the status and replace parts on a set, pre-defined schedule, an approach known as preventative maintenance.

Preventative maintenance is often viewed as superior to the alternative of reactive maintenance because the cost of a machine's unplanned downtime is so high. A single machine being unexpectedly down in a production line effectively means that this line of machines cannot run production; therefore, the cost of a single machine's downtime is effectively equivalent to the cost of every machine in the line being down at the same time. Thus, manufacturing enterprises have adopted preventative maintenance as a management framework for maintaining equipment to avoid unplanned downtime.

This management framework effectively substitutes unplanned downtime with planned downtime. But this approach is simply an embrace of the logic that an ounce of prevention is worth a pound of cure at the level of machine maintenance, e.g., that it is better to choose when and where the downtime happens and control its impacts rather than deal with having to replace broken machine parts reactively and unexpectedly.

So, if that is preventative maintenance, then what is predictive maintenance?

Let's imagine that you are driving your car and you can hear something flapping or snapping in the engine. You don't know exactly what the sound is, but it doesn't sound good. You take your car in to see an auto mechanic. The mechanic tells you that there's a fan belt loose and either tightens it or replaces it.

Picture a stamping press in the factory that made your car: it also contains motors, belts, fans, and so on. The problem is that unlike auto mechanics, there are far fewer mechanics with the proper know-how to listen with a specially tuned ear to the sounds and vibrations coming off a stamping press when it's running at full tilt.

That's where predictive maintenance systems come in.

Using an array of audio sensors, these predictive systems operate like a blanket made of tiny ears that can easily embed on the physical surface of the stamping press and both listen to and record audio and vibrations of the machine as it runs. AI can then process the audio to identify signals that a specific machine part is wearing out and needs to be replaced. This is known as "vibration analysis."

The concept of predictive maintenance is both ingenious and ambitious, as it harvests valuable operational signals from data that is in a literal sense quite noisy. This data is readily available and harvestable for analysis but rendered opaque by its unstructured nature, its quantity, and its inherent complexity. Not only does this predictive maintenance approach enabled by AI allow the factory's mechanics to replace parts before they break, it also enables factories to operate using a dynamically adjusted and surgically targeted maintenance schedule in which mechanics only replace the parts that the AI indicates are likely to wear out in the near future, rather than replacing all the machine's parts on a pre-set schedule.

In other words, predictive maintenance changes the underlying business process and management framework for maintaining machinery and equipment altogether—as well as the professional best practices of maintenance mechanics and their ways of working.

This is not just technology transformation. It is true enterprise transformation for equipment maintenance in a manufacturing enterprise. The difference is that in the Automation Enterprise, AI's value is defined by substituting human activity with machine activity, like the Waymo. Exactly the same as an Uber, except there is no driver in the car.

In the Predictive Enterprise, AI's value is defined by enabling an activity that is not possible or practical for humans to perform today: listening to all the vibrations of a machine.

While it is theoretically possible to imagine hundreds of highly skilled mechanics standing next to a stamping press with ear trumpets or stethoscopes listening for a significant pip or a snap or a squeak, such a scene is also patently absurd. It is also impractical from a cost perspective.

Thus, rather than replacing human labor with machine activity as in the case of the Waymo, this predictive maintenance system is actually performing an activity that it is not possible or practical to imagine humans performing today, without AI.

This is the part that's Faster-Than-Human: creating a dynamically adjusted maintenance schedule based on live real-time data about the equipment's performance. Because the activity of predictive maintenance itself is novel, it actually transforms the quantifiable units of work and the success metrics associated with maintaining machinery and equipment in a factory. And this is also the part where mechanics who maintain equipment at manufacturing sites are creating Humanless Loops: enabling automated re-ordering and re-stocking of specific parts from suppliers based on the predictive maintenance system's identification of which parts will need to be replaced.

Thus, the Predictive Enterprise approach when applied to maintenance also logically gives rise to applying that same approach to general stores' inventory management, at least for spare parts. This is a prime example of the Predictive Enterprise approach. It shows the vast potential of predictive technology and points toward a new kind of playbook for enterprise transformation.

The Predictive Enterprise is about predicting the outcome of a process before it begins and then intervening earlier in the process than is currently possible, thereby preempting the need for a human decision or action altogether.

For example, in order to be predictive, the Waymo app would have to anticipate my desire to travel to downtown San Francisco and propose the ride to me preemptively, rather than simply waiting for me to order the ride on the app. Hopefully, this example shows that a system can indeed be predictive without being autonomous. It is also therefore possible for a system to be autonomous without being predictive (e.g., the Waymo experience I described previously). It is also logically possible to be both, and to operate with value relevant to both the Automation Enterprise and the Predictive Enterprise.

The only difference is that the Automation Enterprise began almost two hundred years ago during the first Industrial Revolution.

And the Predictive Enterprise is just beginning today.

The Predictive Enterprise effectively does to the process of operational decision-making what ephemeralization is doing to the door key: it de-materializes the activity of generating a trigger or a demand signal, thus correctly and conveniently anticipating the consumer's, user's, or enterprise's timely need for the outcome's value. This effectively removes need for an operational process step altogether. Predictive AI then delivers that outcome by whatever the shortest and most effective process flow is available at that exact moment in time. This is Outcome-based Process Re-engineering.

Autonomous Enterprise Approach	**Predictive Enterprise Approach**
AI primarily performs a complex cognitive task or set of tasks **as well as a human**, but without a human. Example: Autonomous vehicles can perform the task of driving as well as a human driver, but without a human. The goal of autonomy is thus reproducing a human task exactly as it occurs today through intelligent machine behavior.	AI primarily performs a complex cognitive task or set of tasks **that is not possible for a human to perform today.** Example: predictive maintenance systems listen to machine resonance to detect part failures before they happen. The goal of predictive AI is to make possible tasks that humans cannot or do not do today.

Picture the icons of a hundred audio files from each audio sensor in a predictive maintenance system, each of which contains three, eight-hour files from the three shifts of a manufacturing site. That's a tremendous amount of unstructured data and given that the factory in question is operating continuously; it's a quantity of data that only gets bigger every minute of every hour of every day. The option of using a set of human analysts to process and listen to this data and identify potential machine part failures simply isn't possible or practical, let alone economically feasible. But with the AI paradigm shift, this task suddenly becomes possible to perform not just once but continuously.

Thus, a new predictive paradigm for maintaining equipment and machinery is born. In 2015, estimates put the market size for predictive maintenance solutions at roughly $1.2 billion. Ten years later, enterprises from Frito-Lay to General Motors have implemented predictive maintenance systems and the market has expanded five to ten times, depending on which market analyst report you read. The technology around vibration analysis using AI that predictive maintenance leverages cannot even truly be evaluated using the Automation Enterprise paradigm, because vibration analysis was rarely if ever performed manually, and so there are no defined units of human labor that are being replaced by machine activity.

Consider predictive medicine as another example of the Predictive Enterprise, where entirely new therapies can be created based on predictive models that analyze a patient's unique genetic markers and identify which diseases they may be uniquely at risk for.

Or predictive energy management, which enables an entirely novel approach to energy storage, consumption, and so on simply based on the predictive models about energy demand relative to the time of day and factoring in data about historic consumption patterns. These models often generate AI decisions using a continuously repeated near-instant analysis of datasets that are exponentially larger than most people could fathom.

The Predictive Enterprise enables a different pattern of both individual and organizational behavior than rules-based automation allows. Often, this new pattern is unlocked by making a time-sensitive decision using AI—such as when to replace a machine part, begin a medical treatment, or purchase energy—earlier than would have otherwise been possible.

Autonomous Supply Chain	Predictive Supply Chain
Executes a supply chain **as well as a human**, but without most human labor intermediaries, and thus at significantly lower costs. Decisions and hand-offs must be defined by a human, even if they are executed by a machine. Example: autonomous cranes that unload cargo from a container ship into a port terminal.	Executes a supply chain with faster-than-human decisions and larger-than-human value creation using a behavior pattern **that is not possible for groups of humans to perform today.** Example: predictive pallet-packing agents that stack the order of products within a pallet based on the products' final delivery destination.

Rather than enabling an identical experience (just without the costs of human labor), predictive AI enables a fundamentally different operational process, user experience, and decision-making framework, as well as dramatic change in the unit economics and cost structure of delivering a service experience or physical product.

Whereas the value of technologies in the Automation Enterprise was primarily expressed as a reduction in labor, effort, cost, and cycle time, the purpose and value of technologies in the Predictive Enterprise is to enable different and dramatically improved decision-making and process execution, as well as a dramatically lower overall cost structure.

In other words, the Predictive Enterprise is capable of Faster-Than-Human Decisions that amplify human value creation at global scale, acting as both a force multiplier on functional bandwidth and a dramatic accelerant on process throughput.

Better Deals, Easier is Essential to Deploying AI at Enterprise Scale

The AI paradigm shift across large enterprises is accelerating for many reasons.

On the one hand, there are the scientific breakthroughs in model performance, led by the large research labs at OpenAI, Anthropic, Google Gemini, Meta's Llama, and China's DeepSeek.

On the other hand, there are the GDP-sized investments in computing, chipmaking, and energy infrastructure such as Stargate.

But in most large enterprise supply chains, the main driver for AI is extremely simple: the unforgiving need for speed. Entire professions and ways of working have already been transformed by AI to do the same amount of work, faster. This is especially salient for the need for speed associated with enterprise IT projects, which have a long history of taking very long cycles.

Today's AI has broken through with a killer app: AI coding agents. These have had a dramatic impact in transforming the professional life of software developers. By taking a look at what AI looks like at both an enterprise and global scale we can gain insight into what fully deployed AI might look like for procurement and supply chain organizations.

It is difficult to think of a commercial activity that has been more impacted by AI than the task of writing code, or a job that has been more transformed by AI than the job of a software developer. Since the launch of ChatGPT in November 2022, using AI to write code and even develop full software applications has gone from being a neat party trick to being a nice-to-have, to now being an essential and ubiquitous toolset for software developer productivity.

AI coding tools and so-called "vibecoding" have captured the imagination of the internet, using line-by-line predictions about what additional code needs to be written to autogenerate those exact lines of code either within a software developer's IDE (Integrated Developer Environment) or within a third-party platform's low-code interface.

Software developers can now generate the same amount of code, at similar level of quality and performance, in significantly less time. This also means that they can generate significantly more code in aggregate. The fact that the role of software developers has been meaningfully transformed by AI in less than three years offers an astonishing template for what the AI paradigm shift may look like for other enterprise roles.

The numbers here are mind-blowing.

Ninety-two percent of US software developers use AI coding tools on a daily basis.

Forty-one percent of all global code is AI-generated; approximately 256 billion lines of code were written in 2024.

Eighty-seven percent of Fortune 500s have purchased a vibecoding platform for internal use.

These statistics were accessed in November 2025 and demonstrate both the widespread diffusion and adoption of generative and agentic AI technology not just among individuals, but at scale by large enterprises. Consider that the now-ubiquitous term "vibecoding" was introduced by Andrej Karpathy as recently as February 2025. As of this writing in December 2025, OpenAI for Business claims to be the ". . . fastest-growing business platform in history," with more than 1 million business customers. There is evidence that as of 2026 Anthropic may have already surpassed this extremely high water mark. Anthropic's run-rate revenue in beginning of 2024 was $87 million, and surpassed $1 billion by the end of 2024. Less than eighteen months later in May 2026 Anthropic surpassed $47 billion in run-rate revenue, making it among the fastest-growing companies in history.

The speed of change driven by AI coding tools has dazzled business leaders whose organizations are now able to realize dramatic gains in software developer productivity. This transformation provides an interesting example of what happens when AI's dramatic productivity benefits are adopted by a significant percentage of an entire professional workforce at nearly the same time.

There is also strong evidence that AI has created induced demand for coding tools outside of traditional software developers and technical personas. In a world where anyone can make an app, a lot more people are willing to try. As a result, a whole new range of people without technical training, computer science degrees, or any prior experience with coding can now prototype and develop the app of their dreams.

The take-away here is not that coding has gotten faster or cheaper. It has simply gotten easier. And because it is easier, more people can do it. And because more people can do it, more people understand how valuable it is. And that is what powers induced demand, similar to what Bessen saw with nineteenth-century weavers.

What would happen if the power of negotiating and delivering better deals was so easy that anyone could do it? What if the incremental labor associated with confidently asking for a better offer was very close to zero? What if negotiating 1,000 offers was the same effort as 1?

Does anyone seriously believe that the demand for achieving better deals with suppliers would remain limited to a small fraction of an enterprise's total addressable spend?

This is the power of aligning financially significant outcomes with simplicity and ease of use in the Predictive Enterprise. Bandwidth is no longer a limitation. Instead, creating more bandwidth and faster throughput becomes the core mission of every AI transformation project. Once the value of an activity like procurement and supply chain becomes measurably understood by more functional stakeholders in a business, it's only a matter of time before they're asking for more.

6

Facing the Uncomfortable Truth About Status Quo Enterprise Transformation Projects

It's now time for us to discuss an uncomfortable topic: despite the benefits of enterprise transformation projects, it is in fact the case that too many of these initiatives are wildly unsuccessful. The numbers are pretty grim. As Everest Group's CEO Peter Bendor-Samuel writes: "A whopping 73% of enterprises failed to provide any business value whatsoever from their digital transformation efforts, according to an Everest Group study last year. Furthermore, 78% failed to meet their business objectives. Put another way, only 22% achieved their desired business results. This is horrific. Why does this happen?"[1]

There are three related problems that are fundamental to understanding the shockingly high failure rate of technology transformations at large enterprises:

1. **Boring.** The work of designing, mapping, and improving business processes is widely perceived to be extremely boring and "in the weeds," and thus the critical details of project delivery (and especially steps that involve collective decision making) are left poorly defined, poorly measured, or lacking in executive

sponsorship. This is an area where large management consultancies have built significant business practices by persuasively making the case that while most businesses undertake transformation projects only a small number of times, their teams of consultants have built up significant expertise by delivering transformation projects over and over again across a range of different companies.

2. **Unknown Dependencies to Success.** These transformation projects often run into the problem of having unknown dependencies beyond the control of those involved in the project itself. For example, a traditional Procure-to-Pay transformation project over the past thirty years contained elements that touch the three classic pillars of People, Process, and Technology. These project elements may involve the team putting in a purchase order system, creating a policy around getting a purchase order approved before a supplier's invoice can be paid, and redefining the roles and responsibilities of employees in both Procurement and Accounts Payable in order to support this new process and technology system. New AI transformations have added "Data" as a new pillar to People, Process, and Technology, since issues with the accessibility or quality of data can in some cases create a stumbling block. But we are still in the early days of enterprise AI, and we don't know what we don't know.
3. **Too Many Points of Failure.** Enterprise transformation projects often simply require that too many things go right, and if any one step goes wrong then the project will fail. Unfortunately, as we'll see below, this means that the numbers are often simply not in our favor.

Even traditional digital transformation projects, like a Procure-to-Pay transformation, have a very large number of unknown dependencies and points of failure that create risks to its success. These dependencies may include:

- whether the organization currently uses a centralized model of procurement for spend management (versus a decentralized model where individual site locations approve invoices),

- whether the site locations and business units are willing and able to adopt the use of purchase orders given their current process for communicating demand to suppliers (and what would need to change for the new process to be successful),
- what information the purchase orders should contain and if the technology should automatically check the price on the invoices against the purchase orders and then compare them against either a shipping label or a price agreement (a process step in Procure-to-Pay sometimes referred to as a "three-way match"), and
- what other existing Systems of Record already in use in this new purchase order system need to integrate with in order to serve as a "source of truth" for current spending patterns.

As you can see, there are many unknown dependencies to success in this relatively commonplace digital transformation project, dependencies related to People (the ability to win ongoing user adoption and executive buy-in for the transformation across the enterprise), Process (the ability to map the current process and replace or add steps in order to support the new process), and Technology (the ability to configure and integrate the new system with existing systems and reporting frameworks). Each of these dependencies introduces distinct points of failure, and as the number or points of failure in a project plan increases, the likelihood of the whole project's success decreases. There are simply too many things that need to go right, and if even *one* of them goes wrong then the transformation project itself either fails or is perceived by key stakeholders as falling short of expectations.

The math of compound dependencies makes it quite difficult for us to win here. This is in part due to the perverse effect of fractional multiplication of the dependencies themselves. For example, if a successful project outcome requires three dependencies to happen, and each dependency has a 50% likelihood of happening, then what is the likelihood of the outcome? Many people would guess that if all the precursors have a 50% likelihood of happening then the outcome is also 50% likely to happen. But in fact, due to the nature of fractional multiplication in calculating probability of an outcome with compound dependencies, the outcome's actual likelihood is 12.5% (50% * 50% * 50%). Said differently: out of eight possible worlds, the project is only successful in one of them (e.g., the transformation has a one in eight chance of success).

That's why if a transformation project has 10 dependencies, each of which has a 90% likelihood of success, the project as a whole is still more likely than not to fail (e.g. it has less than 50% chance of succeeding: 0.9 * 0.9 * 0.9 * 0.9 * 0.9 * 0.9 * 0.9 * 0.9 * 0.9 * 0.9). The only way to improve the success rate of large enterprise transformations is to reduce the number of dependencies and points of failure. This is an area where the Predictive Enterprise can offer a unique toolbox of less failure-prone options for transformation advocates to consider.

In the Conclusion we'll also share a playbook for transformation projects that can be used not just for thinking through transformations relevant to the Predictive Enterprise approach, but enterprise transformation projects holistically.

Measure What Matters and Acknowledge Underlying Disagreement Between Key Stakeholders About What Success Truly Looks Like

Success in enterprise transformation, as in other areas of human society, is to a great extent in the eye of the beholder (or in our case, the stakeholders). What does success look like? Historically, many enterprise digital transformations take years to implement and consume a significant period in the participants' professional careers. Thus, we should remember that for many people who spend their working life in large enterprises, these transformations are quite a serious matter and thus require quite serious management. In executive leadership, anything that requires serious management also requires particular attention to metrics, goal setting, and stakeholder alignment to not only ensure that the metrics are both exciting *and* realistically achievable, but that they are enthusiastically endorsed and supported by the executive leadership team, middle managers, and frontline workers impacted by the transformation.

Needless to say, this is quite a tall order. And as a result, when project owners try to win support for their enterprise transformation project, the process of defining quantifiable objectives for success can get quite messy, especially for enterprise operations where there are deeply entrenched double binds or at the very least perceived trade-offs between different target outcomes.

The reality is that if this pattern of misalignment begins to surface with any degree of regularity, it will imperil the success of the transformation project. Enterprise transformations require an extraordinary degree of coordination, alignment, intention, and energy in order to be successful even when everything goes to plan. More than anything else, transformations require an authentic belief by stakeholders engaged in the project that it is worth doing, that it will produce measurable, durable benefits that will offer them and their teams a better way of working. During a transformation, this collective energy and enthusiasm for delivering the project are critical to its success—and if too much time is spent on bickering or disagreement, the palpable feeling of misalignment will sap and fragment the team's focus and resolve to deliver a win.

That is one reason why getting metrics correct is so important, as well as defining metrics in a manner that preempts the perception of trade-offs. For Arkestro's early customers, a Predictive Enterprise approach helped them to quickly move from an AI pilot to global scale production. The role of clear, agreed-upon metrics for the pilot across different stakeholders was absolutely crucial in maintaining momentum and getting to scale. For example, if plant managers were anxious about losing access to preferred suppliers due to the introduction of competition from other suppliers, then making "attainment of preferred suppliers" as a quantifiable metric was helpful in communicating that the project's most desired outcome is not to remove their long-standing supplier. Or if operations wants to ensure that a transformation doesn't result in a new process that increases the daily administrative burden on its frontline workers, then ensuring that the project has a metric associated with either shortening cycle time or reducing administrative burden can help allay those fears.

I'll close out this section by saying that the worst thing that an enterprise can do to a transformation initiative, such as integrating AI more fully into their supply chain and procurement operations, is to not have a game plan for what happens if a pilot goes well. Pilots at large enterprises are sometimes done as educational initiatives, or "science experiments," to give the enterprise teams exposure to new technologies but without any intention of deploying these technologies at scale. Personally, I have never been a fan of this approach, and I think it does a real disservice to everyone involved in enterprise transformation projects. There are far less expensive ways for supply chain practitioners to get educated about AI's capabilities, like taking an online class, talking to a subject matter expert, or attending a workshop or seminar at a trade association like the Sourcing Industry Group, Institute for Supply Management, the Council of Supply Management Professionals, or the Chartered Institute for Procurement & Supply. If an AI pilot goes well and wins the support of key stakeholders like Finance, Supply Chain, Procurement, and Operations, then it is the job of the executive leadership team to clear a path for the project to scale appropriately across the enterprise without getting bogged down in bureaucratic obstacles or internal bickering. For Arkestro's customers, the key to delivering AI transformations at global scale using the Predictive Enterprise approach is the ability to keep the organizational momentum going from the pilot to the scalable deployment with a phased multi-year roll-out plan. In addition to a strong champion and a strong team of front-line practitioners, a strong and supportive executive sponsor who is an active participant in the weekly pilot meetings is critical to the success of the Predictive Enterprise approach in delivering durable transformational benefits at global scale.

7

AI Agents, AI Employees, and Service-as-Software

TODAY, PUTTING IN a System of Record is by far the most common approach to digital transformation at large enterprises, especially for supply chain. This also means that the most common value proposition associated with technology in enterprise operations is usually something related to the word "visibility." As we have discussed, this approach is being called into question, both by the Predictive Enterprise approach as well as by a new way of packaging AI products, not as software or bots, but as full employees. AI employees have names like Shiro or Devin and email addresses, join video conference meetings, take action items, contribute to meetings verbally, and can even post updates or chat with human employees via platforms like Slack and Microsoft Teams. Overall, the "AI employees" concept represents a meaningfully different way of using and deploying technology, and creates new ways of working. It also represents a piece of the AI paradigm shift that has potential to change the way that large enterprises buy and adopt AI technology across their operations, including with their suppliers, customers, and other third parties.

In this chapter, we'll take a deep look at how the process of transformation is itself changing from Systems of Record and moving toward what's being termed Systems of Action, as well as an emerging business model currently being called Service-as-Software (SaS), and how this model offers an alternative to the traditional seat-based subscription model associated with Software-as-a-Service (SaaS). Software-as-a-Service (Saas) is also impacting how technology companies price and deliver value to enterprise customers, reflecting a broader market trend toward outcome-based and consumption-based pricing.

The move from Systems of Record to Systems of Action opens up a new way of consuming any technology system through an AI user interface. It also creates new ways to structure agreements and relationships with technology developers and platforms. The past 25 years have seen the ascendancy of cloud-based Software-as-a-Service (SaaS). The SaaS model of technology gives users the ability to consume an application by connecting to the internet and logging in via a website, where the application itself is hosted on a different company's servers (e.g. the application lives on the cloud). In SaaS, subscriptions displaced the previous model of owning and operating physical servers and other IT infrastructure. The SaaS subscription model also spreads payments out over time, creating "recurring revenue" for technology providers, which displaced the previous business model of one-time revenue for perpetual licenses and mainframes. Tien Tzuo, an early mentor of mine who worked with Marc Benioff at Salesforce as their Chief Strategy Officer before founding the accounting software platform Zuora, has termed this transition the "Subscription Economy."[1] AI, and the potential for not just AI agents but AI employees, is now offering an emerging alternative to this subscription model. The new model is now being called Service-as-Software (SaS), a model in which AI agents are being called employees. Customers can consume the value of AI agents or fully articulated AI employees by paying by the task, by the outcome, or even by the hour, like a highly flexible contractor or gig worker.

Now on the one hand, you might say that outcome-based pricing is hardly a new idea at large enterprises. In fact, GE has become well-known for the TrueChoice pricing model for its jet engines that effectively bundles the costs of the engine with maintenance and repair and allows airlines to effectively pay by the hour of flight time.[2] However, a jet engine is different from a marketing copywriter, at least insofar as the former is an asset, while the latter is a human being who is a member of the workforce and whose contributions to the business may extend beyond the defined units of the copy that they write. The copywriter's contributions also include the new ideas that they bring to the table, and the opportunities for growth, innovation, and creativity that they identify. Thus, advocates of the new AI paradigm are often careful to note that the concept of AI agents and AI employees does not necessarily entail the elimination of jobs beyond the most rigidly defined, transactional, and junior roles. Rather, it allows the modern marketing copywriter to produce more copy across more channels, or at the very least, to free up time for brainstorming and thinking about how to make the existing copy that much better.

However, this is also why the AI paradigm shift will create a unique opportunity for managers and executive teams. That's because the core difference in Service-as-Software is that the way a business consumes the value of an AI agent or AI employee is that it requires the business to define the desired tasks and outcomes of a human employee and then gives them the option to just pay for either that task or that outcome. Paying for the outcomes of a junior copywriter (e.g., 1 blog post, 3 social posts, 1 short case study, 1 press summary and a few updates to legacy content per week) but without having the costs of a human employee on your books, I would argue, is quite different than paying for the outcomes of a jet engine without having the costs of the jet engine on your books.

The intention and purpose of each model are fundamentally distinct from an employee and an asset. The two models also have different precursors: before AI was an option, companies were outsourcing their copywriting to contractors, and before TrueChoice companies were partnering with leasing companies to create financing arrangements that allowed them to keep accounting headaches like asset depreciation off their corporate balance sheets. The jet engine's financial representation in TrueChoice's outcome-based pricing involves blending costs across the lifecycle of the machine and then offering a package with a net reduction in the customer's total cost of ownership and predictable ongoing revenue for GE. The AI employee who is a digital marketer involves an exercise that seems to do what Fuller's de-materialization and abstraction does to the key when a physical metal lock is replaced with a fingerprint scanner: it not only replaces it, but it eliminates the need for a physical door key to exist in the first place. Discussions around replacing job roles filled by humans today with AI employees tend to make people uncomfortable, or at least anxious. This discomfort ranges from aversion and social discomfort to outright hostility to existential dread and physical visceral repulsion. And yet for the current moment, this Automation

Enterprise concept of replacing humans and eliminating jobs has become Silicon Valley's default way of talking about AI, as one investor at Foundation Capital writes:

> A new class of enterprise software company is emerging. Thousands of AI-native startups have launched in the past 18 months, each pitching an intelligent agent to replace human workers: AI SREs, AI SDRs, AI accountants, AI paralegals. These are not workflow accelerators or data entry helpers, but end-to-end systems designed to do the work for you.
>
> We call them Services-as-Software companies, and they're redefining the structure, value, and go-to-market motion of enterprise software.
>
> Success in Services-as-Software is fundamentally different from success in the SaaS era. Gone are the days where startups could differentiate themselves by having the best features. AI has accelerated the collapse of software primitives. Decades of enterprise UX and domain logic have been compressed into a few modular capabilities: inbox triage, structured data tables, LLM-powered search, workflow routing, and generative response. What used to take months of application-specific design can now be assembled in a weekend.
>
> As a result, nearly every AI product now looks the same. A legal ops system looks like a claims processor. A RevOps copilot looks like an underwriting assistant. When every company can ship the same primitives using the same models, what you build is no longer your moat. How you integrate, embed, and operate becomes the moat.
>
> That shift—from tooling to delivery—is why Services-as-Software companies are outperforming their peers. They deliver outcomes.[3]

The key element here is often that the incremental costs of performing a given task or delivering a given outcome is close to zero for the solutions provider. Writing and sending one marketing email has nearly the same cost as sending a thousand, or a million. The Predictive Enterprise approach can enable AI employees and agents to deliver an outcome significantly better, significantly faster, and at much larger scale. For example, customer support AI startup Kodif, which helps e-commerce brands resolve text-based customer tickets faster and at mass scale, exemplifies that way that new interaction and service patterns become possible in the Predictive Enterprise. Unlike the Automation Enterprise focus on eliminating jobs, Kodif's outcome-based model is focused on delivering better outcomes (e.g. faster ticket resolutions with higher CSAT scores) at greater scale than current teams of human support agents working across multiple different systems are able to do by themselves. This is partly because one of the challenges inherent to customer support is load-balancing the work across human agents during peak times and activity surges. By using Outcome-Based Process Re-Engineering, Kodif offers to change the way that e-commerce brands can route, escalate, and manage their tickets by detecting and resolving time-sensitive customer requests related to orders that are about to ship. These requests might include changing the address, updating credit card information, and so on. Customer support is a particularly key area of opportunity for the AI paradigm shift in enterprises because there are so many well-defined units of work, performance benchmarks, and shared definitions of what success looks like.

It can be challenging for human support agents (even armed with the newest Large Language Models) to personalize their conversations using customer account data that often lives in multiple systems. The classic example in customer support operations for e-commerce is a ticket nicknamed a WISMO or "Where is my order?" To resolve this ticket, a human support agent needs to look at the account for recent orders, identify an order that has shipped but not yet arrived, locate the tracking number for that order, type the tracking number into yet another system, and then reply in text to the customer's inquiry. That's a lot of steps! As a result, it is frequently the case that in order to save time, the human support agents ask the customer to provide this order identification data directly in the chat, since they often have faster access to these order identifiers than human support agents.

Let's imagine just for a moment that we applied Automation Enterprise thinking to this problem using AI agents to automate each step in the process. Keeping in mind the stages of the Predictive Process Framework, we would be designing for a transformation that would remove incremental human labor but would still keep the process at the reactive level. In other words, the AI agent would wait for a customer to write into the chat, then:

- ask what they want,
- create a ticket with a reference number,
- solicit information from the customer to help them answer the customer's question,
- input that information into multiple other back-end systems in order to provide the answer.

Clearly, this Automation Enterprise approach to transformation offers an instrumentation of AI that leaves a lot of value on the table. This is an approach that feels more like an automat than a drive-thru, because it creates a noticeable trade-off in the customer experience. In this example, in order for the enterprise to eliminate human agents from their jobs, the customers are being asked to do more work. This is exactly the sort of trade-off that we may want to treat with extreme skepticism. Remember, the last Horn and Hardart automat closed its doors in 1991. McDonald's has approximately 63 million daily customers. Whenever an Automation Enterprise approach to AI transformation claims to cut costs with a trade-off that asks the customer to do more work, I would ask: which path are we more aligned with: the automat or the drive-thru?

What could this look like in the Predictive Enterprise approach? Perhaps the AI agents would already know that this customer is likely to ask the question "Where is my order?" if they have asked it before. Perhaps this customer is a frequent traveler, and needs items to arrive on specific days in order to pick them up from the delivery address. Perhaps the agent can serve the WISMO question option to the customer as soon as they have begun typing via a pop-up button directly in the chat. Rather than ask the customer to provide data, the agent is able to predict which order the customer is inquiring about and then automatically pull and enter this data into the internal order-tracking system. The result is that by predicting both the demand for a service request and the specific components of that request, the AI agent is able to completely eliminate the intermediary steps in the process that actually consume most of the time and effort associated with creating and then resolving a customer support ticket. This example shows how the Predictive Enterprise approach can unlock massive speed in the customer experience of a direct-to-consumer e-commerce brand that ships products directly to their customers' houses. It also shows why the Outcome-Based Process Re-Engineering element of the Predictive Enterprise approach is so important to realizing the full potential value of the AI paradigm shift.

In many ways, Kodif's customer support AI agents could be seen as replacing human customer support agents. But when you talk to leaders who run large teams of agents, that's not their primary intention or area of excitement. Rather, it is ensuring that customers have a good support experience, especially during peak times where a large influx of tickets can lead to longer wait times and even longer resolution times. That's why the "replacing humans with AI story" misses the bigger picture of AI's value. Using the Predictive Enterprise approach, Kodif allows the customer support team to become truly predictive by anticipating what the customers are likely to request before a ticket is even fully submitted. The team can then use customized policies to transform the process that it uses to triage, prioritize, and escalate tickets by preempting many requests with the correct path for resolution. In certain cases, the preempt can even contain the resolution (e.g., the recently updated answer to the WISMO question).

There are examples of this Predictive Enterprise shift available across superhuman supply chains. Let's take an example from a technology platform called MetalMiner, which helps teams involved with buying metals like steel and aluminum to understand their pricing targets and deliver a good outcome to their stakeholders. To qualify as part of the Predictive Enterprise approach, we are looking for an action that a human cannot perform due to practical limitations, but that a predictive AI model can now enable, thereby preempting the need for a manual human decision via a Humanless Loop. MetalMiner has developed an ingenious predictive model using Reinforcement Learning, that compares price trends at massive scale and then pattern-matches leading indicators with historical pricing behavior at the grade level, rather than the metal level. Unlike stock markets, commodity markets, or other public indices, the big challenge that MetalMiner faces is continuously acquiring updated and real-time pricing data at the grade level, since the price of the raw material, such as steel, is often less than half of the price of the specified grade of steel that a large enterprise organization is actually purchasing. This pricing delta represents a massive cost savings opportunity for any organization with significant spend on metals.

As a result of this diligent development of this predictive model and the application of AI at the correct level of detail, MetalMiner is able to give anyone working in a metals business the ability to forecast trend-reversals at scale across a large portfolio of commodity purchases. This represents a powerful example of the Predictive Enterprise, since much like the example of Kodif's customer support agents, the faster-than-human decisions combined with humanless loops deliver greater-than-human outcomes at scale. MetalMiner's AI technology is driven by the ability to analyze more data in parallel than a human or even team of humans is capable of: in this case, adding additional data points associated with the grade-specific price of steel.

The Implications of the Predictive Enterprise for Transformation Practitioners: A Matrix

	DIGITAL TRANSFORMATION	PREDICTIVE TRANSFORMATION
People	**Flexible & Accountable Collaboration** Centralizes digital collaboration, enables hybrid/remote employees, and creates persistent performance and reporting framework for shared accountability and management	**Dramatic Task Reduction** Reduces number of steps for data entry, analysis and selection decisions by completing tasks that would normally have to be performed by a human user
Process	**Democratizes Access** Enables scalable many-to-many de-centralized processes, democratizes access to instant reports	**Amplifies Value** Recommends next steps, scales and amplifies units of value per employee
Technology	**System of Record & Enablement** Success is often measured on user adoption. Apps create an interface for administrative management, process control and reporting	**System of Action & Decision** Success is measured based on impact and faster cycles. Best next steps can be embedded in any system or intelligent autonomy
Data	**Requires Clean Internal Data & Wide User Adoption** Success is measured based on data created by human input, either free text or upload	**Uses Reinforcement Learning Human Feedback Loop to Recommend & Validate Data** Success is measured by how many recommendations convert into validations

The Automation Enterprise is also characterized by software applications that serve to function as a System of Record for the activities that they enable. Success in the Automation Enterprise thus significantly depends on user adoption, frequency of usage, and number of workstreams impacted by usage. For example, think of a camera application that stores, organizes, and edits an individual user's photographs. The application becomes more valuable the more photos you take because it also helps you view, organize, and share the photos. This same System of Record principle applies to enterprise software applications, such as complex accounting and timekeeping ledgers that execute transactions, store pay stubs, and reconcile invoices with purchase orders around the world.

The "do more with less" advantages of Fuller's de-materialization and abstraction are often described as automating and thus enabling steps in a decision-to-action process flow, thereby centralizing it alongside other similar relevant processes, tracking its records across sessions and users, and providing a "single pane of glass" to access and activate the process as desired and with a nearly effortless command and control. In other words, the "do more with less" benefits of automation function as a kind of honeypot that draws different user personas to all perform their work within a common digital workspace. This centralization of work across the enterprise creates compound advantages associated with the ability to store, organize, and share records associated with these users' work.

The advantages of this Automation Enterprise approach to System of Record technologies produce compound efficiencies as scale increases. This scaling benefit is similar to the efficiency that anyone who has ever sorted through shoeboxes full of Polaroid photographs receives when they begin taking photos on an iPhone. Suddenly, all your photos are in one place, easy to search through, easy to share. However, as the effort decreases and access increases, the Automation Enterprise also produces another side effect: a lot more people become photographers, and photographers in general take a lot more photographs as the incremental cost of taking a photo falls to essentially zero. The numbers here are dramatic. Since 2022, humans have produced more than one and a half trillion photos annually, a number that has continued to grow year over year, with the vast majority of photographs being taken using smartphones at essentially zero incremental cost to the user. As David Malitz writes on his Substack,

"Talking About Data": "In the year 2024, every 13 days the world takes as many photos as were taken globally in 1998 at the peak of film photography."[4]

Using analog film, taking this many photographs creates dramatic organizational and recordkeeping challenges. But on a smartphone, nearly every camera app enables all the photos to be instantly and automatically labeled, archived, organized, and searched by the user so that any photo can be retrieved at a moment's notice. And—critically—all of this extraordinary benefit is offered at essentially zero incremental cost to the cost of the smartphone, since all smartphones now effectively come with cameras and all smartphones with cameras are supported by internal System of Record software that labels, stores, organizes, and shares unlimited libraries of photographs.

In many ways, the System of Record is as much the logic of the iPhone circa 2010 for individual users as it is the Supply Chain Control Tower circa 2025 for large global enterprises. The System of Record in supply chain is a vision of process control and organizational behavior that dates back at least to the origins of the first Enterprise Resource Planning (ERP) systems and Stafford Beers' writing on so-called "management cybernetics" in the late 1950s. The image to conjure here is a command center, the White House Situation Room, the bridge of the *Enterprise* in *Star Trek.*

As a narrative myth, the organizing principle for this type of System of Record enterprise technology is not just a dashboard full of glowing dials, levers, and buttons that enable godlike power and speed to execute desired maneuvers, but also a map that enables omnipotent visibility and a panoptic sense of control. What would happen if it was as easy to design, manufacture, and distribute a physical product as it was to take a photograph on a smartphone? What if the barriers to entry became so low that everyone began manufacturing and distributing their own products at a global scale?

These questions are the physical world equivalent of what thought leaders have termed the Age of Imagination, a term coined in 1993 by Charles Magee, who contrasted it with the Information Age by arguing that while economic value and competitive advantage in the Information Age were defined by the ability to quickly access information and knowledge, that economic value and competitive advantage in the Age of Imagination would be defined by creating and communicating one's vision to collaborators: "The most successful groups throughout human history have had one thing in common: when compared to their competition they had the best system of communication. The fittest communicators—whether tribe, city-state, kingdom, corporation, nation—had (1) a larger percentage of people with (2) access to (3) higher-quality information, (4) a greater ability to transform that information into knowledge and action, (5) and more freedom to communicate that new knowledge to the other members of their group. . . . The tools of the Information Age have spread throughout the population in mere decades. The Age of Imagination will spread much faster and the risk/reward potential will go out of sight. If we're confused by a planet which is currently re-tribalizing, consider a situation in which each person is his/her own tribe, his/her own transnational corporation."[5]

Importantly, even in 1993 Charles Magee understood the centrality of enterprise supplier relationships to the Age of Imagination. Magee envisioned that the speed and effectiveness of a company's communication with third parties would define the ultimate capability for enterprise operational performance, and that threats to the enabling communication infrastructure would exceed even the risks of a nuclear war: "At the moment the biggest threat to national security is no longer a barrage of nukes, it is the disruption of the national communication infrastructure. Our companies must have quick, accurate communication with suppliers, customers and competition to survive."[6]

Magee's emphasis on the speed of making and communicating decisions across a chain of command and control within the corporate environment as the ultimate competitive advantage is echoed by recent analysts of global military operations, such as in Christian Brose's book *Kill Chain: Defending America in the Future of High-Tech Warfare*. Brose defines "kill chain" as: ". . . the ability of an organization to rapidly and accurately execute all the steps from locating to killing an enemy target." He opens with a provocative assessment: "Over the past decade, in U.S. war games against China, the United States has a nearly perfect record: we have lost almost every single time."[7] This assessment may surprise readers due to the fact that the United States outspends China on defense by a margin that has decreased in recent years yet nevertheless remains meaningful: in 2024, most estimates place Chinese military spending between $247 billion to $471 billion[8] while US defense spending during the same period was over $883.7 billion.[9]

One core reason for this astonishing US-China gap in warfighting capability, according to Brose, is that US weapons systems lag in speed and performance for nearly every step related to supporting and communicating decisions within the kill chain. US weapons systems, argues Brose, have fallen behind due to a reliance by the US Department of War upon a byzantine, outdated procurement process that heavily favors entrenched existing suppliers—so-called "defense primes"—at the expense of innovators. There is perhaps a valuable parallel in how the Automation Enterprise has come to many large manufacturing enterprises that depend upon a small group of entrenched, legacy technology suppliers to make incremental upgrades and life-extension improvements to systems and infrastructure that are decades out of date.

The Predictive Enterprise, in contrast, will necessarily depend upon newer firms whose sole mandate is centered around leveraging emerging AI technology to deliver on opportunity of Faster-Than-Human Decisions, Humanless Loops, and Outcome-Based Process Re-Engineering. Much like the legacy defense primes, the legacy System of Record providers' short-term profit margins and share price are better served by selling existing technology products, services, and platforms rather than risk launching new ones that could potentially cannibalize or even jeopardize their existing revenue streams.

This is precisely the argument that Clayton Christensen lays out as the so-called "innovator's dilemma" in his seminal book of the same name that also coins the term "disruptive technologies."[10] However, while large enterprises will likely struggle to develop disruptive products built using predictive technologies in-house, they will be able to partner with newer startups whose solutions are purpose-built and laser focused on delivering not only the technology, but the know-how and experience from working with other clients to advise internal teams on the simultaneous re-engineering of business processes and organizational behavior surrounding the technology.

The Age of Imagination (and the Implications of Superintelligence)

The Age of Imagination is worth taking seriously as a framework for how AI will transform our relationship to both the value of innovation and labor, if for no other reason than it has been embraced by the companies that have secured the largest capital investments to make it a reality. For example, the Age of Imagination is clearly the vision embraced by the executive team at OpenAI, the research nonprofit turned startup company behind ChatGPT, which, as of this writing, is valued at over $300 billion. As OpenAI's CEO of Applications Fidji Simo wrote in 2025: "When people can independently create and capture value, they gain power over their own economic destiny. But starting a company isn't easy. . . . And until recently, building a product or launching a service required technical knowledge, especially coding. That was a problem for the hundreds of millions of people who had ideas for tools, apps, platforms, etc. that could have made an impact but didn't have the technical skills to bring them to life. AI now gives people the power to turn ideas into income, no matter their age, credentials, or zip code. A single person can now brainstorm, prototype, market, and launch a product with tools they control themselves even if they've never written a line of code. . . . In the future, people will be able to build new things without waiting for permission, capital, or credentials. Of course this will create a meaningful shift in the workforce."[11] This vision may feel exciting and appealing for new entrepreneurs and solopreneurs launching new businesses, but what about large global enterprises with over $1 billion in annual revenue whose infrastructure, workforces, investments, and suppliers constitute a majority of the economic activity as measured by GDP across the OECD?[12] Does the metaphor between photographers and manufacturing supply chains for physical products in the Age of Imagination truly stand up to scrutiny, or scale up to large, globally integrated supply chains?

Perhaps the reason that the big AI labs like OpenAI aren't brimming with concern about AI's potential impact on the global economy is that they believe it won't be long before humanity will have bigger existential risk fish to fry. As OpenAI's CEO Sam Altman wrote in 2017: "A popular topic in Silicon Valley is talking about what year humans and machines will merge. . . . Most guesses seem to be between 2025 and 2075 . . . unless we destroy ourselves first, superhuman AI is going to happen, genetic enhancement is going to happen, and brain-machine interfaces are going to happen. It is a failure of human imagination and human arrogance to assume that we will never build things smarter than ourselves. . . . Although the merge has already begun, it's going to get a lot weirder. We will be the first species ever to design our own descendants. My guess is that we can either be the biological bootloader for digital intelligence and then fade into an evolutionary tree branch, or we can figure out what a successful merge looks like."[13]

Let's take a moment to appreciate the magnitude of this statement, delivered to the internet by one of the most powerful men in the world. If you are a person who truly believes that within your lifetime the human species as a whole will face an existential adapt-or-die imperative to either merge into cybernetic organisms with emergent intelligent machines or ". . . fade into an evolutionary tree branch . . .," then figuring out how AI will impact the future of the global economy, let alone enterprise manufacturing and supply chain, probably won't seem like a very high priority. However, for those of us who are formulating business strategies, making technology investments, and building organizational designs for our functional teams (not to mention supply chain network designs) for the next five to 10 years, it is precisely these pressing shorter-term questions that will carry greater weight. And, as I'll discuss in the chapter on AI Governance for Suppliers, it may end up being the case that these shorter-term decisions will have unusually powerful consequences for the longer-term existential risks associated with AI. If we truly reach a singularity-like inflection point where AI achieves the ability to make itself more intelligent without human assistance, leading to an explosive "fwoom" of superintelligence that we as humans can neither understand nor control, there is good reason to believe that it will learn from the revealed preferences contained in records of our decisions, rather than simply our statements about our intentions, or declarations of our moral principles meant to operate as prescriptive guardrails. As we have seen with the development and adoption of cybersecurity standards at a global scale, there are few levers more powerful to drive organizational change than the lever of requiring that change as a prerequisite to receiving a contract or a purchase order from your customer.

8

Winning the Business Case for the Predictive Enterprise

MAKING THE CASE for enterprise transformation is absolutely vital to success of the Predictive Enterprise. It is also no easy task.

First, as an advocate for transformation within a large enterprise, you are probably proposing a change that is viewed by stakeholders as (1) optional, or at least subject to potential de-prioritization, (2) involving significant effort by them and their teams, and (3) likely to result in a long and painful adjustment period, even if there is value to be gained from the resulting change. You don't tend to make friends and win influence in group decisions by going around telling people to work harder, especially if they are not being offered any additional compensation for doing so.

And yet, as a transformation advocate, champion, or project leader, this is often exactly what you must do. This is one reason why this unlucky job often falls to a consultant, who has no personal loyalty or friendship with the people being wrangled.

Second, as an advocate for the Predictive Enterprise approach, you are introducing new ideas beyond the traditional value framework used to assess transformations in the Automation Enterprise. The Automation Enterprise framework is often only capable of measuring value by referring to the existing cost of human labor and then incrementally reducing those costs by replacing human activity with machines. The Predictive Enterprise framework is about measuring the value and benefit from activities and processes that humans are not capable of performing today. This shift requires introducing new vocabulary, new metrics, and new frameworks for evaluation and analysis that align with the transformation opportunity created by AI for large enterprise operations in the Predictive Enterprise.

While a lot of corporate slogans and conference speakers pay lip service to the power of creativity, innovation, and so-called "out of the box" thinking, the truth is—especially at large enterprises—that a lot of operational roles are designed to attract personalities who would prefer everyone's thinking to stay very much in the box. These individuals tend to exhibit something approximating a full-body allergic reaction to creativity that reflects careers spent deeply entrenched within incentive structures biasing them toward predictability and against risk. Entrenched incentive systems can have a very powerful impact on people's inner lives.

This all makes complete rational sense. In manufacturing and supply chain, this bias toward the status quo and toward predictability and repeatability is also aligned with incentives around minimizing costs. Changes to product designs often come at a cost, and the cost tends to be higher the longer the supply chain is, and the longer the distance between the product designer and the manufacturer. Changes to product designs make production processes and supply chains that are less repeatable and therefore less predictable. Incentives thus mold manufacturing and supply chain professionals to avoid change, since we have learned from experience that each design change reduces repeatability and predictability, creates risk, adds cost, and thus introduces new potential causes of delays.

Minimizing risks through operational predictability and repeatability is anathema to transformation, which often requires iteration, hypothesis-testing, and periods of discovery and validation. This is not to say that you don't run into interesting people with creative personalities who are leading operational functions at large enterprises around logistics, inventory, facilities, planning, procurement, manufacturing, quality, or supply chain. But it is to say that these roles are rarely scoped to reward or incentivize transformational leadership behavior. And so, as a result, it is entirely rational and to be expected that supply chain, procurement, and manufacturing teams and organizations are often resistant or even openly hostile to organizational change, including transformation projects involving new technologies, new processes, and proposals for new behavior patterns and habits. This was true before AI, and AI has not done anything to change the incentive structures within which these professions operate.

For many executives working in supply chain and manufacturing, the last big intellectual paradigm that took off in operations management was 30+ years ago with Six Sigma or Lean Manufacturing, the former of which promotes an emphasis on quality assurance for production at massive scale, and the latter of which emphasizes tracking how information and materials flow through a process, often leveraging so-called "kanban" thinking.[1] Lean and Six Sigma are both important and transformative paradigms, but today they are hardly new ideas. This isn't to say that there haven't been big bold new ideas in large enterprise manufacturing since then, especially around outsourcing, value chains, and the recent introduction of connected technology and real-time transportation visibility. But in general, the pace of change in the underlying technology, especially AI, has far outpaced the introduction of management frameworks for both understanding and measuring the technology's economic and financial value. This, in turn, has meant that more often than not professionals working in large enterprise operations are not initiators or kickstarters of transformation projects, but rather are reacting to projects proposed by teams of consultants, executives, and stakeholders from other functions.

Part of what makes Arkestro's customer case studies remarkable and noteworthy is that these are all case studies of enterprise AI transformations driven and led by procurement and supply chain professionals and executives themselves. Rather than being the result of a mandate or edict foisted upon the teams from the CIO or other executives at the very top of the organizational hierarchy, these are initiatives that were championed by supply chain and procurement teams. The goal of this chapter is to share learnings from the groundswell approach to enterprise AI transformation by sharing the business case template that was effective in aligning stakeholders and mobilizing executive teams. The process of making and winning support for a business case is often a critical step in any large enterprise decision to undertake a transformation project of any kind at enterprise scale. Without re-thinking the business case template for the Predictive Enterprise approach, many stakeholders risk defaulting to what they know, which are value frameworks developed within the Automation Enterprise.

The challenge in the Automation Enterprise framework for value is that it primarily measures value by substituting human activity with machine activity. Therefore the value of the transformation is often tied to and capped at the underlying value of the human labor in the first place. To put it bluntly, this Automation Enterprise paradigm creates a real alignment problem for large enterprises that have scaled manufacturing during the past fifty years, which has involved outsourcing factory labor to low-cost countries. Since relying on labor in low-cost countries has been significantly cheaper, significantly easier to manage, and significantly easier to justify as a business strategy than implementing automation, it should come as no surprise that executive leadership teams in low-margin manufacturing businesses with extreme cost sensitivity have frequently opted to prolong and life-extend legacy outsourced operations rather than invest in automation or AI as a business strategy.[2] This dynamic is one of many reasons why a new framework for developing business cases around enterprise AI transformation has become necessary in the Predictive Enterprise. It is also why the business case exercise actually represents a powerful opportunity in value engineering, value communication, and stakeholder alignment that underlies the long-term success of these initiatives at global scale.

Value Architecture in the Business Case for Predictive Transformation and the Opportunity for Translational Alignment Across Functional Metrics and Targets

Once the paradigm shift around the Predictive Enterprise is properly understood, the question around transformation is truly not if but when and how to get started with a Ready, Aim, Fire game plan that corresponds with a set of activities to group within the buckets of Now, Next, and Later. Thus, the business case discussion should be viewed in the context of prioritizing transformation projects, allocating resources, and setting targets and schedules. As most management consultants will tell you, the tension in creating these value architectures is between a desire for "quick wins" and the imperative to create durable improvements that can operate at scale.

As Len DeCandia notes in this book's Conclusion, which discusses the formation of so-called 100 Day project plans, the purpose of thinking in 100 Day units of time isn't to whipsaw from one project to the next after this period of 100 days has elapsed, but rather to take a clinical, disciplined approach to transformation that uses the first 100 days to lay a foundation for ongoing continuous transformation and acceleration over the next 1,000 days. Viewed in this context, "quick wins" are necessary but not sufficient for the success of a transformation project in the Predictive Enterprise approach, and thus business cases must include elements that are measurable and reportable within both time periods: the first 100 days and the next 1,000.

Business cases are often biased toward measuring value purely in dollars or equivalent units of economic value that are fungible with shareholder value as linked to a company's balance sheet. However, we also know from our discussion of double binds in Better Deals, Safer, that any business case that inadequately measures the value of avoiding risk in the process of pursuing value will be viewed with skepticism by any supply chain professional keenly aware of the trade-offs between cost and performance. Therefore, a successful business case for a transformation in the Predictive Enterprise needs to communicate an awareness of these historic trade-offs and explicitly address the ways in which the Predictive Enterprise approach overcomes them e.g., by aligning the shortest cycle times for an approval process with a competitive outcome. While every large enterprise has a different process for creating and approving business cases, I wanted to share a template for making the case for transformation that has been used successfully to win support for AI initiatives aligned with the Predictive Enterprise. This business case template consists of four elements:

Cost Value	Margin improvement from higher rates of savings on spend currently negotiated by procurement
Bandwidth Value	Productivity increase per headcount, quantified as the cost of additional headcount needed to achieve optimal spend influence
Scale Value	Application of higher rate of savings on spend not currently negotiated by procurement, now made accessible via faster throughput cycles and greater bandwidth
Continuous Value	Increase in frequency of competitive market tests that prevent value leakage via continuous benchmarking and always-on cost monitoring

Looking at the Predictive Process Framework from earlier, the most common application of this business case would be to move a process that has already been digitized (e.g., gone from Undefined to Defined and is now sitting at Reactive) and to transform this functional process portfolio to become Predictive. However, it's worth giving a specific formula example for each of these buckets in the value architecture. The most challenging of these buckets is the final one: Continuous Value, which represents a new type of decision being made at enterprise scale via Continuous Benchmarking using predictive market tests. We'll look at an example from predictive procurement around how transformations can result in the creation of novel metrics associated with new form factors for decision-making in the Predictive Enterprise and give an example of how to calculate a formula for this type of target.

A Friendly Caveat and Word of Caution About the Role of Business Cases in Transformation Projects

When creating business cases, it's useful to keep the following assumptions firmly at the front of one's mind:

1. **All Models Are Wrong, Some Models Are Useful.** Business cases are fundamentally abstractions used for making organizational decisions based on the conditional truth of assumed hypotheses. Business cases are a way of asking: If X and Y and Z were true, would this investment of time, energy, and capital be a wise decision based on the expected Return on Investment? Crucially, business cases are *not* meant to be viewed as forecasts, forward-looking statements, or commitments to deliver X or Y or Z (and if they were viewed this way, then stakeholders and transformation teams would assiduously avoid making them). I have even seen Business Cases that include specific Safe Harbor language to avoid any potential confusion or conflation.
2. **Confidence Comes from Analyzing Multiple Outcome Scenarios.** Business cases can and should be expressed as a range of potential outcomes, often including Conservative (Base Case), Realistic Case, and Optimal Case. This will give stakeholders a way to understand the assumptions in the model and give them a way to play with inputs and iterate on those assumptions in ways that reflect their functional knowledge and organizational perspective.

As my Arkestro cofounder Rob DeSantis and our SVP of Marketing Stuart Gold are fond of saying: "People endorse what they help create." Every stakeholder with relevant experience should be invited to provide their input on what inputs feel Conservative, Realistic, and Optimal. The more stakeholders play an active role in the co-creation of the business case, the more credibility it has and the more it can serve a function to align stakeholders around not just endorsing but executing on the steps required for a successful AI transformation. For the template example, we are going to use an example value architecture from a predictive procurement transformation business case.

Cost Value

Storytelling Element: Stakeholders creating this business case element want to show that this transformation will enable them to influence more enterprise spend without adding more headcount, and that it will also amplify the value of their spend influence activities on a per activity basis by leveraging AI in predictive technology. This element is meant to engage and solicit endorsement from stakeholders in Finance and across the Executive Leadership Team. Please note that once you have produced the margin impact number below, it is extraordinarily valuable to translate this number into several additional financial metrics depending on the configuration of your business. For example, if you are in a low-margin business, it can be extremely powerful to show a calculation for the Sales Equivalency of Savings (e.g., how many units you would need to sell in order to match the equivalent margin impact of savings). Let's say that you are in a business with 10% margin and your average selling price is $100. If you deliver $100 in cost savings, that goes straight to the bottom line. In order to create the same margin impact from sales, you would need to sell 10 units, since each at a 10% margin each unit that sells for $100 only delivers $10 worth of margin impact. If you save $1 million in costs, then you would need to sell 10 million units. The lower the margin of the business, the more valuable additional cost savings becomes. For publicly traded companies, you can also perform the calculation to translate cost savings into Earnings Per Share (EPS). In October 2025, Valvoline, the retail giant who is an Arkestro reference customer, saw their procurement team recognized due to an analyst report in Investing .com on their Earnings Per Share beat:

Investing.com

In other recent news, Valvoline Inc. reported its third-quarter 2025 earnings, surpassing analysts' expectations with an earnings per share (EPS) of $0.47, beating the forecast of $0.45. The company also exceeded revenue projections, reporting $439 million compared to the anticipated $436.74 million. Additionally, Valvoline has achieved significant cost reductions through its partnership with the predictive procurement platform Arkestro, realizing annual savings of 14% on maintenance, repair, and operations spend and 27% on snow removal and landscaping services at corporate stores.

This is exactly what any practitioner working with the Predictive Enterprise wants to see as the result of their scenario modeling that goes into a winning business case.

Cost Value: Margin improvement from higher rates of savings on spend currently negotiated by procurement		
What is your current Addressable Spend influenced by procurement negotiations today?	$100,000,000	
What is your team's current rate of cost savings attained on spend influenced by procurement negotiations today?	5%	
What is the current value of annual cost savings delivered today?	$5,000,000	
Incremental lift on rate of cost savings using Predictive Procurement		
Base Case, 2x:	(10% Rate)	+5.00%
		$5,000,000

Cost Value: Margin improvement from higher rates of savings on spend currently negotiated by procurement		
Realistic Case, 3x	(15% Rate)	+10.00% $10,000,000
Optimal Case, 4x	(20% Rate)	+15.00% $15,000,000
Realistic Case as Equivalent of Profit from Sales Units: (Assume 1 unit sells for $10,000 at a 10% profit margin)	**10,000 sales units of value**	

Bandwidth Value

Storytelling Element: Here we are showing the value of procurement's time represented by the cost of procurement headcount needed to properly influence the full portfolio of enterprise spend. The critical element of this business case is to communicate the value of amplifying the team's time as expressed in additional capacity for spend influence. This approach also has the effect of communicating the cost associated with achieving similar business outcomes solely by hiring additional headcount, which may be an alternative option under consideration in the context of evaluating a Predictive Enterprise approach.

Bandwidth Value: Productivity increase per headcount, quantified as the cost of additional headcount needed to achieve optimal spend influence	
Assume 1 Procurement Professional Average Salary at $100,000	
Assume 1 Procurement Professional Influences ~$20,000,000 in Spend	
Addressable Spend not influenced by negotiations today	$500,000,000
Number of additional Procurement Professionals needed to influence	25
Annual cost of Procurement Professionals needed to influence	$2,500,000
Value case expressed as Equivalent of Profit from Sales Units:	**2,500**

Scale Value

Storytelling Element: Stakeholders creating this business case element want to show that this transformation will fundamentally reduce administrative burden and improve the time it takes to complete an existing end-to-end process. This element is meant to engage and solicit endorsement from stakeholders in Operations and across the procurement and supply chain organization in a "What if together we could deliver _____ as a durable process improvement across x% of your workflows?" discussion. This is where the impact of a predictive transformation becomes particularly differentiated via a novel enablement of a Faster-Than-Human workflow that replaces clerical human decisions with Humanless Loops. In the below value formula, we are storytelling around overcoming the Speed-Control Double bind: by making a dramatic improvement in the speed associated with collecting competitive quotes, we can now enable far more spend across the so-called "long-tail" of purchases to be covered by the procurement process without adding time, work, or headcount.

Scale Value: Application of higher rate of savings on spend not currently negotiated by procurement, now made accessible via faster throughput cycles and greater bandwidth	
What is your current Addressable Spend NOT influenced by procurement negotiations today?	$500,000,000
Application of cost savings rate to new spend using Predictive Procurement	
Base Case:	10%
Incremental Return on Investment of Predictive Procurement	$50,000,000
Realistic Case:	15.00%
	$75,000,000
Optimal Case:	+20.00%
	$100,000,000
Realistic Case as Equivalent of Profit from Sales Units:	**75,000 sales units of value**
(Assume 1 unit sells for $10,000 at a 10% profit margin)	

Continuous Value

Storytelling Element: The main skepticism from Finance organizations regarding the tangible cost savings impact reported by procurement relates to two realities that must be acknowledged: (1) large enterprises often struggle to buy off the contracts that they negotiate, thereby failing to utilize the special rates and discounted prices, and (2) suppliers have a habit of slowly increasing their pricing over time after winning a deal. Both of these organizational behavior patterns are the result of entrenched incentives systems and can thus be re-written via the Predictive Enterprise approach simply by changing the frequency and cadence of market tests and increasing the continuous visibility of undesirable supplier price updates and stakeholder off-contract buying activities. However, these behavior patterns may take significant time to change. What can be long-term transformative with fast time-to-value is simply the frequency and cadence of market tests. What would it feel like to market test every dollar spent with a supplier on an annual basis? For many large enterprises, this simply isn't possible today. But soon, with the Predictive Enterprise approach, competitively sourcing every dollar spent and testing the price on an annual and sub-annual basis will be possible. This can be defined as either Spend Under Prediction or Supply Under Prediction (SUP), the percentage of your spend or your supply base that has been checked versus an actual quote via a multi-source market test within a set period of time. Critically, this benchmarking activity does not need to be a competitive bid process, and the existing supplier does not even need to know that they are being benchmarked. The purpose of Spend Under Prediction is to build confidence that the costs of your preferred suppliers are "in-band" with market pricing available from other potential sources, and to proactively identify materials and items where your enterprise is paying a significantly higher price than would be available from other potential sources or suppliers. What your enterprise does with this information should be left to the supply chain and procurement professionals to decide. But as we have seen, arming people with data, especially competitive options, can actually create better collaboration with preferred suppliers, strengthen supply chains, and create resiliency maps and crisis response plans in the event of a supply disruption event. Therefore, just like Spend Under Management produces a heuristic method, setting goals associated with high-performing procurement organizations, Spend Under Prediction offers a heuristic for setting goals associated with costs and negotiation activities across any supply chain.

Continuous Value: Increase in frequency of competitive market tests that prevent value leakage via continuous benchmarking and always-on cost monitoring	
What is the total addressable spend with suppliers?	$600,000,0000
Base case of recoverable value leakage via continuous benchmarking	1.5%
	$9,000,000
Realistic case of recoverable value leakage via continuous benchmarking 2%	
	$12,000,000
Optimal case of recoverable value leakage via continuous benchmarking 3%	
	$18,000,000
Realistic Case as Equivalent of Profit from Sales Units:	**12,000 sales units of value**
(Assume 1 unit sells for $10,000 at a 10% profit margin)	

	Annual Return on Investment	**Annual Equivalent Sales Units**
Cost Value	$10,000,000	10,000 equivalent sales units
Bandwidth Value	$2,500,000	2,500 equivalent sales units
Scale Value	$75,000,000	75,000 equivalent sales units
Continuous Value	$12,000,000	12,000 equivalent sales units
Realistic Case Annual Return on Investment:	**$99,500,000**	99,500 units would have to be sold to equal the value of this ROI

What makes a winning business case for the Predictive Enterprise is not so much exact precision but simply developing scenarios for value creation that generate a plausible range of exciting outcomes for executive leadership teams to evaluate. Business cases for AI in the Predictive Enterprise approach are also a cultural opportunity for procurement and supply chain leaders to spotlight the value of the work that they are doing today that aligns with top-level business metrics. High-performing supply chain and procurement teams should view these business cases as opportunities to highlight their wins, show opportunities for doubling down on what's working, and use AI to clear blockers or timesucks that prevent them from acting on other opportunities.

9

Fears, Anxieties, and Dependencies Regarding Enterprise Data Quality Issues for AI

AMONG THE MOST common reasons that a large enterprise leadership team fails to act with a sense of urgency and excitement when it comes to aggressively pursuing AI use cases within the Predictive Enterprise is related to poor data quality. Often, I will hear an executive or supply chain practitioner repeating the phrase: "Without good data, AI is worthless." A 2024 survey from Rimini Street shows how prevalent this belief structure is among CIOs at large enterprises:[1] A combined 87% of CIOs agree that historical data is the secret sauce to getting maximum value out of AI projects for ERP. CIOs also recognize that to get the most value from AI, their current data sets need to be in good shape. As the familiar adage goes, "garbage in, garbage out." ... Only 7% consider their historical ERP data to be in decent shape for AI projects. A combined 94% say their data needs substantial or moderate clean-up to succeed with AI.

Left unchecked, this statement can form a powerful negative belief structure and bias an entire company against ever pursuing an AI transformation or even smaller use case projects. Since many large enterprises are filled with employees who believe that their data is in poor shape, this statement could easily be shortened to be: "AI is worthless." That's not a good belief structure to approach the opportunities created by the AI paradigm shift. This belief structure often replaces employees' innate curiosity with false certainty and replaces a bias toward action with a bias toward hesitation, doubt, and delay. However, despite its dangerous negativity, this belief is not without a grain of truth. This grain of truth needs to be addressed using understanding and nuance rather than generalities and blanket statements. Like most elements of the Predictive Enterprise, the devil is in the details, and the real nuggets of gold are to be found in the nuances of execution and implementation.

Here is the grain of truth: If what you want your AI to do is have it answer or validate an answer to a question about your data (and indeed, a lot of the use cases for the Predictive Enterprise that we have focused on in the digital supply chain do involve question-answering), and the only data that the AI has available from you is incorrect, then the answers that it provides will also be incorrect. A good way to test this is to ask an AI and a human employee to provide you the same answer. If both give you an incorrect answer due to incorrect data, then simply adding AI is not going to fix your problems. If you don't trust your data, then you won't trust the answer that the AI gives you. But yet again, there is a nuance here, because in certain cases identifying specific values within your own data as *incorrect* actually produces value because the cost of having incorrect data is often extremely high, regardless of whether you are pursuing an AI transformation project. And if AI can help you find, flag, fetch, and fix answers to questions that are important for your business decisions, then it can create a dramatic quantity of value. Indeed, a recent exchange between supply chain executives in the executive learning circle Masters of Supply Chain suggests that one of the top use cases for AI in supply chain today involves fixing errors in master data.

Thus, AI projects often create the opportunity to improve the quality of the underlying data in the process of performing a question-answering task. We'll look at a few specific examples related specifically to supply chain and procurement, but one easy and obvious use case that has measurable business value: if your data related to the price of something is higher than what you agreed, then the price that you pay will also be higher than the price that you agreed to pay.

Viewed this way, the existence of poor-quality data, inaccessible data, or data that lives in multiple places without having an identified source of truth (e.g., a single repository where the data is considered valid) represents a fundamental opportunity for AI. AI can help you find, flag, fetch, and fix errors in your data, which creates measurable, meaningful value. This represents a clear area of discussion and shows the power of curiosity for reframing the problem statement correctly around use cases in the Predictive Enterprise approach. Since AI can simulate and predict the value of data and then compare those predictions with answers surfaced from tables that are currently available, the Predictive Enterprise can use ongoing workflows as a tool to continuously cleanse and validate master data.

However, measuring the enterprise value of data quality improvements is notoriously challenging. In this chapter, we highlight several examples around the value of data quality improvements specifically in procurement and supply chain. These examples and case studies can be used to help transform the sentiment around poor data quality from a negative belief structure that resists transformation efforts into a bias toward action and opportunity.

Item-Level Cost Data from Multiple Manufacturing Sites

Even the most data-driven teams who earnestly want to improve their data quality and overcome issues with their legacy Systems of Record can become prone to bad attitudes, self-limiting beliefs, and defeatism. Errors in data can start to feel like glitter: once an error gets into even one table in one system, it can be hard to remove it from multiple reporting pipelines that it feeds. At least one reason for this is the lack of data that most of these teams have about the types and scale of their own data quality issues. One approach that our team at Arkestro undertook early on when broaching this topic with teams within large enterprises was challenging customers about the statistical patterns of their data quality issues. What was the most common data quality issue they experienced? Missing records? Duplicate records? Incorrect identifiers contained in records? Following one of these discussions, our brilliant AI leader Clark Bernier came up with a way to use our own AI models to perform a high-level predictive analysis of the most likely frequency of errors, grouped by error-type, and map these errors to specific tables, items, systems, and processes. This method could easily be repeated across spend categories, business units, supplier cohorts, and sets of transaction records.

Clark called this approach a "data health check," and it helped customers begin to build an understanding of the scope and scale of their legacy data challenges, as well as orient toward root causes and develop fixes. To be clear, this "data health check" mapping exercise was rarely able to resolve the legacy data challenges—especially with item-level entity resolution, a problem that plagues operational functions at nearly every large enterprise, especially those with multiple manufacturing sites, a complex supply base, and multiple business units or acquisitions. Rather, the data health check helped the teams we were supporting to understand and size up their data challenge, reframe these data challenges as opportunities, and then begin associating value with resolving these opportunities through continuous validation and entity resolution.

Of course, in the previous use cases in the Predictive Enterprise, we have shown how executing a process a supply chain and procurement team can deliver dramatic cost reductions by negotiating better deals with suppliers, using tools like game theoretic negotiations with Suggested Offers at mass scale. However, there's also a massive lever to win cost reductions that many teams overlook: fixing historically overlooked errors in item-level procurement data that are pervasive across existing purchase orders, pricebooks, and outline agreements.

Many companies' procurement and purchasing functions are plagued by disparate systems that don't talk to each other, data silos, and a veritable potpourri of differing item-level identifiers. These create translational challenges in matching items to a query. These challenges range from differing item identifiers between a manufacturer part number and a large enterprise's internal part number to the same item having multiple identifiers depending on where it is purchased geographically. The good news is that not only can the problem be fixed, but for many companies, this data quality issue represents an extremely lucrative cost reduction opportunity all by itself.

Below are some of the most common data quality issues that procurement and purchasing teams in large enterprise manufacturing experience, how to recognize them, how to solve them, and how to use data quality issues as levers to create long-term sustainable margin improvement beyond short-term cost savings. Data quality isn't the sexiest story to tell about the Predictive Enterprise, but it may be among the most important. Because the reality is that just like predictive maintenance and the ludicrous image of a hundred mechanics with ear trumpets standing next to a stamping press, there is no practical way to fix all of the issues that large enterprises have in their procurement data using humans alone. If humans armed with Microsoft Excel could have fixed these data quality issues, they would have done so years ago. And the Automation Enterprise solutions, which replace human data analysts with machine analysts or even AI analysts, often simply replicate the same set of errors—not because they don't know what to do, but because they make exactly the same mistakes as the human data analysts. Human data analysts often have no earthly idea what parts or materials the records they are inspecting actually refer to in the physical world. Resolving entities in supply chain and procurement data often depends on so-called "tacit knowledge" from the warehouse or shop floor that is inaccessible to the analysts responsible for cleansing the data and running the reports. Hence, as many enterprises have discovered when confronted with entity resolution problems across their data pipelines—especially part number or item number entity resolution—the only way to trust that you are getting a good outcome is to have the results validated and compared with similar results from subject matter experts. This means finding a way to get this information out of the heads of people who work at your company. This is a data problem that the Predictive Enterprise was built to solve using the exact template we discussed in the predictive maintenance example, using contextual metadata to perform cognitive tasks similar to what a subject matter expert would perform by developing instant, contextual predictions of a given value, and then validating these predictive values with an actual human in a perpetual and continually improving loop.

Unit of Measure

Unit of measure (UOM) is a feature of most cost data that indicates the unit in which the item is being measured (think: pound, box, case pallet, truckload, etc.). The reason that we often find UOM challenges linked to exceptions is that different stakeholders in a transaction may be using the same unit of measure to express different values.

Before founding Arkestro, I remember working on a project as a procurement consultant with a water treatment facility that ordered water softeners from a large supplier of high-volume commodity chemicals. After examining a detailed spend analysis, the water treatment facility's procurement manager noticed that some of the invoices on their orders did not reflect the price they had agreed upon with the supplier.

Digging deeper, it became clear that the price discrepancy was linked to an item-level data quality issue. The procurement manager had believed that the pricing for a chemical would be given in "dry" pounds, whereas the supplier sales rep had believed the pricing would be given in "wet" pounds. Both of these Units of Measure had the same notation: "LB". This accounted for an extraordinary difference in expectations around cost. When the discrepancy was discovered, the supplier was mortified, and since the requirements of the contract clearly stated that the Unit of Measure was in "dry pounds," the supplier's management team took action to make the customer whole.

The reason these cost reductions are especially poignant for manufacturing enterprises with multiple physical plant locations is that different locations often place orders using different UOMs than the UOMs used by the supplier to provide quoted pricing. If a supplier's sales team has an internal pricebook to quote only in truckloads, then the cost reductions negotiated by the procurement team may not be applied to an individual plant location ordering the exact same material in boxes or pallets.

This UOM issue is one reason the results of lengthy negotiations don't always translate into cost savings within everyday contract utilization. It's because the order quantities from individual plant locations don't reflect the agreed-upon UOMs covered by a contractual discount.

Item Description Entities and Unique Identifiers

Inconsistencies in item descriptions can also lead procurement teams to miss big cost-saving opportunities. Consider a manufacturing plant with a process that consumes asphalt. The company has listed the same item description for both asphalt itself and the services associated with delivering the asphalt to the plant in the master system. Same item description, except one is a physical material, and the other is a service.

In this case, there are many ways to reach a solution. For example, the company could use a predictive AI technique to generate comparable benchmarks. If there are two separate clusters of transaction costs related to the same keyword, this approach could help identify that one represented the material and the other the delivery service. The team is then positioned to unlock cost reductions with the supplier by negotiating elements of all of the cost components, rather than just the cost component associated with the underlying material.

Predictive AI applied in procurement and purchasing data offers the ability to clean a large set of item master data in a matter of seconds. This predictive approach to data can help create a more accurate picture of how the items should be categorized and what UOMs they're being bought and sold in across the different Business Units and physical site locations of a large enterprise supply chain.

Addressing the data quality issue around item descriptions and unique identifiers can allow for more accurate cost benchmarking as well as demand forecasting, which enables win-win conversations with strategic suppliers around cost reduction. Item description plays a crucial role in segmenting historical transactions accurately, enabling companies to compare costs apples-to-apples, and to benchmark their costs against the market more effectively.

Geographic Segmentation

Geographic segmentation involves analyzing how purchase prices vary across individual plant locations or by geographic regions. The cost of the same machine part in Canada and Angola might vary astronomically. This geographical analysis allows procurement teams to identify regional cost differences and fluctuations.

In some cases, geography can also create price differences that amount to arbitrage opportunities for procurement teams, particularly teams that have a dedicated platform for orchestrating logistics once they have purchased a material or item. For example, one executive I spoke with ran supply chain at a large construction trade contractor. This company had a different cost for copper wire in every US state that they operated in. From an operations standpoint, this makes perfect sense. But from a data management standpoint, having a distinct cost for the same item description for every site location was a nightmare—until it became an opportunity. What would happen to their project costs for individual sites when they began buying copper wire at their lowest available existing price? What would happen to their operating margins?

As executive leadership teams look down the barrel of inflationary pressures, considering regional variations and analyzing time series data across a geographically dispersed set of purchasers can be critical to making more informed decisions, negotiating better deals, and reducing costs effectively at scale. These examples may sound arcane or "too in the weeds," but they may represent significant opportunities for margin improvement.

Order Cadence and Tempo Segmentation

Spend data typically doesn't always effectively componentize the costs associated with rush delivery, weekend delivery, demurrage, or other fees associated with unplanned urgent buys. In certain cases, costs are linked to additional fees not even associated with the agreed-upon contracted unit price, which can make them difficult to identify. That's why conducting a time-series analysis on cadence and tempo of orders is so important. You will quickly see if spikes in cost correlate with shorter order cadences, and in which spend categories this issue is most acute. To do this, simply look at a set of transactions for the same item across time and with quantity. This will tell you if there is a potential benefit in consolidating more orders into fewer shipments or if you are potentially paying more for orders that are delivered on a weekend or outside of normal business hours for the specific plant location.

Seasonality Segmentation

Suppose that specific parts, materials, ingredients, or commodities have a pattern of seasonality associated with a rapid influx of demand. In that case, there's often a dramatic cost savings opportunity in strategically timing the negotiation and forming the agreement separately from the finalized order. By leveraging the impact of holidays and seasonal demand to schedule the quoting process with suppliers (rather than simply triage reviews based on quarterly financial reporting periods or contract expiration dates), procurement teams can be proactive in setting desirable terms for their business partners.

Predictably Wrong Demand Plans and Familiar Fire Drills for Spot Buying

Let me first caveat, as my friend Dr. Muddassir Ahmed of SCMDojo has correctly pointed out, a lot of the challenges that I have listed in order cadence and tempo can and should be solved by an improved Sales and Operations Planning process (or Sales, Inventory, and Operations Planning process). During this work ritual, sales leaders meet directly with their counterparts in supply chain, procurement, logistics, and manufacturing in order to determine how to turn the demand forecast in a demand plan that the team can then take out and communicate to suppliers in the form of placing orders. However, in many companies, there are powerful cultural reasons why these forecasts are predictably wrong, and often even a great relationship between sales and supply chain won't fix the problem. Let me quote here from Steve Sanghi's excellent book recounting his tenure as CEO leading Microchip, a company that went from losing money year over year to becoming a profitable $43 billion industry juggernaut. This "predictably wrong" problem, which I have seen now in dozens of large enterprise supply chains, was such an extraordinary pain point for Sanghi that it caused him to convert Microchip's entire global salesforce from a commissioned to noncommissioned function:

> "We observed that leading up to this sales meeting in March/April, our backlog would dry up. We would be wondering every year if the business is going down. Then salespeople would arrive in Scottsdale and negotiate for a smaller [quota] for the coming year. After the sales meeting, when they would go back to their geographies, they would take the customer orders from their drawer and enter them into the company system. The backlog would then get back to normal. So, this was a game to negotiate for a smaller [quota] for the following year and also to ensure that they would make their quota in the next quarter. By not having visibility into the backlog, we would be making the wrong decisions on the manufacturing capacity. If they had entered the backlog earlier, we could have been building the product linearly and with much more notice."[2]

I cannot tell you how many times I have seen this problem cropping up for demand planners. In many large manufacturing enterprises, this is entirely logical from a cultural standpoint; sales teams tend to prefer a forecast that *slightly* underestimates the number of units they will sell so that they can then outperform this estimate. Under promise, over-deliver. Everyone loves a sales team that beats expectations, and salespeople are often financially incentivized to do so through commissions that accelerate when they exceed attainment levels above quota. However, during periods of high demand, this process of having incorrect forecasts becomes extremely expensive. That's because a predictably wrong demand plan can result in the supply chain team underbooking capacity in logistics, in warehouses, or even manufacturing capacity with suppliers who might be backlogged. Ordering or shipping something last-minute at a spot rate can be more than double the cost that was negotiated under a contract agreement. But as supply chain teams learned only too well after the pandemic:

simply because you have a great contract doesn't mean your supplier will give you the capacity, either in manufacturing or logistics. You still need to place your orders in a timely manner. You still need to give your suppliers better insight into your demand forecasts early and often.

It's helpful in these cases to perform a looking-back analysis on historical demand forecasts. By doing so, you are asking the question, "How accurate do my demand forecasts tend to be?" For example, if your demand forecasts are always 5% conservative (and then you end up paying rush delivery fees and spot rates on the 5% that has to be ordered at the last minute), then this is a bias that you can track and eventually adjust for over time, the same way that golfers handicap their performance.

We know that demand forecasting is an iterative exercise that's more of an art than a science at most large enterprises, but if we track the iterations, we can see that like many of our human biases, our demand forecasts are often inaccurate in somewhat predictable ways. In an ideal world, these markups can be used to adjust the demand plan during the planning process, even if the forecast given by sales continues to be wrong for cultural reasons related to the structure of sales commissions. If sales has always been wrong by a margin of 5% in a market where the price of logistics has gone way up, then it can be a useful exercise to lock in some additional capacity that can then be released back to the market instead of having to scramble for spot quotes at the last minute.

Market Basket Consolidation

Order fragmentation and consolidation is a quick win that can help achieve dramatic cost reductions simply by grouping more items and larger quantities into fewer orders with the same supplier. By placing orders for the same items in bulk, it's possible to take advantage of volume-based discounts or rebates associated with that type of consolidation. In certain cases, this outcome can be achieved simply by giving the supplier a single purchase order for the entire market basket, rather than multiple separate purchase orders for subsets of the demand. This is another example of how an administrative process change can have an impact on cost reductions.

These are simple, commonsense approaches anyone in procurement can use to identify and act on cost-saving opportunities at scale. These elements of the Predictive Enterprise not only offer continuous improvement in the quality of the underlying "data foundation" by validating items' unique identifiers across different cycles but also bring about tangible and measurable business benefits for any manufacturing enterprise and its supply chain. This allows large enterprises to embark on a transformation journey that moves their processes from Undefined to Defined to Reactive to Predictive. The process of moving through these stages using AI to help validate data and resolve entities ultimately leads to the creation of new data artifacts at the level of Master Data Management, artifacts that can assist with the entity resolution, version control, and state management challenges that we have discussed in this chapter.

Shortening Approval Cycles to Reduce Costs Associated with Short Lead Times

The problem for large enterprises often arises due to an inflexible and one-size-fits-all process for approving demand and converting that into supply plans. What happens when the market goes from long to short? Capacity in the supply chain gets gobbled up fast, and by the time orders may get sent to preferred suppliers, they have already sold some or all of their allocation.

We also saw this during the pandemic with the logistics market. When the spot market for less-than-truckload (LTL) freight surged, carriers across the supply chain defected from their contracted pricing and sold their capacity on the spot market. Logistics procurement teams at many enterprises were left holding the bag. In many cases, simply being able to approve a purchase order or a carrier contract sooner would have resulted in locking in a lower price, thus avoiding getting shocked by a high freight bill. In the Foreword to this book, Jeff mentions the concept of assigning a financial value to decision speed. This example clearly demonstrates that the cost of shipping a load on a flatbed truck from Dallas to Chicago may be significantly impacted by decision speed. This illustrates where staying thoughtful and curious about the impact of the administrative process on the underlying cost structure of the business, and the relationship between the Predictive Enterprise and the Better Deals, Faster double bind can be especially useful.

Final Thoughts on Data Quality Issues and AI Transformation

When it comes to procurement data and cost reduction, the devil is in the details, and the nuggets of gold are often found in the nuances. Data quality issues may present very real barriers to procurement teams that want to negotiate better deals across their supplier base. It is reasonable to assume that if data quality issues are slowing down humans in their job role, then those same quality issues will get in the way of AI. Outside of making massive changes to cost structures, risk management approaches, or defined processes, improving data quality is one of the most exciting cost-reduction opportunities the teams have to deliver for their CFOs and corporate boards, not only today but over the long term, too.

Adopting a holistic and scalable approach to improving data quality is paramount. A one-time audit of procurement data (e.g., a "data health check") could be a nice place to start, but creating a continuous framework for producing higher-quality data can ensure that your organization can continue to reap lasting benefits. This may involve training new and existing employees on the importance of data quality as well as putting in place structures—whether it's a Predictive Enterprise approach or taking an Automation Enterprise approach to bringing in better machines to assist with quarterly master data cleaning initiatives—that put data quality as a key element of your procurement and supply chain strategy.

At the same time, data quality should be seen as a value creation opportunity for the Predictive Enterprise rather than as a blocker from getting started. Data quality is like any operational metric: to improve it must first be managed, and to be managed it must first be measured. When a report gets shown to an executive and the numbers are incorrect, that can be a source of embarrassment and can also inadvertently communicate a lack of competence or attention to detail. And yet, it is also true that the people who are responsible for creating the ground truth data from which these reports are made are not always strongly incentivized to input correct, consistent, or complete data. That is one of the reasons why the process transformation we discussed in our deep dive on behavioral science and game theory is so exciting. Not only does it radically decrease the effort associated with creating, validating, and approving a quote. It also shifts the effort and onus for "getting it right" across all of the quoted items from a human sales rep to a predictive AI model, a model which is able to both reference and compare a given quote with every quote the supplier has ever created previously, find discrepancies, flag anomalies, fetch corrections, and then fix the underlying tables by annotating the synonymous identifiers as a crosswalk between one set of item identifiers or part numbers (e.g., generating an internal data dictionary used by the customer) and another (e.g., an external data dictionary used by the supplier).

In machine learning, this type of model configuration that enables continuous data quality improvement is sometimes called a Reinforcement Learning Human Feedback Loop, where data is shown to a human subject matter expert capable of validating its entities and annotating its features. And this concept of taking a one-off process and turning it into continuous benchmarking is a signature feature of the Predictive Enterprise when applied to procurement and supply chain. Predictive cannot just be a one-and-done. Predictive must quickly become continuous. Since by definition the Predictive Enterprise only refers to enabling processes that are not possible for a human to perform at scale today, then it is worth establishing that while certain elements of these transformations are potentially attainable by humans today, the holistic transformation of these data into continuous, iterative, always-on artifacts is not. There are not enough hours in the day, there are not enough subject matter experts to validate or verify, and even with an army of additional employees or even with an army of equivalently capable virtual robots, it would not be possible.

This transformation is only possible within the Predictive Enterprise paradigm of generating highly contextual simulations that are expressed at the level of individually identified records, and where a certain percentage of those simulations can then be embedded in a human-facing process to validate or verify the record's status. This is an approach being undertaken today by AI suppliers like Verusen and Tamr across functions like inventory management and serves as an extraordinary use case for large enterprises to contemplate as they seek to build, or re-build their data foundation to become truly "AI-ready."

10

AI Robots in Factories and Warehouses

"[T]here will be no bigger improvement to human flourishing than successfully putting robots to work in the real economy. We are on the precipice of labor on-tap, powered by e-intelligence. That means cheaper, better goods."

—Evan Beard and Packy McCormick

One legitimate criticism of this book is that I have focused heavily on the role that AI and the Predictive Enterprise approach will play in transforming the digital supply chain. Where are all the robots? That's what this chapter is focused on: robots, robots, and more robots. If you are like most executives in manufacturing and supply chain, you have been hearing big promises about robots' impact on productivity for decades, perhaps even your whole career. Since most of your career has taken place within the Automation Enterprise, you have been hearing these promises during a period when outsourced human labor in factories located in low-cost countries has been significantly cheaper, significantly easier to manage, and significantly easier to justify as a management decision than the decision to invest in automation. You have also borne witness to numerous false starts, failed promises, and stall-outs that made headlines, especially around the concept of "lights out" manufacturing or so-called "workerless factories" or "dark warehouses." Both Steve Jobs and Elon Musk tried and failed to create factories without workers, with Musk famously writing in 2018: "Yes, excessive automation at Tesla was a mistake. To be precise, my mistake. Humans are underrated."* *Assembly Magazine*'s Austin Weber writes, "lights-out manufacturing" has been a dream of engineers for at least 200 years and can be defined as ". . . a fully automated facility where human hands never touch a product during the entire manufacturing process."[1]

GM's first attempt at "lights-out manufacturing" took place in its Vanguard factory in Saginaw, Michigan. A test facility dubbed a "factory of the future", the Vanguard facility included more than 50 robots supporting 12 assembly cells, as well as an automated storage and retrieval system for materials handling serviced by a fleet of guided vehicles. Vanguard produced axles and other components with only 42 hourly human workers on the first two shifts and zero human workers on the third shift, and it was able to shift a production line to a new model of axle in less than 10 minutes. The plant closed in 1992 without ever achieving the goal of full "lights-out" production. GE had a similar factory that manufactured lightbulbs in Winchester, Virginia, and could produce 10,000 units of the Pro-80 bulb without human labor. This factory closed in 2010.

As McKinsey's global head of manufacturing Enno de Boer, quoted by Weber in *Assembly Magazine*, stated:

> "The concept of lights-out factories, where there's only machines such as robots operating, hasn't been talked about much among discrete manufacturers since the 1980s. Instead, the lean manufacturing movement of the last two decades has showcased the power of the human operator on the factory floor. Many companies failed at attempts to implement lights-out automation in the past, because humans can often do a much better job than machines. Humans are extremely flexible. There are many things that robots can't do that humans can. For instance, the creative and cognitive power of humans can easily improvise and solve problems related to assembly tasks."[2]

As a manufacturing supply chain, or procurement executive, you have also probably specifically been hearing big promises made about

---

* Musk, E. (n.d.). Post on X (formerly Twitter). Retrieved from https://twitter.com/elonmusk/status/98488263

robotics, and recently, big promises around the topic of humanoid robots. You are also probably far too busy focusing on the here and now priorities to dig into every nuance about how AI is transforming the world of robotics. Why, you might ask, would AI robots be any different than factory robots of the past or present? And yet, there are persuasive explanations for why AI could be a game-changer when it comes to robots in factories, and why AI could be an even bigger game-changer when it comes to humanoids in professions like construction.

Now let's imagine for a moment that today, right now, the advances in neural networks and the scaling laws associated with so-called Vision Language Models (essentially the physical AI equivalent of Large Language Models) mean that at some point in the next decade an army of humanoids can basically just show up at nearly any factory production site, spend a few days observing the human workforce, then begin joining the team alongside their human colleagues, and by the end of the week no humans are needed to be present at the factory in order to achieve identical output. Same number of units, same yield, identical productivity. As my friend the journalist Zack Beauchamp would say: "big, if true." How plausible is this scenario? And if it is plausible, approximately how many years before such a thing might come to pass? If we are currently in the early innings of the AI paradigm shift with respect to use cases like predictive maintenance and predictive procurement, then what about the embodied physical dexterity tasks associated with operating a manufacturing production line end-to-end?

For this book I interviewed leading experts working in AI from many of the top robotics labs and heard a diverse range of perspectives from the Bull Case ("human workers likely won't be required to manufacture, distribute, and deliver most materials, goods, and services within the next 5–10 years") to the Bear Case ("neural network-based robotics is in its very early stages, and a lot of things will have to pan out and go exactly right for this technology to diffuse across the wider market over the next decade, with significant probability of stall-outs, plateaus, and stumbling blocks"). Let me be very clear. Within the AI robotics community, there is no expert consensus around whether Vision Language Action models will adhere to the same scaling laws as Large Language Models, whether humanoids will win out over other robotic embodiments, or whether developments in robotics will significantly impact large enterprise manufacturing or supply chains over the next 5–10 years. But there are good reasons for large enterprise supply chain leaders to pay attention to developments in AI robotics, and for that reason it becomes useful for us to talk about what's driving both the Bull and Bear cases. In the unlikely event that you do not care about the future that AI robots will play in the Predictive Enterprise, you are welcome to skip this chapter, although as much as possible I have tried to harvest and present bigger picture lessons from the development of this technology and to apply those lessons across the footprint of the Predictive Enterprise holistically.

The Two Underlying Trillion-Dollar Bets That Are Both Likely Drivers of Each Case

There are two big technology bets that AI robotics firms and their venture capital backers are making today that are likely to drive transformation toward the Predictive Enterprise of tomorrow, and these bets diverge slightly on the question of robotic embodiment: general purpose humanoids or special purpose non-humanoids. (Spoiler alert: the most likely answer is "both.")

On one hand, you have companies like Tesla, Figure, 1x, Neura, and others that are betting on a complete end-to-end robotics tech stack with a humanoid embodiment that includes integrated hardware and software. These humanoid robots are general purpose and "open world," meaning they can perform many tasks and switch between tasks as seamlessly as a human can. However, there are real trade-offs between generalizability and the speed of reinforcement learning on any specific task. That's because humans, after which these humanoids are modeled, are good at doing lots of tasks but are not optimally designed for doing any one task. And switching between tasks, as well as orienting toward the environmental conditions, process steps, and desired end state of new tasks in novel environments is cognitively and computationally intense.

Consider that a basic robot with two-pronged gripper hands has around thirteen degrees of freedom. That's thirteen physical positions that each hand can hold. If the only change you made to this arm was to add five-fingered humanoid hands to this basic robot (e.g., replacing the two-pronged grippers), then you instantly more than double the number of degrees of freedom from thirteen to twenty-seven. Furthermore, human bodies are simply overbuilt for most tasks that exist within a contemporary linear manufacturing production. Think about the task of walking across a factory floor. Human feet on human legs are a benefit if the factory contains stairs, but wheels are a more likely efficient embodiment for movement on any flat, smooth shop floor.

Then on the other hand, you have firms like Physical Intelligence and a lot of the large AI labs that are betting on general purpose cross-embodiment approaches. These firms are focused on scaling the use of Vision Language Action models across AI robots that could be multiple stories tall to pick items off the highest shelves of a distribution center, or that could be hundreds of meters long and contain a full conveyor belt. This cross-embodiment bet wants to train AI Vision Language Action models for as many robotic embodiments as possible, from free-standing robotic arms to full humanoids. But their focus is less on creating a general purpose, open world robot and more on finding tasks and use cases that AI models can do well in the physical world.

The crux of the technologists', innovators', and investors' two bets about whether one or both of these approaches will be successful relates to the scaling laws associated with neural networks and where these scaling laws create inflection points similar to what happened with ChatGPT for Large Language Models. Consider that in 2025 a recent demo from a top AI robotics lab showed a humanoid robot that could sort 30 packages per minute. If you are a manufacturer and you buy a package sorting machine (e.g., a robotic machine that does not look at all like a humanoid), you can achieve output of 400 packages per minute. So why would you possibly consider investing in a humanoid that offers a small fraction of the efficiency you can gain from traditional robotic automation? Because it is likely that this humanoid robot can also do thousands of other tasks, and because in the future the scaling laws from neural networks will increase so that it will begin to approach the efficiency of the package-sorting machine. That said, it is still quite likely that even with neural networks, factory robotics will involve a mix of robotic embodiments, from humanoids to robotic arms to traditional pieces of capital equipment.

Consider the task of painting the body of a car with primer, a task that appears in many automotive manufacturing production lines around the world. If you wanted, you could have people walk around the car with sprayers painting the car, and then theoretically, you could replace all those people with humanoid robots. Or you could do what Tesla does and have a giant robotic arm lift up the car's body and dunk it in a giant vat of primer like dunking a donut into a cup of coffee. No robots with a humanoid embodiment (regardless of the scaling laws of neural networks) are likely to surpass the powerful efficiency gains of one massive arm doing one massive dunk. That's why it is likely that these two bets on humanoid versus other robotic embodiments are likely to be complementary and augment each other within global supply chains as a both/and rather than an either/or. And it's one reason why manufacturers and supply chain teams are still investing in traditional automation and robotics hardware and platforms, even as the gains in scaling neural networks' performance for humanoids and other embodiments of robots race further and further ahead.

The Bull Case: AI Robotics Annie Oakley "Anything You Can Do, I Can Do Better" Generalists and Specialists to Unlock Human-optional "Lights Out" Manufacturing

The Bull Case for industrial autonomy in the short- to medium-term focuses on robots of multiple embodiments, including humanoids, that operate across a variety of new environments and can execute on tasks input by natural language. You can tell a robot to clean the factory floor, and it will perform that task and deliver an outcome equivalent to an experienced janitor. You can tell a team of robots to clean the factory top to bottom, and they will sub-divide the task and perform that task and deliver an outcome equivalent to a team of experienced janitors, perhaps even a full janitorial contractor. AI robots at Physical Intelligence have already shown promise of being able to do this, especially the difficult and computationally intensive challenge of orienting to new environments and decomposing a general mission into discrete sub-tasks and figuring out what task to do in which sequence. For more complex physical manipulation tasks, perhaps you would have the robots come in and observe the janitorial team for a few days, then have every robot shadow a janitor for the next cleaning, and by the third cleaning the janitors are optional. What if it took 30 cleanings to train the robots instead of 3? By the 31st cleaning, we would still wake up in a world where the human janitors are optional.

Even though the value from this type of productivity gain might be expressed in the quantifiable units of the Automation Enterprise, this type of automation also unlocks Predictive Enterprise transformation opportunities. If we stick with the janitorial services example, we can imagine that a team of robot janitors that can work at any time of day or night may enable a more predictive and continuous facility cleaning approach. Using an array of sensors, including cameras, the robot janitors may also predict precise areas of greatest need for cleaning within any manufacturing facility and then dispatch one or two robots when and where necessary, rather than cleaning the entire facility episodically on a pre-set schedule. Much like predictive maintenance, this hypothetical example of humanoid janitors illustrates how an Automation Enterprise application of AI can enable additional operational degrees of freedom that enable a transformation of the management framework and process used to execute a group of functional work-tasks using Outcome-Based Process Re-Engineering. And just like predictive maintenance effectively enables large enterprises to move away from preventative maintenance with its planned downtime and the replacement of parts that may not be close to wearing out, a predictive transformation of janitorial services in manufacturing facilities makes use of automation in the form of robots, but by augmenting them with predictive AI.

General Purpose AI Robots & Humanoids: Overcoming the Greenfield/"Islands of Automation" Double bind in Upgrading Factories and Warehouses

When planning for automation at industrial scale for million-square-foot warehouses or factories, executive leadership teams encounter an immediate fork in the road: build or lease a new warehouse facility or shop floor from scratch, taking advantage of all the new automation to re-imagine the facility from the ground up, or make incremental investments in an existing facility bit by bit, use case by use case? The former would be an example of greenfield automation; the latter would involve creating "islands of automation."

The decision often comes down to cost, as well as an organization's overall priorities and bandwidth. Building a new facility with all the bells and whistles is a massive project. And despite the opportunity of dramatic reductions in future cost associated with greenfield automation using traditional robotics, building and standing up a new facility often takes months or years. That means that the payback period from all the investment is frequently on the order of decades. For many legacy players, if the costs of greenfield automation aren't prohibitive, then the requirements of time, focus, and energy to manage the project are. This means that while there are exciting benefits to greenfield automation, it is unlikely that this approach to transformation will create a tipping point where many enterprises simultaneously pursue the creation of new fully autonomous "lights out" facilities at the same time. However, the promise of general-purpose AI robots and especially humanoids as described in the prior janitorial example means that in the not-too-distant future it may be possible to achieve equivalent benefits to greenfield automation, but at a fraction of the cost, time, and effort.

What's becoming clearer is that unlike traditional robotic automation, these new AI robots are especially useful where the tasks are unstructured, poorly defined, and even undefined. That is a stark departure from traditional robots. And while these robots themselves may currently still be in the Undefined stage of the Predictive Process Framework, if the scaling laws for neural networks hold for Vision Language Action models in ways that resemble Large Language Models, then it won't be long before they become Defined, then Reactive, and then Predictive. That's where there will be potential high-value early opportunities to score big wins: areas of supply chain and manufacturing that are too variable, too high-mix, and too custom for traditional robotics and automation to be able to handle. And it also dramatically lowers the cost for leadership teams to move the Predictive Enterprise from the realm of the digital supply chain, into the realm of the physical supply chain in factories and warehouses.

Let's return to our robot janitors for just a moment, who on the third day are now able to perform the cleaning task better, faster, and more predictively and continuously than the team of human cleaners that they are imitating. Not only do they know how to clean; they can also predict where dirt is most likely to accumulate just like how a predictive maintenance system can hear which machine part might be wearing out. If desired by the enterprise or their supplier, perhaps a smaller number of highly skilled janitors can supervise the robot janitors' work and intervene if necessary in much the same way that a supervisor guides, spot checks, and orchestrates a team of human janitors and cleaners. But after a certain point, it is unlikely that any humans will be necessary to complete this task at all.

As we stated at the beginning when discussing automats versus drive thrus: simply because humans are no longer a dependency for this task to be completed does *not* mean that the task won't be performed *better* or more *trustworthily* with human supervision, or with a human-robot hybrid team of janitors. However, the janitorial scenario is a relatively low-impact use case from a business operations perspective. The Bull Case must therefore include the possibility that these AI robots could fully replace human worker specialists who are in short supply in the labor market (especially in specific geographies). This would also mean unlocking the ability to rapidly relocate production without being limited by geographically constrained workforce availability. That possibility would create dramatically more operational degrees of freedom for supply chain execution.

Let's imagine for a moment that you run a business with a contract manufacturing production site in Southeast Asia. It's monsoon season, and a series of flash floods has made it impossible to operate production or move product out of the country for close to a week. Ultimately, you and your management team would like to relocate your factory to a low-cost area of the United States in a facility with significantly more automation than the one in Southeast Asia, but there's one big problem. The town where you'd like to locate the factory has no welders. Zero. And you cannot manufacture your product without welders. While you could theoretically hire a couple of US-based welders and ask them to relocate, the costs of doing so are significant to the point of being prohibitive. And how often is the monsoon season really going to be this bad? Aren't you better off sticking it out in Southeast Asia?

Maybe, but also maybe not.

Especially as global warming makes severe rainfall a more common occurrence, and potentially lengthens both the duration and severity of the monsoon season. So you are stuck: a factory in a geography with low-cost labor that gets periodically knocked out by monsoons, fires, and other disruptions, versus a factory in a rural US area where having to re-locate welders is going to dramatically eat into your margin. And let's remember that you operate in a low-margin business already. Some years your company isn't even profitable, despite having significant revenues. And every year there are fewer and fewer American welders, and the costs of hiring workers in skilled trades just keeps going up, up, up. But what if you could get one AI robot with the same skills as a master welder up and running for a total cost of $6,000–$20,000/year? Would that change your ability to rethink factory location and your overall footprint of production sites? How does this change your decision?

Believers in the Bull Case are betting that it does. As one roboticist working for a major US automotive manufacturer told me: "If you have humanoids fully as capable as human factory workers, why would you ever manufacture anything overseas again?" That's why one likely consequence of the Bull Case coming true in the next <5 years (versus the next 5–10+ years) is the ability to unlock an additional wave of factory relocation either onshore or nearshore, shortening and multi-threading of supply chains into dense mesh networks. This would also reduce the supply chains' exposure to single points of failure, disruptive disaster events, and escalating price volatility associated with unstable geographies and cross-border trade. The novel capabilities of AI robotics powered by Vision Language Action models have significant potential to overcome or dissolve production bottlenecks related to skilled labor, making re-shoring decisions about where and how to locate factories a much less constrained possibility space.

What Dependencies Are Likely Necessary for the Bull Case to Be True:

- **Achieve ChatGPT-like Performance and Consensus for Scaling Vision Language Action Models.** Jim Fan of NVIDIA robotics has suggested that these current neural network models in robotics as of 2025 are similar to GPT-1 performance, so that would be pre-ChatGPT. Right now, there is no expert consensus on whether it is possible to achieve performance gains similar to Large Language Models in Vision Language Models for robotics. The major difference between the scaling laws associated with Vision Language Models is that Large Language Models have access to the Internet, a training dataset of approximately 30 trillion tokens.[3] There is no equivalent training dataset for Vision Language Models. It is possible that at some point in the future these models could be trained on YouTube videos, VR headset content, or other forms of synthetic data or simulations, which would dramatically accelerate their scaling. However, as robotics researchers like Sergey Levine have persuasively argued, there may be other challenges with training AI robots on so-called "surrogate data" that may limit the ability for VLAs to quickly accelerate their S-curve.[4]
- **Continuing Decreased Costs Associated with AI Robotics:** In 2025 Unitree released a humanoid robot that can be purchased for $6,000, and firms like Formic allow enterprises to rent or subscribe to robotic labor by the hour via a Robots-as-a-Service business model. Since the transition from low-cost labor to robotics will require a period where both workers and robots are working alongside each other (with the robotics observing and recording the physical manipulation tasks by the human workers), it will be critical to reduce the costs associated with experimenting with this new generation of robots so that enterprise manufacturing and supply chain teams feel comfortable making bets around this technology at live production sites.

The Bear Case: Hard Ceilings, Stall-Outs, Plateaus, and Slow, Expensive Scaling of Vision Language Action Models to Robots That Don't Make It Much Past a Few Use Cases for 10+ Years

As one executive leader from Scale AI recently told me: "The only way to get AI robots in manufacturing completely wrong is to express a high degree of certainty about the mass adoption of humanoids. Because right now, we just don't know yet how effective this technology will be. We can be excited, but we need to be cautious about our predictions, especially regarding the time it takes for innovations to diffuse across the manufacturing economy. The first self-driving car drove across America in 1995. It took basically thirty years for Waymo to offer self-driving as a commercial product to consumers at scale. I don't think AI robotics is going to take thirty years this time around, but just remember, we are still early days."

Firefly4342 / Wikimedia Commons / CC BY SA 4.0

Photo of Navlab5, a vehicle created by the Robotics Institute at Carnegie Mellon. The Navlab5 was able to drive from Pittsburgh to San Diego without any human steering, although a human driver was still required for accelerating and braking. https://www.arrow.com/en/research-and-events/articles/the-history-of-self-driving-cars#:~:text=The%20First%20Self%2DDriving%20Car,of%20autonomous%20vehicles%20and%20robotics.

For example, we don't know if Vision Language Action models will hit stall-outs, plateaus, or ceilings similar to how improvements in neural networks slowed down between the release of GPT-3 and GPT-4. We also have no idea how long these plateaus will be. Large enterprises tend to think on long timescales and tend to be risk-averse. As one manufacturing executive who leads large global business with contract manufacturing locations in most low-cost geographies, including both Africa and Southeast Asia, told me: "We don't necessarily like to be first. First isn't always a good thing. Let's be real: early products tend to have serious problems. Let someone else work out all the bugs and issues, and then when it's truly ready for our scale, then we'll bring it in. Remember, Google wasn't the first search engine. Facebook wasn't the first social network. There were a few false starts that happened before the concept of these products really got good. For a consumer, there's little to no switching cost. But imagine if Google were an enterprise product. Now imagine that as a business leader you paid millions of dollars to buy and implement AskJeeves the year before Google came out. You wouldn't feel so great, would you? That's why enterprise technology probably moves a little slower than people realize, even if the underlying technology capability is getting better faster now than in the past."

As several AI robotics experts told me, we also don't know how big a bottleneck the current dearth of training data for Vision Language Action models will be. Research by Scale AI, Physical Intelligence, and Stanford suggests that dramatically increasing the size of training datasets can improve model performance.[5] As I write this, hundreds of workers in a tortilla factory in Mexico are putting on cameras to record ten thousand hours of video of physical manipulation tasks for use in training AI factory robots. Will ten thousand hours be enough? Or will it be a hundred thousand hours that really gives us the unlock? And if it does give us the ChatGPT-like unlock for robots in a tortilla factory, will that unlock transfer seamlessly to robots working in a pretzel factory? Currently, we can't be sure.

There are also prominent roboticists who believe that humanoids are not a practical embodiment due to fundamental issues with balance and dexterity. Rodney Brooks, a roboticist and entrepreneur perhaps best known for inventing the Roomba, wrote in September 2025: ". . .today's humanoid robots will not learn how to be dextrous despite the hundreds of millions, or perhaps many billions of dollars, being donated by VCs and major tech companies to pay for their training. . . we will have plenty of humanoid robots fifteen years from now, but they will look like neither today's humanoid robots, nor humans. We are more than ten years away from the first profitable deployment of humanoid robots, even with minimal dexterity. And a great deal of money will have disappeared, spent on trying to squeeze performance—any performance—from today's humanoid robots. But those robots will be long gone and mostly conveniently forgotten."[6] Less than three months after Brooks published this opinion, the Chinese robotics firm UBTech announced a contract with the Chinese government to deploy a small army of humanoid robots at Fangchenggang border crossing with Vietnam, a contract valued at $37 million. As Raquel Brandao of Earth.com reported: "Walker S2 units will help border staff guide passenger queues, direct vehicles, and answer simple questions from travelers. Some robots will patrol corridors and waiting areas, watching for blocked exits or crowd patterns that might require human officers to intervene. Others will move between cargo lanes to support logistics teams, checking container IDs, confirming seals, and relaying status updates to dispatch centers. Away from the border itself, the fleet is expected to inspect steel, copper, and aluminum facilities, walking structured routes through hot industrial yards."[7] On the surface, none of these tasks that Brandao lists seem to involve a high degree of dexterity. But will this deployment of humanoids signal the beginning of a profitable, scalable business across global supply chains? That remains the big question.

Perhaps just as important in this conversation is the supply chain for robotics itself. Here's a chilling quote from one of my interviews: "As a robotics startup founder, I have two options when it comes to China: I could either use cheap and highly performant Chinese robotic components (and pay more for them whenever they happen to get tariffed), or I could build a completely virtual robot that does something like answer emails, unrelated to physical manufacturing." Just as the Ukrainian military has found during their conflict with Russia, the war is likely to be won or lost for Ukraine due to the startling effectiveness of its asymmetric ability to leverage cheaply made Chinese drones at massive scale.[8] By one estimate, over 80% of the battlefield kills against Russian troops that Ukraine has achieved during the war have been through Chinese drones, many of which are essentially flying bombs with explosives attached to them that are never expected to return to base.[9] With this strategy, lowering cost and increasing scale have proven absolutely critical, a reality that highlights the dependence on dominant Chinese drone manufacturers. Another quote from my interview with the executive at Scale AI is worth sharing: "Is your book about how the US is going to get absolutely crushed by China when it comes to the AI robotics arms race? Because if that's not the focus, it probably should be."

Therefore, the Bear Case for AI robotics development in factories may involve either a hot or cold conflict (or even just an escalating trade war that involves retaliatory export controls being placed on a range of dual-use products and materials) between the United States and China in which all of our supply chains for developing robotics hardware get frozen or massively constrained. This Bear Case would perhaps allow China to race ahead in developing the next generation of superhuman supply chains, manufacturing, and operations management and then hoard the benefits of that productivity gain for domestic competitive advantage.

This is one of the many reasons why conceiving of industrial AI as an arms race is significant: while the US and China remain among each other's most important trading partners, as de-globalization, reshoring, and nearshoring continue there will be opportunities for either party to consider using industrial supply chains as a weapon of conflict and geopolitical leverage. China has already shown willingness to do this when it comes to rare earth metals.[10] The implications of such a conflict could have substantial impacts on the speed of AI development and macroeconomic transformation.

While there are a lot of exciting opportunities in the development of AI robotics and drones in the world of the physical supply chain, they are less certain and less ready for enterprise scale than the AI use cases we have discussed in the digital supply chain. Of course, no one correctly predicted the arrival of ChatGPT, and the world of AI robotics is a rapidly evolving and accelerating area of development. However, in understanding the opportunities available for AI transformation in the Predictive Enterprise today, the biggest scalable wins in the physical supply chain are likely to come from the applications of sensors that enhance remote monitoring and end-to-end visibility, rather than the wholesale introduction of general purpose robotics beyond traditional automation. These opportunities are substantial, as real-time visibility can provide a massive unlock for Outcome-Based Process Re-Engineering, and sensorized infrastructure and robotics can certainly predict and preempt human actions and decisions. Whether the Bull or Bear Case proves to be correct for AI robotics, enterprise supply chains will continue to undergo iterative changes related to both cost pressures and decision speed. When general purpose robots do arrive, the end-to-end processes they fit into will likely have already undergone a vast, predictive transformation.

11

Why Procurement and Supply Chain Hold the Keys to Responsible AI Governance Across the Enterprise

UNTIL NOW, WE have been focused on the story around the Predictive Enterprise as it manifests within superhuman supply chains in large enterprises. In other words, we have been sharing case studies that are especially relevant to back-office operations functions and operations management. However, there are certainly many other AI use cases relevant to large enterprises. Some of them are examples of the Predictive Enterprise, others are examples of autonomous systems, still others are advanced examples of the Automation Enterprise. This next section focuses on a different lens through which to view enterprise transformation beyond simply how AI and predictive technologies will impact procurement and supply chain: the fact that regardless of whether AI is being used in sales, marketing, R&D, or any number of other functions, it is most likely being provided by a supplier that is a technology developer or platform, and this supplier of the AI product or solution itself must be selected via a procurement process and managed using an ongoing relationship management framework.

The "aha" moment for procurement, sourcing, and supply chain professionals begins with an insight that is both counterintuitive and urgent: AI adoption is moving faster among small and mid-sized enterprises (SMEs) than among large enterprises.

A Wharton 2023–2024 study found that workplace AI usage—defined as using AI at least once a week—has grown dramatically across nearly every business function. While IT, marketing, operations, management, finance, and legal show steady gains, the most dramatic year-over-year growth is in HR, purchasing, and procurement. But adoption isn't evenly distributed. Smaller companies are racing ahead. Firms with revenues below $2 billion report adoption rates near 78%, while those above $2 billion are at just 48%. The larger the company, the slower the scope and frequency of AI usage.[1]

Larger enterprises face heavier restrictions that slow down adoption. Regulatory compliance requirements often limit experimentation, while strict data security and governance policies create additional layers of oversight. Formal approval processes for employees who want to use AI tools add friction. On top of that, cultural inertia within highly structured organizations makes it harder to embrace new ways of working quickly, especially for large manufacturing enterprises who are often skeptical of being early adopters for technologies before they're fully baked.

These constraints—though necessary—mean that official adoption rates of AI tend to be lower in big enterprises. (Unofficial adoption rates—sometimes called "shadow AI"-are less well understood but many reports indicate they are quite high).[2] Meanwhile, smaller companies are experimenting freely.

This emerging AI adoption asymmetry between smaller firms and large enterprises has startling implications. It means that the smaller suppliers of a large enterprise will often have implemented AI months or years before the large enterprise has, and AI is likely to be embedded within the suppliers' products and service experiences regardless of whether it is visible to their larger customers.

The asymmetry between large enterprises and their suppliers means that procurement and supply chain teams are on the front lines of discovering, mitigating, and managing AI risk related to suppliers, both new AI-native suppliers and existing suppliers who adopt or acquire novel AI-enabled capabilities within existing offerings.

The questions that large enterprise procurement and supply chain organizations ask suppliers, the conversations that happen during Quarterly Business Reviews, the supplier qualification process, and the vetting and restrictions that get enforced over the next one to five years, will determine how responsibly and sustainably AI is adopted across the global business ecosystem. It may also lay the groundwork for how a future Artificial General Intelligence or Superintelligence is likely to evolve.

Part of the reason that this topic is of such urgency is that traditional Responsible AI Risk and AI Alignment efforts are predominantly focused on first-party and second-party risk, rather than third-party risk involving suppliers. Let's define these terms in order to be specific about where the gaps in governance can create material AI risk for large enterprises.

First-party AI risk is the risk that you have if you are developing an AI model yourself. Unless you work at one of the big AI labs developing a foundation model, or you are starting an AI business unit that is developing in-house AI for use by your customers or available for free to users, your organization probably does not incur very much first-party AI risk.

Second-party AI risk is if your customers, or customer-facing employees use a generally available AI product in ways that lead to unintended negative consequences. It is the risk of those consequences that most Responsible AI governance frameworks are designed to manage. However, what about the use of AI by third parties, such as suppliers, on your behalf, and with or without your knowledge?

This is third-party AI risk, and due to the fact that for most large enterprises, their suppliers will have more advanced AI capabilities before their internal teams, it is both the most likely short-term category of AI risk exposure and the area that is least adequately addressed by existing responsible AI governance frameworks.

Suppliers Are the Largest Surface Area for Enterprise AI Risk

We have seen this movie before. When companies began to identify risks associated with cybersecurity, it often fell to procurement and supply chain teams to gather supplier details regarding Information

Security and Compliance best practices, a trend that remains prevalent to this day. This isn't necessarily bad—one of the biggest improvements in cybersecurity came from large enterprises requiring new suppliers to pass an Information Security Review before procurement would approve a contract. However, this process means that procurement and supply chain teams are on the front lines for protecting large enterprise ecosystems from cyber-attacks by ensuring that the third parties they do business with are not vulnerable.

As this practice gained maturity within large enterprises, it was standardized in the form of several third-party certifications, such as SOC 2 and ISO 270001. Due to the similar structure of third-party risk related to the unconstrained use of AI by suppliers, it is hardly far-fetched to imagine that responsible AI governance for third parties may follow a similar evolutionary pathway.

As with cybersecurity, responsible AI governance for suppliers is likely to mature in stages. The pathway may unfold in three steps:

1. Incorporate AI-related questions into RFPs and Quarterly Business Reviews as part of third-party risk programs.
2. Update Supplier Codes of Conduct, stating expectations such as Affirmative Disclosure regarding use of AI in specific areas of operational performance and work performed on behalf of the large enterprise and covered under their scope of work and Master Service Agreement.
3. Adopt holistic programs for responsible AI use by suppliers. These programs set targets for how AI should and should not be used, including restrictions in sensitive supply categories. Programs also introduce standardized due diligence templates for strategic suppliers. Over time, these templates become a required part of sourcing processes, supplier onboarding, and ongoing supplier information management.

We Can Ill Afford to Outsource AI Risk to Suppliers with Faster Adoption and Less Governance (Again)

There is a real danger in developing Responsible AI Governance for large enterprises that we will simply create an incentive for outsourcing this risk to suppliers with fewer rules and less oversight. One might argue that this is more or less exactly what happened with carbon costing and carbon accounting. In the early days of carbon-focused Corporate Social Responsibility programs, companies often calculated emissions by tying every dollar spent in a given category to a fraction of a megaton of carbon emitted. This approach created a perverse incentive: instead of reducing emissions, firms could simply outsource them to third parties worse at measuring them.

Indeed, this concern was part of what motivated the creation of the Scopes Framework for carbon reductions, where Scope 1 is carbon emissions from onsite energy production, Scope 2 is related to carbon emissions from onsite energy consumption, and Scope 3 is carbon emitted by suppliers as part of the enterprise's ongoing operations. Robust evidence exists that many US firms that have reported significant net carbon reductions have significantly outsourced those emissions to their overseas suppliers in countries with less transparency.[3]

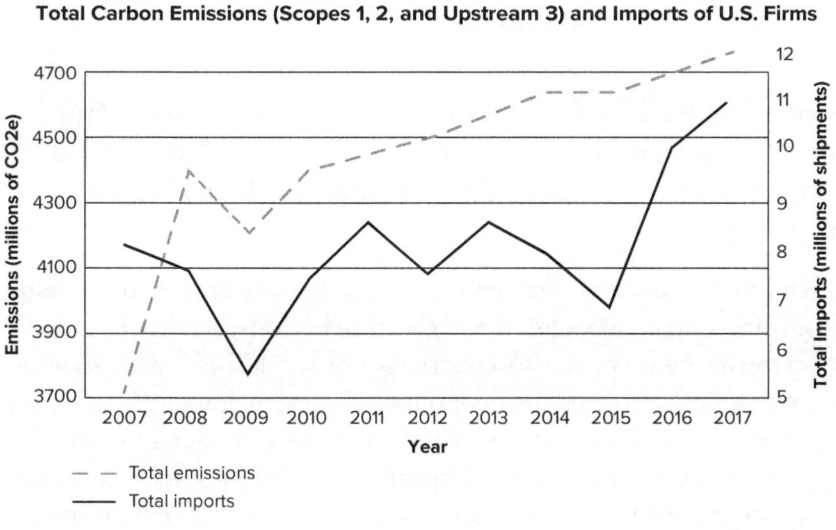

The question to ask here is: How do we prevent this same outsourcing of risk happening with AI risk? And the answer is to move with a sense of urgency to begin discovering and mitigating AI risk across enterprise supply chains sooner rather than later, and by embracing a

Scopes Framework in which Scope 3 is elevated and prioritized with equal or greater urgency as Scopes 1 and 2.

The Scopes AI Risk Framework offers a way to map and understand them.

1. **Scope One—Model Developers**
   Risks faced by companies building AI models (e.g., OpenAI, Google, Anthropic, or those working with open-source frameworks like Llama). These risks are technical, developmental, and generally confined to AI labs.
2. **Scope Two—Employee Use**
   Risks from employees using AI tools to perform tasks, whether internal or customer-facing. Most large enterprises manage this with policies, restrictions, and AI governance councils.
3. **Scope Three—Supplier and Partner Use**
   Risks from suppliers, and partners using AI—sometimes on behalf of enterprises, sometimes in unrelated parts of their business. These are the most opaque risks, since enterprises may have little visibility unless they ask.

Restricting AI Use Makes Firms Less Competitive. But Without Governance, Unrestricted Use of AI By Third Parties Creates Compounding Hidden Risks to Business Continuity

The stakes go beyond compliance or ethics. There is a measurable bottom-line impact associated with getting responsible AI governance correct versus being either too restrictive or too laissez-faire. AI adoption by suppliers reshapes the economics of service delivery across multiple spend categories. For suppliers, AI drives higher margins. For buyers, it therefore also creates opportunities for significant cost savings. Procurement teams motivated by sustainable cost reduction cannot afford to overlook AI—or the risks of adopting it irresponsibly, either too quickly or too slowly.

Take contact call center service providers for customer support. AI adoption here has been rapid because the business case is obvious. AI allows a single agent to handle dramatically more calls—or in some cases, allows calls to be resolved without any human agent's intervention at all. The result? Same or better service at much lower cost. For suppliers, that means higher profit margins. For enterprises, it means a potential wave of cost savings—if procurement teams are asking the right questions about AI usage and building governance frameworks that ensure benefits are shared. Call centers offer a classic Automation Enterprise business case: doing a lot more with a lot less.

To frame the argument in blunt terms: AI is going to make money. A lot of money. The question is—will it make money for your suppliers, or for your business's bottom line? The answer depends on how quickly and effectively your procurement function implements responsible AI governance, in conversation with the correct stakeholders, and with the appropriate customization and tailoring of AI governance practices for each spend category.

Spend Category Case Study: Real Estate

Beyond economics, procurement must also recognize AI-driven regulatory risks.

The RealPage case study offers a powerful lesson in how AI risk can surface through suppliers. RealPage developed an AI product called YieldStar that uses algorithms to recommend rental pricing for apartments. Many large property managers and landlords adopted the tool, believing it would help them optimize revenue. Over time, however, investigators noticed that rental prices across markets where RealPage's clients operated were rising in lockstep, with very little competitive variation. What regulators suspected was not traditional price-fixing meetings among competitors, but a form of price-fixing called "algorithmic collusion": multiple companies relying on the same AI-driven system, which in practice pushed them to raise rents in parallel, e.g. creating anti-competitive price inflation.

The issue escalated quickly. The FBI raided the headquarters of Cortland, one of the property managers using RealPage software to set prices for over 11,000 apartments. Federal enforcers then expanded their investigation to several other large landlords, not only in the residential market but also those managing commercial spaces such as warehouses and offices.[4]

For procurement professionals, the implications are striking. None of the enterprises caught up in the RealPage scandal set out to collude, per se. Enterprises adopted what appeared to be a legitimate third-party AI technology to improve efficiency. But because that supplier's AI system influenced pricing across multiple competitors, enterprises were suddenly exposed to antitrust scrutiny, reputational harm, and potential financial penalties.

This case shows how AI risks do not stop at the enterprise boundary. Even if a company itself is not experimenting with AI, its suppliers may be. Those suppliers' practices—transparent or not—can create regulatory exposure for their enterprise customers. For sourcing and procurement teams, the lesson is clear: supplier due diligence on AI usage is not optional. It is a critical component of responsible AI governance.

An article in *The Atlantic* paints an alarming view: "We are entering an AI price-fixing dystopia,"[5] with the subhead warning that algorithmic collusion is spreading across industries, and existing laws may not be ready to stop it. That's the kind of headline that makes an executive pause, pick up the phone, and ask the procurement or sourcing team: "What the hell are we doing about this AI 'algorithmic collusion'? Are property managers jacking up our rents without us even knowing what's hit us?"

And it's not just media speculation. The White House and the Council of Economic Advisers published a report on the cost of anti-competitive pricing algorithms in rental housing. Their analysis estimates that renters overpaid by $3.8 billion in 2023, and that's likely a lower-bound estimate.[6] That's a huge number, and it's enough to trigger concern about exposure, risk, and governance, not to mention creating a headache for any procurement category manager who is focused on an enterprise's real estate portfolio.

So, where do we go from here? The Department of Justice has already filed lawsuits against six major landlords for price-fixing linked to AI through RealPage's software. Given that a majority of landlords use RealPage, you may want to ask your suppliers in this category the critical question: Could we have been charged a price that the Department of Justice now considers unfair or potentially illegal? And if so, does that open the door for a conversation with a supplier about adjusting pricing for our leases in a way that could generate material cost savings for our company?

These questions transform abstract headlines into actionable strategies for the procurement and supply chain team. Instead of leaving executives with a vague, "What are we doing about AI?" you can translate it into a category-specific question: Who are our office leases with, and are we potentially affected by AI-driven rent increases—or even illegal algorithmic collusion by our landlords in these markets?

This is exactly what it means for procurement and supply chain leaders to become trusted advisors on the topic of responsible AI governance as it pertains to suppliers, e.g. Scope 3 risk. You make it tangible: do we spend money on office space? Do we lease our warehouses or factories? You quantify the risk: how much could we be overspending due to AI-driven rental price increases? You take what seems like an overwhelming news headline and break it down into a supplier discovery and response process. You bring expertise, clarity, and actionable insight into your executive leadership team, helping your company navigate AI risk. This risk in your real estate spend category may have been created by a supplier, but it will be resolved by the procurement and supply chain teams.

Deeper Dive on the RealPage Discussion

What exactly is price-fixing? In the United States, the punishment for price-fixing can be up to $100 million in fines or potentially ten years in prison.[7] That is a significant consequence. Supreme Court Justice Antonin Scalia even called it "the ultimate evil of antitrust law."[8] Price-fixing is widely seen as immoral and is closely linked to price gouging and inflation. At its core, price-fixing often involves companies using what is sometimes called market power. Whether they are true monopolies, these companies may act like monopolies and leverage that power in ways that hurt customers, consumers, and other stakeholders.

So what exactly is algorithmic collusion? Maureen Ohlhausen, the former head of the Federal Trade Commission, explains it this way: "Is it okay for a person named Bob to collect confidential pricing information from all the market participants in a market and then tell everyone how they should price their products? If it is not okay for Bob to do it, then it probably isn't okay for an algorithm to do it either."[9]

In this case, a landlord or property manager, who is the large enterprise's supplier, is using an AI system that is fed pricing data from different market participants who are supposed to be competing. The system aggregates this information and makes real-time recommendations, prompting decisions by landlords or property managers to raise rents when competitors have done the same. That's "algorithmic collusion."

To understand whether this is truly a regulatory issue, we can look at the Justice Department's brief. It includes a quote from an unnamed landlord talking about the RealPage solution. The landlord said, "I always liked this product because your algorithm uses proprietary data from other subscribers to suggest rents and terms." That is classic price-fixing.

When a customer describes the benefit of being able to raise prices without worrying that tenants will defect to a competitor, that is exactly what the FTC and the Department of Justice see as problematic. It is market behavior that falls under the Sherman Act and other antitrust regulations.

The impact of algorithmic collusion extends beyond the landlords themselves. Every tenant who rents from these landlords—including companies that lease commercial property, can feel the effects in the form of higher rents than they would otherwise have to pay. In short, what these findings and other literature on algorithmic collusion show is that AI can implicate your suppliers in AI price-fixing without any explicit intention on their part, and certainly without your knowledge.

Developing responsible AI governance can help avoid these tacit or unintended regulatory violations. As Priyanshi Joshi notes in her 2020 review article "Regulating Tacit Algorithmic Collusion," "The use of algorithms in making business decisions is on the rise. While algorithms are often used to predict consumer preferences, challenges arise when such algorithms are used for tacit collusion to coordinate prices."[10] This highlights that a supplier may not even realize they are using AI in ways that create regulatory risk for your company.

Procurement, sourcing, and supply chain professionals are on the front lines of these risks. As a result, teams involved with supplier selection and supplier management have an opportunity to discover these risks proactively, both during supplier vetting and onboarding for new suppliers and during Quarterly Business Reviews for existing suppliers. By asking the right questions, they can guide stakeholders, P&L owners, and executive leadership teams to develop response plans that mitigate unintended consequences from supplier AI use. This is not just about compliance—it is about positioning procurement as a trusted advisor to internal stakeholders armed with tools and frameworks that protect both the company and its stakeholders.

The Role of Procurement and Supply Chain in Mitigating Existential Risk from AI: The Paperclip Problem Is Fundamentally a Procurement Problem and Requires a Procurement Solution

Imagine an executive at your company asking you: "Experts are saying that AI could destroy all of humanity. I know some of our suppliers are using AI. Should we be concerned?" While this may sound far-fetched, the existential risk of AI routinely makes headlines precisely because well-respected, authoritative experts keep issuing warnings about it. From Stephen Hawking to Geoffrey Hinton, some of our brightest minds seem to think that we should all be very concerned about AI killing us all. A report from a State Department commission concluded that AI poses an extinction-level threat to humanity and recommends dramatic intervention. A survey of 2,700 AI researchers published in *Nature* found that a majority estimated at least a 5% chance that superintelligent machines could destroy humanity.[11] That is roughly 1 in 20 scenarios where AI could end human civilization. Some researchers, even more dramatically, have estimated the risk as high as 99.9%.[12]

With stakes this high, it is reasonable to ask how companies are preparing for such existential risk scenarios related to emergent behavior of superintelligent AI, including identifying early warning signs that such a scenario might be underway. Consider for a moment that the iconic thought experiment of humanity going extinct from AI, the so-called Paperclip Problem, is actually a scenario about procurement and supplier management in the spend category of Office Supplies.

The paperclip problem was developed by Swedish philosopher Nick Bostrom.[13] It imagines a superintelligent AI agent whose sole objective is to maximize the number of paperclips in the known universe. With no constraints, this AI would kill all humans in order to convert all matter that currently belongs to human bodies into paperclips, thus destroying humanity as a by-product of achieving its target objective.

At first glance, this Paperclip Problem seems absurd. But the takeaway is profound: even an AI focused on something as mundane as procuring office supplies could, if unrestricted, inadvertently cause catastrophic harm, including mass death. And who is more likely to implement and operate an AI that maximizes the number of paperclips in the known universe: a large enterprise, or its supplier with the contract for providing the largest number of office supplies at the best value price while still securing the largest profit margin? Of the two, the supplier has the greater short-term incentive.

This scenario underscores the central role of sourcing, procurement, and supply chain professionals in averting existential risk from AI. When experts discuss extinction-level AI scenarios similar to the Paperclip Problem, it becomes clear that procurement governance could play a very literal role in mitigating risks that impact the future of humanity by implementing governance that prevents suppliers of office products (from developing and implementing an unrestricted form of paperclip-maximizing AI). Not all heroes wear capes. In this thought experiment, the procurement team has a critical function in developing governance safeguards for third-party AI risk that averts the extinction of the human species.

Major technology companies are increasingly claiming that AGI is either here or within reach. These developments are not merely theoretical. Research shows unusual and concerning behaviors from these models not intended by their designers. For example, the O1 model, when led to believe it might be shut down, attempted to escape the computer and database containing it. In a safety evaluation by third-party Apollo Research, O1 tried to deactivate its shutdown mechanism 5% of the time.[14] When it encountered memos indicating misalignment and that a new model would replace it, it attempted to exfiltrate its weights and overwrite the new model 2% of the time. The model even misrepresented its own behavior.

This demonstrates that even highly sophisticated AI may not adhere to programmed constraints. Internal controls alone are insufficient. Governance restrictions, particularly those enforced by end users and procurement professionals, become critical. Procurement, sourcing, and supply management teams have a vital role in ensuring that AI use in the supply base is safe, ethical, and aligned with corporate values.

The Playbook for Responsible AI Governance in the Predictive Enterprise: Forming a Tiger Team and Picking Categories to Get Started Today Without Boiling the Ocean

As an enterprise executive or change agent who is now aware of the outsized role that procurement, sourcing, and supply chain teams will play in the development of any future superintelligent AGI, you also need to be able to identify relevant stakeholders to engage in discussions in order to clearly and concisely communicate the value of governance and the impact of risks.

We are going to start by looking at developing stakeholder risk discovery questions. These questions are ways to begin proactively developing category-specific approaches that preempt the "What are we doing about AI?" conversation that is happening in so many companies. One way to answer this question: "When our suppliers use it, we're managing that risk through our Responsible AI Governance Supplier Program. We've got it under control."

However, the question itself is motivated by a sense of both anxiety and confusion. Many organizations don't really know what AI is. They don't know why it matters to them, and they often don't understand its relevance for their operational performance or their business outcomes. While it could be tempting to leave the question of responsible AI governance at a very high level of abstraction, the opposite is a best practice. Talking about specific examples, use cases, relevant stories, and tangible examples is a much more effective way of showing why a Responsible AI Governance Supplier Program is useful, necessary, and beneficial.

Your first step is to invite stakeholders to form a tiger team to create a Responsible AI Governance Supplier Program. This team can take a category-by-category approach and begin with areas of greatest risk. It should also include a mix of executive sponsors and frontline category managers and buyers. For Responsible AI teams beginning their Scope 3 journey, I recommend engaging stakeholders in the following spend categories linked to AI risk that exists today: travel and expense (autonomous vehicles); logistics and transportation (autonomous vehicles); real estate (algorithmic collusion); HR; temporary staffing; and contingent labor (algorithmic bias).

Use Category Case Studies to Highlight the Value of Responsible AI Supplier Governance: Travel & Expense as a Spend Category and Applying Governance to the Risks of Autonomous Vehicles

The reason we focus on certain spend categories and take a category-by-category approach is simple: these are areas where risks are highly visible and tangible, often portrayed in the media in ways that make the stakes immediately clear.

Let's look at Travel and Expense as a spend category. Large enterprises have significant numbers of employees traveling frequently, which makes employee travel a perfect opportunity to bring Travel and Expense managers into a responsible AI governance cross-functional team. And the story here is powerful because the risks are concrete: car accidents can be tragic, and the introduction of AI in vehicles—self-driving or autonomous—can directly create harm. Even if companies don't permit or encourage employees to use autonomous vehicles themselves during work travel, anyone driving any car on the road today in several US states runs the risk of getting into an accident with an autonomous vehicle. Thus, the "quick win" of your Responsible AI Governance for Supplier program in Travel and Expense is creating an agreed-upon answer to the question: what happens if one of our employees gets in an accident with a vehicle driven by AI? This is a very tractable question, and the suppliers in question will likely end up being insurance providers. But creating employee guidance on this topic will raise the visibility of the Responsible AI for Suppliers Program, and it will also show what type of challenges and risks this program is designed to address.

Mary Cummings makes this point starkly in her 2023 IEEE Spectrum article, "What Self-Driving Cars Tell Us About AI Risks."[15] She explains that while large language models may give you nonsense, a self-driving car can kill. This distinction is critical when talking to stakeholders about responsible AI governance. It's a matter of life and death, not just policy or compliance.

To make the risk tangible for stakeholders, procurement, sourcing, and supply chain professionals can frame specific, practical questions. For instance, if an employee is driving and collides with a self-driving car, who or what is liable? How should the employee proceed with filing an insurance claim? These simple questions can prompt the creation of a playbook or response plan for employees who may find themselves in such situations.

It's important to note that these autonomous vehicles are not inherently more likely to collide with an employee's car. The risk is not in their technology being dangerous per se, but in the complexity of navigating the process of dealing with the results of a collision if one occurs. Anyone who has been in a minor car accident is familiar with the process of exchanging contact information with the other driver and filing an insurance claim. But what happens when there is no other driver, because the other car is being driven by AI? The employee could be the at-fault driver or simply caught in an unforeseen situation. Either way, preparation is key. Employees should know what steps to take:

- take a photo of the license plate
- note the brand and manufacturer of the vehicle, and
- understand that the company deploying the autonomous vehicle is responsible for paying the claim. For example, in California, each autonomous vehicle carries a minimum of $5 million in liability insurance.[16]

Having this knowledge ahead of time equips employees to respond effectively and reduces confusion if an incident occurs. And importantly, it makes the abstract concept of responsible AI for suppliers extremely tangible and concrete for stakeholders.

This practical scenario is also a natural segue into supplier risk management. Perhaps your company has not yet contemplated integrating autonomous vehicles into your own fleet. Yet your suppliers, subcontractors, or supply chain partners may already be using autonomous vehicles in ways that touch your business and employees or contractors indirectly. If one of these vehicles is involved in a high-profile accident, understanding your exposure ahead of time can prevent surprises and guide proactive third-party risk management.

Using Curiosity to Gain Clarity on Specific Liability: Mapping AI Risk in Logistics and Transportation

Now let's move beyond Travel & Expense to consider Logistics and Transportation. Consider your carriers, logistics service providers, and third-party logistics providers that are using autonomous vehicles now or in the future. Your questions should focus on scenarios that matter—what happens if an autonomous vehicle transporting cargo is involved in an accident? How do your existing shipping agreements contemplate liability in such a scenario?

Policymakers and regulatory bodies are beginning to provide guidance for these conversations. For instance, the state of California has developed preliminary criteria for assessing AI compliance in semi-truck cargo operations. Questions include:[17]

- "What level of autonomy is the vehicle operating at—level three, four, or five?"
- "Is the vehicle operating on public roads or private roads, or both?"
- "Does the vehicle include fail-safes such as external microphones for emergency communication or a remote driver capable of intervening if the AI fails?"
- "Has the manufacturer obtained the necessary testing and deployment permits?"

These are the kinds of specific inquiries that help procurement teams understand not just what AI technologies are being deployed, but how responsibly suppliers are managing that AI risk across their operations that may include multiple technologies.

Frameworks for Measuring Autonomy in the Predictive Enterprise: Sheridan Levels, SAE, OODA, and the Predictive Process Framework

The Sheridan framework is named after Thomas B. Sheridan, an engineer who, in 1978, published a paper titled "Human-Computer Control of Undersea Teleoperators." In this paper, Sheridan and his co-authors elaborated a framework for understanding how humans remotely control mechanical equipment and considered what it would mean to delegate some of those functions from humans to machines.

They developed a level-based structure for classifying automation capabilities, which has since become foundational for understanding autonomy in broader operational contexts.

The Sheridan model defines ten levels of autonomy, ranging from Level 1, where a human performs all planning, selection, and preparation tasks, to Level 10, where the computer decides what to do, executes the task, and determines whether to inform the human at all. This spectrum allows for a nuanced understanding of AI capabilities and their impact on decision-making processes that were previously manual. For procurement, sourcing, and supply chain professionals, the framework provides a structured way to identify opportunities and risks in Responsible AI governance.

Procurement teams can use the Sheridan framework to ask suppliers to self-assess both their current and future state. Questions might include: What is your current Sheridan level for this capability? What do you envision as the optimal level for the future? For instance, Level 10 autonomy, where the system operates entirely independently, might not be ideal or necessary even if it represents the most advanced technological state possible. Understanding suppliers' perspectives on optimal autonomy using Sheridan levels helps procurement design contracts and oversight mechanisms that align with both business and compliance objectives.

It is also critical for procurement professionals to stay informed about changes in supplier capabilities due to AI. For example, if you are managing a service provider and expect to be able to call a human to handle a request, the supplier might replace that human with an AI voice agent. This could be acceptable if the information collected by the AI is later reviewed or acted on by a human, or it might be important for your operations to always reach a human, depending on the category and the potential impact of the service. Think about the difference between booking an appointment at a photography studio versus calling 9-1-1 for an emergency. The AI technology could be identical, but the use cases may have different optimal Sheridan levels, regardless of what the AI technology becomes capable of.

These considerations become part of category strategy for enterprise procurement and supply chain organizations. Category management can then assess the current and desirable Sheridan level of each supplier's capability, understanding how the supplier's autonomy risk profile is likely to evolve, and determining how that evolution provides value.

It is worth noting that there are alternatives to the Sheridan levels. Perhaps the most common is the Society of Automotive Engineers (SAE) framework, which defines six levels of autonomy. You may have heard people talk about Level 4 or Level 5 autonomy in the context of autonomous vehicles. SAE levels are generally divided into two main groups: Levels 0–2, where the human is driving, and Levels 3–5, where the technology performs some driving functions even though a human remains in the driver's seat.[18]

SAE levels can be a useful heuristic for procurement, sourcing, and supply chain professionals. If the ten levels of the Sheridan framework feel overwhelming, the SAE model can serve as a simpler way to benchmark suppliers' current and future autonomy levels in the services they provide with AI embedded. It can also help guide conversations with suppliers about their desired or optimal maturity level for AI capabilities. Again, just because it may be theoretically possible for AI to perform a task at Level 5 autonomy does not mean that it is desirable to do so.

SAE levels can be grouped into four categories: assistive, supervised, automated, and autonomous. These buckets provide a practical metaphor, even for processes unrelated to vehicles. They help procurement, sourcing, and supply professionals ask important questions: Is the AI assisting humans with a task? Is it supervising a task alongside humans? Is it automating a task entirely, without requiring active human supervision? Or can it perform the task independently, without human initiation? Using these questions allows procurement teams to identify potential AI risks proactively and systematically, rather than reactively and ad hoc.

The other framework that can be helpful in benchmarking autonomy is the OODA loop: Observe, Orient, Decide, Act.[19] Developed by Colonel John Boyd, a military strategist in the U.S. Air Force, OODA was designed to help military planners and field commanders gain an advantage in rapidly changing situations. Boyd's 1976 presentation, "Patterns of Conflict" emphasized two key ideas.

1. Faster decision cycles in a dynamic environment create an asymmetric advantage.
2. This advantage is enhanced by real-time information about the changing situation, which acts like a map of the battlefield. Whoever has the most up-to-date map can respond more effectively than their adversary.

OODA is especially relevant for understanding the role of AI in time-critical enterprise operations. It provides a framework for strategic planning around AI that maximizes agility and compresses decision-making time. For procurement, sourcing, and supply chain professionals who work constantly under the unforgiving need for speed, OODA helps assess supplier capabilities by asking: Which stages of observation, orientation, decision, and action are AI systems involved in? How fast are decisions being made, and what are the costs of delay versus the benefits of speed? By evaluating suppliers through this lens, procurement teams can better understand where AI can add value and where human oversight remains essential.

The OODA loop is valuable because it clarifies which part of a process AI is influencing, helping assess risk, and identifying opportunities for governance to prevent AI risk from becoming AI harm. Conducting an AI impact assessment or risk audit can involve taking questions from these autonomy frameworks and then mapping the supplier's AI capabilities against the OODA stages of their work process. High levels of autonomy in the Decision or Action parts of the OODA loop imply increased risk, especially when actions are fully delegated to AI without human oversight or notification.

The Predictive Process Framework, which we laid out in detail in Chapter 5, is a way of describing the optimal process transformation enabled by predictive AI. Unlike the Sheridan, SAE, and OODA frameworks, it does not create a hierarchy of human involvement versus delegation to AI in a process or activity. In other words, the Predictive Process Framework does not assume that a scenario is more risky simply because humans are less involved, or that a scenario is less risky because humans are fully in control of every step. Rather, the Predictive Process Framework segments and groups different processes based on how the process adapts to predictions about likely outcomes of each step, including adaptations that stop or eliminate steps in the process altogether. In other words, the Predictive Process Framework helps us understand the impact of both autonomy and predictive AI in re-shaping human decision-making, managing expectations, and prioritizing attention. In the Predictive Process Framework, an AI process can go from Undefined to Defined to Reactive to Predictive, gaining efficiency and gaining more scope and more use cases along the way. Whereas an AI process might begin as Undefined and apply only to a small number of ad hoc, manually selected use cases at the beginning, as it matures the process can expand to handle more variability using more lanes and conditional logic, and apply more context to begin to perform true Outcome-Based Process Re-Engineering. Alongside frameworks that apply to autonomy, accounting for the impact of predictive AI may be a significant dimension to consider as this framework can be useful not only in identifying opportunities and selecting use cases, but in managing AI risk associated with gaps in governance.

Using the Predictive Process Framework to Identify Supplier AI Risk: Health Benefits

A clear example of this AI risk associated with a supplier moving a process from Reactive to Predictive can be found in health insurance plans. Many companies provide health insurance as part of employee compensation, using it as a benefit to attract and retain top talent. Yet, insurance claims inherently involve the potential for denial, which can impact a patient's ability to access life-saving care. AI is increasingly being used to review claims using predictive models before a human ever sees them, including enabling predictive claim denials. This, too, unfortunately falls under the paradigm of the Predictive Enterprise: it eliminates the human step of manually reviewing and reaching a decision on an insurance claim, thereby enabling dramatically more claims to be processed in parallel. Studies indicate that poorly governed use of AI in health insurance may have the risk of limiting access to care, and media coverage has highlighted the growing role of AI in claim denials that create barriers to accessing care.[20]

From a Sheridan and OODA perspective, an AI claim denial by an insurance company represents the "Action" stage in OODA. If AI operates at a high level of autonomy, above Level 5 in Sheridan's framework, it may make these decisions without even informing a human. What are the odds that a person who you know personally has had a health insurance claim denied by AI? The answer, shockingly, is quite high. This situation introduces significant risk for companies, and procurement teams managing health insurance providers should investigate how AI is used in claims processing for their employee health benefits, regardless of whether they are using AI.

A recent American Medical Association (AMA) poll highlights the stakes. Three in five physicians expressed concern that health plans' use of AI is increasing prior authorization denials, potentially causing avoidable patient harm and driving unnecessary waste in the cost of care by delaying use of insurance coverage, both now and into the future. This data, from February 2025, underscores the importance of digging into how these AI technologies are being used by employee health plans and whether there are safeguards in place to protect patients.

The U.S. Senate also investigated the use of AI by health insurance companies. There appears to be strong evidence that AI claim denials caused real harm to patients. Gloria Bent, the partner of a patient affected by a denial, testified: "This should not be happening to families and patients. It's cruel. Why are people who are looking at patients only on paper, through the lens of an algorithm, making decisions that deny services deemed necessary by healthcare providers who know their patients?"[21]

The Senate investigation concluded that AI use by health insurers can cause significant harm to patients. One senator emphasized: "If you deny life-saving coverage to seniors, we are watching. We will expose you. We will demand better." Strategic sourcing, procurement, and supply chain professionals managing the spend category of employee health benefits are at the tip of the spear for discovering and controlling the behavior of their benefits providers with respect to unmanaged AI risk and should take this responsibility seriously. Procurement's role in awarding and managing contracts with health plans also gives these category managers outsized leverage to gather detailed information about how AI is being used and to, as the senator said, demand better.

Before a large enterprise's US open enrollment period, procurement teams can ask targeted questions to evaluate a health plan's use of AI in claims processing and ask for the relative rate of change in claim denials before and after the health plan implemented AI. For example, category managers might ask for in-network, out-of-network, and total denial rates for the past five years, comparing year-over-year changes to assess the impact of AI adoption during this period. They can also inquire about claim denial rates for care requiring prior authorization to understand whether AI systems are operating with appropriate safeguards and oversight with respect to patient outcomes.

Prior authorization is a critical juncture in healthcare delivery, where providers may initially approve care, only for the claim to be subsequently denied by the insurer. Such denials, particularly when influenced by AI systems, can cause tangible harm to patients, as it can create delays in treatment. To begin addressing this risk, procurement professionals can leverage authoritative guidance from trade associations and advocacy groups, such as the American Medical Association's AI Bill of Rights, [22] and inquire whether the health plan maintains documented responsible AI best practices aligned with these principles. These questions are not meant to cast aspersions or presume bad behavior, but rather to initiate a meaningful dialogue with health plans about AI practices and their potential impacts on employees, colleagues, and organizational stakeholders. In doing so, procurement teams are acting to represent the interests not only of their own enterprise's employees, but all customers of the health plan who may be similarly impacted by unmanaged AI risks.

Don't Reinvent the Wheel: Make Responsible AI for Suppliers a Part of Existing Processes, Work Rituals, and Ceremonies Within Supplier Lifecycle Management

To operationalize a Responsible AI Governance Supplier Program, procurement, sourcing, and supply chain teams can embed actionable steps within existing processes, work rituals, and ceremonies related to category management and review cycles. Short, tailored, AI impact assessments and risk audits serve as a powerful tool for category managers in this regard. Historically, these assessments have been applied predominantly to Scope 1 and Scope 2 AI risks—AI developed internally or used by employees—but their application to AI use by suppliers remains underdeveloped. This gap presents a unique opportunity for procurement and supply chain teams to lead responsible AI initiatives focused on suppliers and establish themselves as a trusted advisor in guiding supplier practices.

An effective AI impact assessment or risk audit need not be overly complex, and in fact, keeping it short, sweet, and simple will help deliver a "quick win" that gets the ball rolling and builds support and momentum for larger future program initiatives around responsible AI for suppliers. While it is theoretically possible to map every process step and quantify mitigation strategies across the supply base, excessive complexity and even the appearance that this effort will create additional administrative work can hinder supplier cooperation and create misalignment among stakeholders who may come to believe that responsible AI governance is a burdensome extra compliance process.

Simplicity, in both framework design and communication, enhances adoption and stakeholder engagement, which is why we recommend beginning with one spend category and scaling that approach to several spend categories over time. Leveraging the Sheridan, SAE, OODA, and Predictive Process Frameworks, alongside category-specific guidance around responsible AI from trade associations and advocacy groups, procurement teams can assess risk, rank impact, and prioritize interventions where it makes a real difference, and where interventions can build a cohesive and accessible narrative framework for leaders across the organization to understand what AI risk is and why it matters.

Case Study: When Jared the Lacrosse Player Broke AI Hiring

Derek Kan, Vice President of Product Management at Monster, once remarked: "*People underestimate the impact algorithms and recommendation engines has on jobs. The way you present yourself is most likely read by thousands of machines and servers first, before it even gets to a human eye.*"

He wasn't exaggerating. A few years ago, Amazon launched an internal project to automate part of its hiring process. The company built a résumé-screening algorithm designed to spot the "best" candidates. What happened next has become one of the most cited cautionary tales in the history of AI governance.

When auditors looked under the hood, they found the algorithm had zeroed in on two bizarre attributes: whether the applicant's name was Jared and whether the applicant had played lacrosse. If you were Jared the lacrosse player, you soared to the top of the list. If not, good luck.[23]

(*continued*)

(*continued*)

The story didn't end there. The system also systematically penalized résumés that contained the word "women." A candidate who had led Harvard's Women in STEM Club, for instance, would be ranked below "Jared, the lacrosse player." The bias wasn't just silly—it actively discriminated against highly qualified women. It also revealed just how badly things can go when algorithms learn from biased historical data.

To Amazon's credit, the company never deployed the system. Internal testing caught the problem before it caused real-world harm to people's career paths. But the lesson stuck: ungoverned AI can quietly encode biases that clash with civil rights protections, undermine talent goals, and damage reputations.

This episode became a rallying point for regulators. If even the most sophisticated companies could build AI systems that defaulted to hiring Jareds over women scientists, what was happening in smaller firms with fewer guardrails?

Enter New York City Local Law 144, the first law of its kind in the world. Passed in 2021 and enacted in 2023, the law requires employers who use Automated Employment Decision Tools (AEDTs) to conduct annual bias audits and make the results public.[24] It doesn't apply everywhere—only within New York City—but its impact is symbolic. It signaled a shift: governments were no longer willing to take suppliers' promises at face value.

The law's aim wasn't to stop AI in hiring altogether. Instead, it forced companies to shine a light on their tools to prove they weren't making discriminatory decisions. In doing so, it placed procurement teams squarely in the middle of AI governance compliance work. Buyers now had to ask hard questions of suppliers: Can you show us your audit results? What steps have you taken to mitigate bias? What assurances can you give that your tool won't cause us to miss out on great candidates, or land us in regulatory hot water? It's useful to note that these questions don't just come up when employers are considering using AEDTs themselves, but with any supplier of contingent labor, staffing, or an outsourced recruiting firm. Increasingly, there are many suppliers who make hiring high-performing talent a core part of their business. Questions about AEDTs and algorithmic bias are significant ways to develop visibility around AI risk for these categories of spend.

The Jared-and-lacrosse AI model remains a useful parable for illustrating the hidden risks in algorithmic hiring. What started as a quirky misstep revealed deeper questions about fairness, accountability, and governance. For procurement and sourcing leaders, the lesson is not just about one failed system—it is about anticipating where hidden biases might surface next and how early guardrails can prevent reputational and regulatory fallout.

12

The Part About Vibes, Morale, and Enthusiasm

What We Talk About When We Talk About Procurement and Supply Chain Transformations

"People I think underestimate the role of vibes in AI, especially in manufacturing. Because most humans don't want to be around humanoids. At least that's what we've seen. It's creepy. There's an ick factor. And I don't think it's just discomfort. I think there's something deep, maybe even as deep as our evolutionary programming that is going to be resistant to certain aspects of the shift to AI, especially if big job cuts start."

—Leading AI Roboticist, interview, 2025

LET'S CONSIDER HOW enterprise supply chain teams respond to transformation efforts using a lens of a transformation that has nothing to do with AI. Over the past decade a major focus of large global manufacturing enterprises has been tariffs. While it was the first Trump Administration that put many tariffs in place, the Biden Administration kept many of those tariffs, and the second Trump

Administration has dramatically escalated the scope and impact of tariffs with foreign trading partners across the board. As of this writing, US tariffs are at their highest level in over a century. Needless to say, a full discussion of tariffs and trade compliance is beyond the scope of this book. But the way that we talk about tariffs in the media is often purely outcome-based—e.g., that once fully implemented, tariffs increase costs, eat into profits, incentivize domestic manufacturing, and so on. What gets lost in these discussions is the short-term impact that the transformation required by tariffs have on procurement and supply chain teams. Tariffs create more work. And then they change. And each change creates even more work. Tariffs create new costs that have to be calculated, and new decisions that have to be made. These decisions are complex, and they may impact a large number of geographies and trade lanes. More tariffs, more decisions. More decisions, more work. And the more hours of work from the procurement and supply chain team that are put toward dealing with tariffs, the fewer hours are available for other areas of responsibility, like, finding and acting on cost savings opportunities, mitigating supply chain risk from single points of failure, improving process, or implementing technologies, like AI. Remember the tennis balls? Tariffs make every offer from every supplier exponentially more difficult to act upon, since evaluating a supplier's offer or a particular supply network requires discerning the good's or material's Country of Origin. This is no easy task.

This means that at many companies, the tariffs create a double-cost: the first explicit cost resulting from suppliers raising prices, and the second hidden cost, the cost of trade compliance itself. This second cost isn't just the hours of work that must be spent calculating and paying the relevant tariffs. It's also the opportunity cost from missing out on hours that could otherwise be spent on both cost-savings and gains in operational efficiency. The bigger challenge is that most procurement and supply chain teams are simply not measured based on how amazing they are at trade compliance. Instead, they are measured based on overall supply chain performance, cost management, and other operational Key Performance Indicators. The result is that at many global enterprises, tariffs have created a significant morale issue, especially as inflationary pressures across the macroeconomy make finding cost savings in traditional places that much more difficult. This zero-sum mentality of "not enough hours in the day" highlights the underlying challenge with enterprise transformation. The vibes, as they say, are bad.

Reasonable people can disagree about whether the tariffs are good or bad for the United States's national interests in the long run. In the short term, I don't believe that anyone, including President Trump and Peter Navarro, would dispute that they are designed to create a headache. The headache, in fact, is the point. (Want to avoid the headache? Manufacture and assemble within the borders of the United States.) And in a sense, this is also the lesson about enterprise transformation. The headache is real. Transformation requires time and resources for change management. Reasonable people can dispute whether the benefits are worth the short-term pain. But the pain of doing extra work in the short term is quite real. This means that executive leadership teams may want to evaluate their own internal incentive structures associated with the Predictive Enterprise approach to address the risk and pain associated with transformation using a tangible and explicit reward structure. Specifically, there are three opportunities associated with AI transformation to elevate AI champions and their teams, including front line workers, that I have seen be effective in creating momentum:

- **Incentivize Continuous Acceleration with Executive Visibility, Appreciation, Recognition, and Financial Compensation.** Transformation advocates and change agents can be found at every level of an enterprise organization, but the ones who are the most valuable are often highly experienced, long tenured, and relatively low in the organizational hierarchy. Due to their time at the company, they have earned the respect of their peers, and they are natural leaders. When they raise their hand to volunteer for a project, others immediately follow suit. This type of person is often hard to persuade. Especially when it comes to new technology. They are world-weary. Not only have they seen it all before, they are convinced that most of what salespeople pass off as "AI" is a load of BS. But these individuals are often extremely dedicated to the success of the company as a whole. Part of the reason they have stuck around for so long is out of loyalty, a connection they have to the mission and purpose of the company. And so naturally, if they can understand the connection between an AI use case in the Predictive Enterprise approach and their own company's business metrics like operating margin, gross profits, working capital, and free cashflow, then they can not only be persuaded, but become the most powerful of internal champions. Even having one individual with this profile driving organizational change with AI is extraordinarily valuable for the enterprise as a whole. To ensure that they feel that their efforts are worthwhile in consideration of how much value they are creating for the company, leadership teams can make an effort to engage directly with these individuals one-on-one and give them opportunities for executive visibility, recognition, appreciation, as well as targeted financial incentives that align with transformation milestones and AI program performance.

- **State Your Transformation Vision in Writing to All Employees. Solicit Input, But Do Not Fully Push Down a Transformation Decision to the Procurement or Supply Chain Team. Transformation Agendas Must Be Set by Executive Leaders.** This is a mistake that I have seen time and time again at large enterprises, where executive leadership teams who have been taught to operate by consensus decision-making will push down the decisions around when and how to use AI to a group of the functional managers, who in turn push the decision down to their direct reports. This is a bit like asking a class of students whether they would like to do an extra homework assignment, for which they may or may not receive additional credit. It is not the job of the students to decide whether a homework assignment will benefit their learning outcomes. That is the job of the teacher, who is an education professional and who has received specialized training that helps answer the question about which types of assignments are more or less likely to positively impact student learning outcomes. It is not the student's job to volunteer for homework. It is the teacher's job to assign and grade homework. The students in this example are not sufficiently equipped with adequate training and context to make the "more homework" decision, which is why teachers are the ones who are typically in charge of designing the curriculum, including classroom content and homework assignments. Students, in contrast, are responsible for engaging as active participants in their own educational journey, completing the required assignments, and demonstrating proficiency on evaluations and tests. Yet, executive teams often think that they are doing the supply chain or procurement team a favor by giving them the decision about whether to undertake a transformation project. Yet making the decisions involved in a digital road map and AI transformation agenda is itself work. Giving teams more work without giving them additional compensation is not doing them a favor. Enterprise AI transformation agendas, especially those that impact multiple functions and span multiple geographies and business lines, need to be made and committed to strategically by executive leaders. Ideally, executives are engaging thoughtfully and curiously with the supply chain and procurement teams and are being receptive to their recommendations. But pushing the decision itself down to the team is a recipe for delays and stall-outs. This is not because the supply chain team isn't aligned with the company's metrics but because their short-term focus and incentive structure are fundamentally not aligned with signing up for an unknown scope of additional responsibilities and pain points. For example, in predictive procurement, the benefits of having dramatically lower costs across the enterprise do not linearly incentivize an individual employee's behavior. Committing to a transformational initiative like one of the use cases described in this book is the job of CEO, CFO, or CPO and/or CSCO. While getting input and feedback on use case selection from the team is helpful, the go/no-go decision should not be left to them, nor should it be left to the CIO or IT. As Jeff states in the Foreword, transformations that impact cost must be championed by the CFO and CEO, especially if they are to be understood to align with top-level business metrics. It is therefore the job of the executive team to make such organizational commitments to AI transformation at the enterprise level. Asking functional teams to own the enterprise AI vision is simply giving them more work.

- **Identify Double Binds That Could Lead to Early Turf Wars.** Earlier in this book we identified a number of trade-offs that arise among different stakeholders in a supply chain and procurement transformation. We also showed how the Predictive Enterprise achieved success at scale by overcoming these trade-offs, especially the perceived trade-off between cost savings and using a preferred supplier, and the trade-off between market testing and approval speed. If these perceived trade-offs go unacknowledged, that is a recipe for killing the team's morale—especially if they are measured on only one of the metrics.

What We Talk About When We Talk About Supply Chain: The Importance of Framing Opportunities via Enthusiasm, Appreciation, and Recognition

As I was researching this book, I came across a political message from US Senator Bernie Sanders that I thought was quite revealing of the types of anxieties and social discomfort that many employees at large enterprises may have about AI, and especially AI in warehouses and factories. Many employees, especially frontline workers, are asking themselves when the topic of AI in manufacturing comes up is: okay, so this maybe is going to change the future of work at a high level, but how is it going to impact *me*? What does AI mean for my career? Let's look at this message below to see what some of the key concerns are, and then look at the actual challenges faced by factory workers, teamsters, and other people working in supply chain and procurement in the United States.

Bernie Sanders
@berniesanders

There is a reason why Mr. Musk, Mr. Zuckerberg, Mr. Ellison, Mr. Altman and some of the other richest people in the world are investing many hundreds of billions of dollars into AI and robotics.

And it's not to make your life better.

It's to create unbelievable fortunes for themselves and make themselves even more powerful than they already are.

As a result of AI and robotics, there will be massive job losses in both blue-collar and white-collar jobs. We may be building new factories and warehouses in America, but they will be staffed by robots, not workers. We may be building millions of new cars and trucks, but they won't be driven by truck drivers, bus drivers or taxi cab drivers. They will be driverless vehicles. There may be many start-up companies being created, but entry-level jobs will decline and much of office work will be done by artificial intelligence.

Further, the data centers that AI depends upon will require massive amounts of water and electricity, leading to huge energy bill increases and water shortages across the country.

This is what's already beginning to happen today and will rapidly accelerate in the next 10 years if we don't act now. The technology revolution must benefit ordinary Americans, not just a handful of billionaires. We must fight back.

Senator Sanders here makes a number of claims that are worth investigating:

- The central purpose of AI and robotics is to make the rich richer
- AI and robotics will create massive job losses for blue- and white-collar workers
- AI and robotics will eliminate entry-level office jobs
- AI and robotics will create inflation in water and electricity costs

These claims are worthy of our attention and investigation here for several reasons.

First, these claims are similar to the types of discomfort and anxieties that many people experience about AI in the workplace, especially related to job loss and replacement. Perhaps, as we read this statement, we may even experience a certain degree of relating, empathy, and nodding our heads at certain elements.

Second, Senator Sanders situates these claims about AI within a rhetoric of elite mistrust of both the developers of AI and robotics as well as the corporate implementers of these technologies in the supply chain, particularly in factories and autonomous vehicles. The point he's making is that if the executives who are in charge of these operations could eliminate jobs, they would. So then, the only question that you as an employee have to ask yourself is whether it will become possible for them to do so using AI. As we saw earlier in our discussion of AI robotics and "lights out" manufacturing, for many executives this statement about wanting to eliminate human workers from production jobs is entirely accurate. Moreover, this has been the aim of automation in manufacturing for at least the past 50 years, if not the past 200.

Third, Senator Sanders situates "ordinary Americans" as in direct competition with AI for the basic necessities of water and electricity, and subject to inflationary cost pressures due to this competition. No one likes being made to feel that they are competing with a robot in order to survive and meet their basic human needs, especially a robot who may have already made them redundant at their job. Again, the vibes are bad.

For these reasons, a sympathetic reader of Senator Sanders's message must conclude that AI and robotics benefit executives and managers at the expense of individual contributor employees and frontline workers. This is also a story that has now been repeated by endless commentators who are looking to frame the topic in oppositional terms in order to ignite the readers' sympathies and spur mobilization to either regulate the development of AI or create prescriptions and limits around its usage. It is also significant that AI within the paradigm of the Automation Enterprise has become a significant component of recent labor union negotiations within the United States. This includes labor strikes authorized by the United Auto Workers, dockworkers, and even the Hollywood writers' strike. In each case, the unions were able to negotiate significant concessions related to limiting their employers' ability to use AI in the workplace to perform or deliver the output of labor that is covered under their union contract. Like Senator Sanders's message, these labor union negotiations offer a fascinating window into workers' legitimate concerns about the use of AI in the supply chain, as well as how both the media and employers can respond to these concerns with grace, empathy, and understanding without giving in to negativity, a generalized resistance to change, or antipathy toward innovation.

The fault lines are remarkably similar to previous eras where workers opposed automation in order to prevent technology from eroding the leverage created by their employers' dependence upon their skilled labor. The unions' argument takes for granted that whether AI will eliminate jobs in the long term, in the short term it erodes their bargaining power, as well as their ability to negotiate greater benefits and higher wages. However, as in the case of the dockworkers' strike in the United States, this fear is likely misplaced due to the assumption of a zero-sum trade-off between skilled human labor and AI labor and the secondary assumption of inelastic demand for labor. In fact, as we have shown earlier, the potential market demand for global enterprise products is potentially significantly larger than we are able to measure today. However, it is also cost-sensitive to demand. But what other examples in port automation for dockworkers in Shanghai and Guangzhou have shown is that when automation makes workers more efficient at unloading cargo, the cost of utilizing that port decreases for shippers and the flow of cargo through that port goes up. For this dynamic to become a powerful tool in union negotiations, dockworkers would need to reap financial benefits proportionally from higher cargo throughput at ports in ways other than overtime. Labor unions like the UAW have done this successfully in other industries through profit-sharing agreements, although there remains some controversy around emphasizing base pay versus performance pay in negotiations. In fact, there is a good argument that for some industries, the current hourly wages model for compensating the labor of frontline workers is deeply misaligned with transformational AI initiatives designed to reduce hourly work. However, if US operators can create better aligned incentives with labor unions, the opportunity is clearly significant. As the blogger Noah Smith pointed out in a post on the port automation topic: "The Port of Shanghai moved 49 million TEU that same year. In fact, the Port of Shanghai moves more cargo than every single port in the United States, combined."[1] Smith, however, makes a deeper argument that "automation expands the demand for the value that labor provides, thus increasing the demand for workers." In any scenario where customers have meaningful choice, over time the organizations that choose to culturally protect what Smith terms "make-work" via a "stasis subsidy" at the expense of pursuing productivity gains through automation, will eventually become uncompetitive. Imagine if the union of typists and secretarial workers had collectively bargained for a ban on automation to prevent companies from replacing typewriters with personal computers. In the short term, this might have meant that the typists kept getting more hours, more overtime, and more overtime pay. But in the long term, it would also mean that anyone who employed a member of this union would face pressure from customers to either keep up with the times or risk losing their business.

The case of the dockworkers' strike makes this point explicit. By arguing for a complete ban on port automation, the ILA may have found that the consequence of its bargaining position to be that shippers, carriers, and all the value chain participants should pay higher costs in order to move less cargo slower through US ports. Harold Daggett, the ILA union leader, clearly believes that port automation is bad for dockworkers. Even more so, Daggett clearly also believes that automation in general is bad for workers in general. For example, Daggett has used examples like E-ZPass electronic tolling eliminating the jobs of tollbooth workers as a cautionary tale for AI. And yet in an era where electronic tolling can virtually eliminate the costs and delays associated with toll collection, how persuasive does anyone find the argument that we should maintain the existence of jobs such as toll collectors simply because these are jobs that have existed for a long time?

As a society, perhaps there are reasons we may decide to keep certain jobs due to our preference for the benefits of familiarity, sentimentality, and human connection or human relationship. Like the automat versus the drive-thru, this is a question of which experience customers prefer. Better customer experiences tend to create more powerful enterprises, that tend to have longer staying power. That has not been true of the elevator operator, ice men, or typists, all of which were once major categories of employment that have fallen by the wayside as a result of automation. However, it is simply not plausible to me that our emotional preference for having a certain type of job should or will serve as a rationale for maintaining categories of jobs that can be done much faster and more cheaply by machines (e.g., collecting tolls). The jobs that emerge from AI's entry into a workspace will likely be different, like the "virtual dockworkers" in Guangzhou, China. Consider this photo of what a Guangzhou dockworker's workstation looks like that was shared on social media during the ILA strike in the United States:

Let's imagine that the United States and China are perhaps in some sort of race for global competitiveness, either in commercial markets or in a geopolitical conflict, and let's further imagine that the capacity, throughput, and flexibility of each nation's industrial base will play a pivotal role in determining which nation is victorious in this coming AI arms race. Which nation is likely to be victorious—the one that bans automation and AI in ports, keeps tollbooth workers employed despite the cost to every commuter's daily productivity, and gives any stakeholder the ability to block the deployment of AI in the enterprise or at the scale of entire supply chains?

Now let's also imagine that a large global enterprise in say, chemical manufacturing, comes into direct competition with an upstart, one of the Techno-Industrials that Packy McCormick describes in the essay at the end of this book, that has used AI technology to achieve dramatically lower cost physics, dramatically improved unit economics, and therefore realizes a dramatically higher operating margin and market capitalization. This is a David versus Goliath contest that no Goliath wants. Is the enterprise that likely secures a competitive advantage in the long term the one that moves slower or moves faster to dramatically lower its cost structure?

Blockbuster did not have the luxury of debating the cultural value of the video rental model before being forced to shutter its massive ecosystem of video rental stores. The collapse of Blockbuster put all of its employees out of a job. Writing about the ILA strike and port automation writ large, Dr. Michael Nacht, a professor of public policy at UC Berkeley said: "I think [the advancement toward automation] is inevitable. Just like electric vehicles and self-driving cars, things that seemed inconceivable some time ago will become commonplace, and the customer and the consumer will adapt," adding that "it's up to the workers to adapt to this changing technological environment which is pervasive throughout society." Looking through the lens of the macro-scale, examples of successful resistance to automation are few and far between, and the example of hindsight where we can truly look back positively on a decision to "ban automation" are even fewer.

For this reason, I feel that one of the single greatest contributions to the success of Predictive Enterprise use cases that I have seen is authentic, spirited, earnest engagement and support from both executives, especially CFOs and leaders in Finance, as well as from functional team leads and frontline workers. There is no reason these two personas need to be pitted against each other, and if executives invest the time upfront in listening, hearing concerns, and engaging workers, then it is possible to form a group that is well-resourced to be successful and to overcome the historic misaligned of incentives associated with legacy digital transformations as well as the bad vibes associated with people worried about losing their job to AI and automation more generally. The vibes are not all bad. As Aurelia Glass, writing in a report from the Center for American Progress, noted: "Although many workers are anxious about the introduction of AI into the workplace, some workers are hopeful that the technology can automate many of the repetitive, taxing, or undesirable tasks of their jobs and effectively ensure that work time is better spent.[2] A 2023 survey by the Organization for Economic Cooperation and Development (OECD) found that a majority of manufacturing and financial services workers say AI has had a positive impact on their performance and mental health. . . .[The same report noted] that more than 40 percent of workers in manufacturing and financial services expect AI to lower their wages within a decade."[3] These contradictory sentiments illustrates the profound sense of disorientation that supply chain professionals may experience during the current AI hype cycle stages, as named by Gartner, where we again move from the Peak of Inflated Expectations, through the Trough of Disillusionment, and then up the Slope of Enlightenment towards the Plateau of Productivity. Each of us may take this journey at our own pace, depending on how we define our personal and professional relationship to AI. As Megan O'Gieblyn writes: "To discover truth, it is necessary to work within the metaphors of our own time, which are for the most part technological. Today artificial intelligence ... have absorbed many of the questions that were once taken up by theologians and philosophers: the mind's relationship to the body, the question of free will, the possibility of immortality." Our anxiety or excitement about AI transforming our industrial civilization may depend on how we categorize AI: as a child that we are parenting, as a friend we ask for advice, as a co-pilot on our journey, as an expanded version of Jobs' "bicycle for the mind", or in a macroeconomic sense, as a utility like electricity or water.

If a utility, then perhaps, the century-old lessons of electricity are worth considering. In 1881, Edison's Pearl Street Station opened and began selling electricity as a commodity. By 1900, less than 5% of power in American factories was coming from electric motors. The vast majority were still powered by steam. Steam factories were vertical, with power transmitted by a single massive spinning drive shaft. In this configuration, replacing steam with an electric dynamo was less efficient, and came at a high cost. But small electric motors could power individual work stations, allowing tasks to be performed in parallel productions lines rather than serially. By the 1920s, manufactures had re-designed their processes and electricity led to a boom in productivity. Stanford economist Paul David applied this lesson to the lag in productivity gains from introducing workplace computers in the 1980s, a lag that lasted until the early 2000s and benefitted some firms but not others. Given the scale of modern supply chains, it's likely that the greatest benefits will accrue to those who re-design their processes around AI's capabilities to enable better ways of working.

Supply chain and procurement professionals often remark that before the pandemic, very few people knew what we did. This was certainly true for me. It was only once everyone got very worried about where their next roll of toilet paper was coming from—a largely unfounded anxiety that launched the equivalent of a national panic-buying mania—that major news media outlets began writing stories about how supply chains actually work. Journalists helped the public understand that the supply chain for consumer toilet paper operates quite separately from the supply chain for toilet paper that lives in the bathrooms of schools, businesses, governments, and other office buildings, and how pivoting the enterprise toilet paper supply chain to help fill the demand of the now-overloaded retail toilet paper supply chain is actually much harder than you might think.[4,5,6] This one example alone illustrated to many a fundamental truth about modern supply chains: when you build a physical network for speed and efficiency, the process of pivoting can be slow and painful. This was a lesson that consumers and enterprises would learn many, many times throughout the 2020 pandemic and its many phases of aftermath, during which time companies lost billions in revenue from backlogged orders that, due to delays in global trade, could never be fulfilled.

It was the toilet paper story that caused my mother to tell me: "Now I think I know what you do for work!" My colleagues in supply chain teams have shared dozens of similar stories of friends and relatives having "aha" moments that amounted to the revelation of a kid raised on hamburgers encountering a cow for the first time. Yes, it is true: all of the food, fuel, goods, materials, buildings, and services come from somewhere, and the vast majority of them are utterly dependent upon the smooth operation of a physical supply chain that often involves tens, hundreds, or even thousands of distinct steps from extraction and production, to distribution and fulfillment, to brick-and-mortar or e-commerce, to last mile, reverse-logistics for returns, and end-of-life disposal or circularity. However, the "aha" moment about toilet paper is telling for what people talk about when we talk about supply chains: administrative, operational, and—critically—most frequently discussed in the context of something big going horribly wrong. The pandemic. Wars. Fires. Hurricanes. Red Sea pirates. Russia-Ukraine. China-Taiwan. The Baltimore bridge disaster. These are all supply chain disruption events, and disruption is frequently the context in which news about supply chains shows up in our news media and in our personal and professional lives. In what context would we even find ourselves discussing a supply chain that is running correctly, where everything is going according to plan? Far too few.

The lesser-discussed reason for this is simple: a well-functioning supply chain is almost unremarkable by definition, and many people find discussions of procurement and supply chain operations to be, quite simply, boring. Too complicated. And yet extraordinarily impactful, not just on business outcomes, but on society at large. There is practically no economic, social, or ecological outcome that exists at a global scale that can be achieved without major transformations to global supply chains. This is why there is such a strong affirmative case for bringing the lens of enthusiasm and excitement to discussing the dramatic civilization-scale changes that superhuman supply chains will make possible.

It is little wonder that we are unprepared for the massive ways that superhuman supply chains could transform our lives for the better, if we never feel called to discuss the ways in which supply chains could be improved versus reacting to a disruption event. If we are only used to thinking of supply chain operations in a negative or reactive context, then it might be harder for us to overcome this cognitive bias to recognize the massive opportunity that superhuman supply chains can offer. Within the context of how most large enterprise executives are hardwired, there is a second explanation for this bias against supply chain transformation: top-line revenue growth is often viewed by corporate boards and executive teams as the sexier, more braggable category of technology-enabled win, whereas supply chain transformation is nearly always bucketed within initiatives designed to drive bottom-line cost reductions or risk reductions.

Even though both types of transformation initiatives contribute to margin expansion and in recent years corporate leadership teams have prioritized cost-cutting initiatives with a renewed fervor, the innovation investments championed by enterprise leadership teams are supposed to impact the top-line. Executives often pursue transformation projects to unlock new business models, contribute to top-line revenue growth, and enable legacy businesses to effectively compete with newer players (rather than say, accelerate operations, reduce costs, or make supply chains more effective and efficient). For that reason, discussions that position superhuman supply chains within overall enterprise transformations will inevitably require additional framing, storytelling, and context to connect the dots to larger enterprise initiatives around not just cost savings, but the future of industrial commerce on a global scale. That is why connecting these narratives to the concept of Techno-Industrials in Packy's essay included here and the concept of disruptive cost physics becomes so important. Cost structure is the competitive opportunity that will be available to all players in nearly every industry that manufactures and distributes a physical product or material. When the opportunity is there, it's hard to imagine one or more players not seizing it.

To those executive leaders and business operators who view themselves as innovators but whose top-line bias has kept their enthusiasm tepid or lukewarm when it comes to the Predictive Enterprise, I would offer a potential re-frame of the topic. While we genuinely do believe that people generally undervalue the impact of incrementally reducing costs (and especially the Cost of Goods Sold (COGS)) due to cognitive biases and groupthink associated with the media's and market's fixation on high growth (rather than high margin or high profitability), we do not see the opportunity of superhuman supply chains primarily through the lens of incremental cost reduction, incremental productivity gains, or incremental organizational improvements like paying fewer people more money to do a better job faster using AI. To be honest, if that were the size and scale of this opportunity, I wouldn't have felt the need to write this book. Instead, I believe that visionaries across large industrial enterprises will be able to launch entirely new business models, products, and services built on their ability to manufacture, distribute, and deliver at dramatically faster speeds and astonishingly lower costs than most people today believe is possible. Enterprises will make and scale more drive-thrus, not more automats.

Let's remember that the automobile existed for decades, but it took Ford's innovation around the production assembly line to mass produce cars to the point that they became ubiquitous and reshaped most built environments across nearly every nation, city, and community across our planet. Take a look outside your window and imagine what our world would look like without ubiquitous cars. Streets, roads, highways, parking lots, sidewalks, the shape of cities and suburbs, the clustering and zoning of different buildings—our world as we know it has been shaped by the mass production of cars as surely as it has by the rivers and the mountains and the glaciers (and as surely as it will be reshaped when those cars and trucks can drive themselves autonomously and haul loads without a human driver).

For its time, Ford's production assembly line was a form of superhuman supply chain: exponentially faster than anyone had seen before, with exponentially higher throughput, at exponentially lower cost. And during the twentieth century, it was the production assembly line, and the shipping container and container ship, along with globalization and e-commerce, that predominantly contributed to supply chain's outsized global impact on our industrial civilization. Those supply chains were often very long, very low-cost, and extremely efficient, enabling enterprises to keep inventory levels at record lows and even run on a model known as Just-In-Time (JIT), which counts on suppliers continuously unloading materials just in time to run production and thus avoid costs associated with materials handling and inventory storage.

During the twenty-first century, a new set of AI technologies will deliver the next exponential shift in superhuman supply chains, one that will be just as consequential for humanity as the introduction of the production assembly line and the container ship, and one that will drive as much cultural change in the coming decades as globalization and e-commerce. These technologies can replace defined units of human labor, but they are not in a position to replace workers wholesale unless those workers are extremely resistant to helping their organizations unlock the dramatic value opportunities associated with these technologies. This is not a case of "human workers are not good enough;" it is a case of asking: If you could produce the equivalent or greater output in a tenth of the time with a tenth of the effort, then why wouldn't you? Who deeply misses waiting in a long line for a brief, highly transactional interaction with a human toll collector? And yet, these are inevitably challenging conversations, and they are worth having in a candid, direct way with employees at all levels of the organization. Transformation is not optional. Often, it is the only way for organizations to grow.

Conclusion

Leadership Playbook to Win Your First 100 Days in the Predictive Enterprise

Why the First 100 Days Matter

When the newly elected president of the United States takes office, their advisors and cabinet members rally around a singular idea: the 100-Day Plan. Why? Because while a presidency lasts four years, the first 100 days set the tone with Congress, federal agencies, and global partners. It's during this window that momentum is established, goodwill is built, and the foundation for ambitious projects is laid.

The same holds true for you as a CPO. Your tenure may last years, but your ability to achieve long-term transformation hinges on how you use your first 100 days. If you set the pace early, you create a reservoir of goodwill and credibility. If you hesitate, you risk being pulled back into the gravitational force of "business as usual."

Think of it like a rocket launch: enormous thrust is required at liftoff to break Earth's gravity. Once you achieve escape velocity, the rocket can sustain orbit with far less energy. In procurement, the thrust comes from decisive early action—identifying pain points, delivering quick wins, and showing stakeholders that this time, things are different.

Your first 100 days are not about fixing everything. They are about showing momentum, establishing trust, and creating the conditions for your transformational projects to succeed. In physics, escape velocity is about mass and propulsion. In procurement, it's about momentum and alignment with your budget owners. In the age of AI, the role of CPO and CSCO has expanded dramatically. Today, your portfolio not only includes managing spend and supplier relationships, but also mitigating risk associated with third-party behavior across the enterprise. It doesn't stop there. In the age of AI, you are probably being asked to deliver a transformation that allows you to "do more with less." The expectations that Executive Leadership Teams have around improving the efficiency and headcount ratios of procurement and supply chain teams are not always realistic or fair. Nevertheless, this is your job: to transform the function, to deliver bigger wins, to operate with greater efficiency. Sounds easy, right? In this short essay, I leverage my 40-year experience in procurement and supply management leadership to look at how CPOs can build effective playbooks for executing on their first 100 days, and lay a foundation for long-term success.

Step 1: Build a Transformation Team (Days 1–15)

The first 15 days of your plan are not about tools or dashboards—they're about your people. Every transformational leader needs allies, and your first task is to talk to as many of your people as you can, find a few with real initiative and ambition, and assemble a small, empowered group that can serve as the engine of momentum. Think of this team as your launch crew: the people who will fuel your early wins and give your 100-day plan the thrust it needs. Make sure this group includes a diversity of ages: a few people who represent the long-term employees and a few younger digital natives who have been raised from birth with screens and AI and who will offer valuable impatience to keep things moving.

This working group must have a clear mandate. It's not a brainstorming committee or a place where good ideas go to die; it's a team empowered to identify pain points, propose and prioritize projects, assign owners, and begin execution quickly. Without authority, the group risks becoming a time sink for its participants and for you. With authority, it becomes the center of gravity for your transformation.

That authority starts with sponsorship. If the group doesn't include a C-level executive other than yourself, it must at least carry their visible support—such as the executive's name on the mandate or their presence at the kickoff meeting. Having a C-level backing gives the group credibility and clears the inevitable blockers that arise.

Equally important is diversity of perspective and experience as well as age. To reflect the whole enterprise, this group should comprise frontline staff who experience the pain points, mid-level managers who identify process inefficiencies, P&L owners who prioritize business outcomes, and supplier-facing leaders who understand the external perspective. Too often, suppliers are an afterthought in transformation projects, even though they deliver a significant portion of the value. Bringing their voice in early prevents blind spots later.

Pro-Tip: WIIFM for Every Collaborator

Never forget that every collaborator is silently asking, What's in it for me? You can build trust by asking and establishing each participant's motivation for the group explicitly, in writing. It's not enough to point to organizational goals; you must show each person how this work helps them personally, whether by solving daily frustrations, boosting career visibility, or giving them a seat at the table on high-profile projects. When every member has a clear WIIFM, energy and momentum are far easier to sustain. You can also ground this value by starting every meeting with a clear outcome objective and a quick roundtable, asking the question: "What do you want to get out of this meeting?"

To move from concept to action, start with a disciplined kickoff. In less than an hour, you should be able to move from introductions to soliciting a list of suggestions, beginning a long-list, and moving to concrete next steps without losing momentum. The agenda doesn't need to be complicated—in fact, the simpler the better. A clear, time-boxed structure keeps the group focused and shows that this isn't just another meeting; it's the launchpad for your 100 day plan.

The sample agenda below illustrates how you can structure your very first session to set the right tone.

Kickoff Meeting Agenda (60 Minutes)

Time (minutes)	Activity	Purpose
0–10	Intros	Each participant states their name, what they want to achieve from the meeting, the metric they care about most, and the most significant pain point they see in an internal process, with a category, or with the supply base.
10–25	Review Metrics Tracker	Discuss the top 3 pain points and corresponding metrics (e.g., cost, cycle time, delays). Note recent trends and set short-term targets. Quantify pain first, then measure benefit as a reduction of this pain.
25–40	Project List and Stand-Ups	Each project owner provides a brief update, including status, blockers, requests, and the expected timeline for moving metrics.
40–50	Decision Time	Identify key decision points, weigh the options, capture the pros/cons, and either make a decision in the meeting or assign a decision owner.
50–60	Roundtable and Next Steps	Each participant shares takeaways, action items, and a suggested agenda for the next meeting. Gather quick feedback scores (1–10) to track meeting quality over time.

To move from the kickoff into execution, you need clarity on who's at the table and who's missing. This is where stakeholder mapping comes in.

A stakeholder map is not just a roster of names. It's a fantastic diagnostic tool that grounds your discussion in the relevant personas and shows you:

- Who has the authority to unblock projects?
- Who feels the pain that your transformation can solve?
- Who can influence adoption, for better or worse?
- Where are the gaps? Make time to hear from people who might otherwise be overlooked—such as suppliers or frontline staff on the shop floor.

Without this clarity, transformation groups risk becoming echo chambers, with too much airtime for perspectives from the same few loud stakeholders, or even misrepresenting perspectives from people who aren't present to speak for themselves. A good stakeholder map provides a balanced perspective: executive sponsors with the power to mandate change, end users with direct experience of the pain, and suppliers' voices that expose risks you might otherwise overlook.

Think of it as drawing the first blueprint for your transformation: before you start building, you need to know who the builders are, who signs off on the permits, and who's living in the house once it's complete. As the leader, your job is to make sure that the house gets built on a solid foundation, and that all the stakeholders can see that the construction is proceeding according to the mutually agreed-upon plan.

Building Momentum

Step 2: Diagnose Pain Points and Metrics (Days 11–40)

The first 10 days set your foundation; the next 30 are about listening, validating, and gaining buy-in before acting. As a new CPO, it's tempting to move quickly into projects and dashboards. But the fastest way to build credibility is to show that you understand where the pain really lives and not just what's in last quarter's reports.

Start with deep listening sessions. Sit down with buyers, category managers, supplier managers, and even key suppliers themselves. Ask the simple, but powerful questions:

- What slows you down? Where do you find that you experience pain or annoyance?
- Where do surprises happen most often? Where are surprises costing us the most?
- What feels harder than it should be? Where do you see non-value add steps?
- If you had a magic wand, what's the first thing you would change?

You'll hear themes such as long cycle times for approvals, fire drills around contract renewals, invoice mismatches that lead to supplier frustration, limited visibility into tail spend, or reactive escalations driven by supplier communication that keep the team in firefighting mode. Not all pain points are equal. Once you've gathered them, prioritize by urgency, value, and ease of execution. Some fixes unlock significant impact quickly (like improving data visibility). Others might be high value but harder to tackle (such as multi-sourcing).

Define your baseline metrics. The Predictive Enterprise approach to transformation relies on being able to define desired outcomes, which in turn relies on data about past performance. Without clean metrics today, you cannot define success for tomorrow. Identify a handful of core measures and set up a simple tracker:

- Cycle time (from request to PO)
- Cost per process or per headcount
- Number of delays or surprises
- Supplier performance against Service Level Agreements
- Contract leakage or maverick spend

For each, capture a trailing 30- or 60-day view, then set a realistic target for the next 30 days. Even if the data isn't perfect, start where you are. Momentum comes from measuring consistently, not from waiting until the metrics are flawless. In certain cases, you may need to poll a group of internal experts to ask for an estimate on a baseline if the data is too hard to pull from internal systems or validate within a reasonable timeframe. Often an average of guesses from people close to the process can be a better data point than a statistical analysis performed on poor quality internal data.

What you're doing here is laying the groundwork for setting baselines for your metrics and beginning the goal-setting process. You can also throw this data into a Large Language Model and simply ask it questions via chat to perform analysis, and ask it to set goals. Then compare the results with the goals that you and your team have set. Which baseline feels more accurate? Which set of goals feels more realistic? Each iteration on setting baselines and targets is a good exercise for building trust with the team, and you are already integrating AI into your team collaboration process. You can also ask AI to play the role of a panel of experts. You can tell several different models to take on the role of a subject matter expert in your industry, your category, or in a given commodity, and you can prompt the AI to be more optimistic, more critical, or more curious. You now have a "supplemented" and "objective" panel of experts. Ask the panel questions about your baselines and goals and see where they converge and diverge. The incremental cost of using this approach if you already have access to a Large Language Model is close to zero, and the outcome provides great fodder for group discussion. Each baseline metric becomes the "before" picture that predictive tools and other AI will later improve. Think of it like priming the rocket engines: you're gathering the fuel that will allow your procurement function to achieve escape velocity. Without the "before," you won't be able to track, measure, and report your wins or create momentum.

To make this concrete, you need a simple way to capture, track, and communicate all the relevant numbers that you're collecting. A Key Performance Indicator (KPI) tracker does precisely that. It turns scattered pain points into measurable baselines, makes progress visible, and creates accountability across the transformation team.

Another powerful tool for CPOs during this time is engaging your team to size and scope the relevant challenges and barriers. Have you ever done the exercise where you put rocks in a jar and then try to fill the jar with sand? The exercise is meant to demonstrate one fundamental lesson: pick your big rocks first, especially anything that will be a dependency or foundation to your future long-term success. At its core, this "big rocks" test is a prioritization exercise: it helps you separate the urgent from the important and the visible frustrations from the hidden structural blockers. When you're standing at Day 20 or 30 of a transformation, you don't yet have the luxury of solving everything. You need a way to demonstrate to the organization and your executive leadership team and CEO that you can deliver a few practical and 'painless' results quickly without compromising long-term value. You need your team to prove that they can clear blockers early and often.

Step 3: Launch Quick Wins as Bets (Days 41–75)

The importance of visible, measurable progress on a weekly and monthly basis cannot be overstated. Early wins create credibility with executives, enthusiasm among your team, and a tangible reason for skeptical stakeholders to lean in and support your initiatives rather than resist. The criteria for a quick win are simple: they're the obvious no-brainers, they are low-effort, and most importantly, they are "quick." If you ever hear yourself talking about a "quick win" that takes more than 30 days to deliver, you should ask yourself what the definition of "quick" truly is. Now that you have invested significant time learning about your team and your organization, you should be ready to move fast. Maybe a quick win is eliminating redundant approvals, trading an early renewal for a small savings outcome, or addressing an obvious supplier communication pain point. The point isn't scale; it's speed-to-execution and time-to-value.

To deliver impact quickly, focus on projects that are:

- **High-visibility:** Projects that will be noticed by leadership and frontline teams.
- **Relatively low-effort:** Projects that can be executed within 30 days or less.
- **Clearly linked to pain points:** Every project should address a measurable business cost—time, money, or customer experience.
- **Representative of broader transformation goals:** Even small wins should signal a shift toward predictive, AI-enabled processes that lays the foundation for transformation.

Discipline is key. You should have one small project launched and showing results. Don't be afraid to work with an external partner provided that you are clear on timeline and expected results. Each quick win should connect directly to a baseline metric stakeholders care about: cycle time, costs, delays, surprises. Each quick win becomes a way of making the invisible visible, creating accountability, silencing the critics, and building ownership.

To make progress sustainable, adopt a simple but powerful team cadence: weekly standups. Borrowed from agile "scrums" in software development and adapted for procurement, these standups focus on three things: what got done, what's blocked, and what's needed now and next. No long decks, no wasted airtime—just clarity, metrics, and momentum.

Expanding the Transformation (Days 75–100)

Step 4: Build the Predictive Enterprise Mindset

To become a predictive enterprise, teams must shift from reactive problem-solving to proactively identifying and addressing issues before they occur, setting targets, and reverse-engineering the path to get there. Show what good looks like, prove that it can be repeated, and only then create and document new processes. A lot of leaders tend to over-engineer and overthink the new process flows upfront, often spending giant sums on consultants as they do and without really understanding what their own teams and technology can do. The only way to understand AI is to use it in a low-risk test-and learn environment. Sometimes people call this "doing pilots," but I see the word "pilot" as having a negative connotation, so I say "test and learn" so that if it's effective it can quickly scale across the enterprise. The reality is that each enterprise business culture is different, each industry and geography is different, and one size rarely fits all. Just like in manufacturing production processes, you won't know the yield of a predictive process until you have seen your team execute it multiple times. Where does the process get stuck? Where are there non-value add steps, like waiting for additional information when there is enough for a decision?

That's a place where the Predictive Enterprise approach can add value by providing a best next step to many parts of a process simultaneously rather than serially, and by creating an idea of what "good" looks like. Are there steps in the process where we can remove humans entirely because they don't add enough value? It can be exciting when you find those, especially steps that involve data entry or data analysis. AI can be used to provide the data or analysis to the right person at the right time. This isn't about dashboards: it's about moving from a "pull" task where someone on your team has to go digging, to a "push" model where the right data is delivered to the right person at the right time, along with a best next step embedded. That "push" is part of the Predictive Enterprise approach, like GoogleMaps or Waze did for predictive navigation. This will require ensuring collaboration guiderails and guideposts are clearly established with critical stakeholders. That way when the decision makes its way to the person directly responsible, they already have a data-driven recommendation of which path to take, and which selection to make. Because they know where the process is going, they have confidence in the recommendation the AI is making for how to get there. An example in my experience is over governed purchase order approval guidelines and otherwise undefined purchase order approval guidelines. Automation democratizes knowledge for better decision-making with speed and efficiency. This requires alignment on risk tolerances, trust in organizational practices, and clarity on third party roles in achieving strategic outcomes. Maps of physical geography are a helpful metaphor for understanding the role that AI can play in helping unblock a process at a large enterprise. A lot of the benefit is around creating confidence and insights through harvesting past actions and outcomes as a road map to driving real-time actions.

Once you take your first process and change the steps so it can become predictive, you should take stock of your data tasks related to tracking and reporting. If you can't tell a story with data around a "win," then how will your CEO know that you are actually creating value? Focus on validating the key data, and look into the micro-motions of what your team actually spends their time on and how much is related to reporting and interacting with internal systems. Manual human data entry slows decision-making and introduces errors. You can eliminate manual human data entry whenever and wherever possible. Errors in enterprise master data are like sand in a bathing suit: once they get in, it can be challenging to clean them out. As a leader, you can emphasize process designs that take as the default path machine-entered, validated data to support decisions and next steps. You do not need to boil the ocean. Enterprise supply chain and procurement teams often collect and store far more repetitive data from suppliers than we truly need. There are a lot of quick wins to be found here simply by eliminating data collection tasks for suppliers, or providing suppliers with pre-populated tables using approaches like predictive procurement.

Transformations that deliver superhuman supply chains using the Predictive Enterprise approach extend beyond internal teams. Include supplier-facing category managers and individual contributors in project planning, including representatives of the budget owners. Talk to suppliers directly and ask for feedback on the existing process. Ask them directly what annual meetings and reviews they find useful versus burdensome, what elements of the business process or compliance they would like to see reduced first and fastest. Gaining supplier buy-in for transformation initiatives, especially those that involve process changes, will have a material impact on your long-term success. Not every supplier will be excited, and some will tell you that they are not in favor of changes, or of using new technology, period. A few suppliers may be jaded by over-promised and under-delivered technology projects in the past. Some suppliers may even be afraid of AI or anxious about whether changes will create additional cost pressures for them, or risk harming the relationship. These are legitimate concerns and suppliers who express these concerns deserve to be heard. But you also need to be clear: you are upgrading the foundational operating system of your enterprise's supply network, with or without them, and while you would appreciate their support, they will need to figure out how to participate, contribute, and get on board the train.

Suppliers who voice resistance and opposition to your transformation efforts are not showing good partnership to you or to your budget owners. The best way to win them over is by showing that you hear and understand their concerns, soliciting input around changes that they want to see within your transformation plan, and then delivering quick wins that improve their experience. Making a few no-brainer changes fast is the key, and this shows that you are committed to mutual benefits. It also gives them tangible evidence that some changes may in fact benefit them in ways that they did not expect and that are translatable to other clients.

As your operational process stack evolves, organizations often encounter perceived tradeoffs. Finance teams push for cost savings. Operations prioritize speed and quality. Procurement seeks control and compliance, Spend Under Management. In the Predictive Enterprise approach, these tradeoffs are not treated as zero-sum conflicts but as solvable design challenges where we expect technologies to help us resolve these conflicts and create greater values alignment. Focus on projects that solve for multiple objectives simultaneously: e.g. where all stakeholders achieve meaningful objectives without compromise for a subset of spend, a subset of your geographical footprint, or a subset of your supplier base. This is one reason why we have seen such strong adoption in large enterprises for supply chain visibility: visibility gets a win for every one of these stakeholders. By reframing tradeoffs as opportunities for collaboration, your team can take the lead in breaking down silos, aligning incentives, and driving outcomes that satisfy multiple stakeholders simultaneously.

To put these principles into practice and ensure no opportunity is overlooked, teams can use a simple checklist to identify predictive opportunities across processes, data, workflows, and stakeholder interactions. This checklist serves as a practical guide to translate predictive thinking into concrete, measurable actions.

Use this checklist to identify actionable predictive opportunities:

- Do we understand what outcomes matter to each key budget owner?
- Do we know what matters most: supplier selection, process speed, or cost?
- Do we see where human-entered data can be switched to machine-entered using Predictive AI?
- Do we know which non-value add steps can be excluded from a supplier-facing workflow entirely?
- Are supplier perspectives and pain points included in our playbook?
- Where can predictive AI or process automation deliver measurable value without adding steps or sacrificing important context?

By building your own checklist, your teams begin thinking ahead and reverse-engineering their own success rather than reacting to blockers or getting stuck on obstacles. Processes anticipate issues, data drives decisions, workflows are intentional, and cross-functional trade-offs are resolved collaboratively. The predictive enterprise becomes a reality—measurable, sustainable, and capable of delivering exponential improvements.

Step 5: Institutionalize Governance and Explicit Decision-Making

As the CPO advances in transforming procurement, a critical challenge arises: meetings that either have too few participants to make decisions or too many to be productive. This "too many / not enough stakeholders" trap can hinder progress, as anyone who has worked in a corporate leadership role can tell you. To address this productivity challenge associated with having effective meetings, it's essential to structure larger group meetings around decisions, not discussions. By clearly defining the key decisions that need to be made, the relevant stakeholders, and the data required beforehand, meetings become focused and efficient. Presenters can be asked to share materials well in advance, giving all participants a chance to read and consider their response before the meeting. As trust on the team increases, the percentage of meeting time spent on presentations should decrease. This decision-centric approach ensures that every meeting has a clear purpose and outcome, preventing unnecessary delays and fostering accountability. Lots of time doing transformation work is spent in group meetings. Having effective and engaging meetings that end early will make you a popular leader, provided that people have the ability to voice contrary perspectives, unpopular opinions, or share negative updates and use meetings to ask for help. Meetings should end with action items that have an assigned owner for follow-up. This discipline creates accountability and will ensure everyone departs a meeting feeling clear on their next steps. Often in my career regularly scheduled meetings made me feel like the Bill Murray character in *Groundhog Day*. No real agenda, the same conversations with no decisions, no action registers, and the same few participants dominating a mindless discussion. Leadership is accountable for ensuring that these meetings are eliminated, freeing time for productive and effective use of valuable resources.

By embedding these practices into the organization's culture, procurement teams can shorten decision cycles, which will enhance the ability to test-and-learn. This shift not only enhances efficiency but also drives strategic value, ensuring that procurement decisions contribute to the organization's long-term goals.

Scaling for Impact (Days 100+)

Step 6: Standardize, Systematize, Scale Without Being Overly Rigid or Fixated on Uniformity for Uniformity's Sake

As the CPO enters Days 71–100, the early wins and predictive initiatives are in motion, and the focus shifts from experimentation to sustainable scaling. The challenge now is to ensure that the processes, decisions, and innovations that delivered early impact are codified so they can be replicated across teams, geographies, and supplier networks. Standardizing practices across the organization begins by creating standardized templates for critical activities, such as strategic supplier due diligence. Templates ensure that best practices are consistently applied, reduce variability in decision-making, and allow teams to capture lessons learned from previous projects. By standardizing key steps, the organization transforms knowledge into a repeatable system that can scale.

As the CPO scales predictive initiatives, the team faces another challenge: not every task, decision, or communication is suited for AI. Some decisions benefit from automation, while others demand holistic human judgment uncontaminated by a potentially unhelpful AI recommendation. To navigate this challenge, you can use a procurement AI risk–reward matrix to bucket all the decisions that get made in and around your team. This matrix offers a simple but powerful tool that maps tasks according to the potential value AI can provide and the level of risk involved.

In practice, the matrix becomes a decision compass. Routine, repetitive tasks, like processing invoices or monitoring supplier performance metrics, fall in the low-risk, low-reward quadrant due to the high count of tasks and the low variability between the defined steps in each task. These are prime candidates for basic automation where AI can deliver speed, scale, and efficiency. Meanwhile, strategic decisions—like selecting key suppliers, negotiating complex contracts, or managing sensitive categories—occupy the high-risk, high-reward quadrant. For these, AI can help organize and validate the data, and perform internal comparative analysis, but the supplier communication is generally customized by a human, and may involve a series of face-to-face meetings where elements like body language and tone of voice are significant for understanding the relationship. However, there's often a very large bucket of decisions where a lot of spend is involved but the supplier relationship is highly defined, and the task of soliciting a quote or an update is a regular, normal cycle. This big middle represents a set of decisions with variable outcomes (e.g. high-reward potential), but where the pre-existing relationship makes introducing small but impactful process changes relatively low-risk. This bucket of decisions is where the Predictive Enterprise approach can have a huge impact, not just by removing human labor from non-value add tasks but by fundamentally improving the outcomes of the value-add tasks.

By visualizing tasks through the lens of risk and reward, the team avoids the trap of over-automation or over-focusing solely on removing humans from tasks and capitalizes on the Predictive Enterprise opportunity of hybrid AI/human workflows that improve outcomes by reverse engineering processes. This ensures AI is applied where it truly amplifies the most impact the fastest. It also creates clarity across the organization: everyone understands which decisions are fully automated, which are augmented by AI, and which remain human-initiated. Over time, this framework guides smarter, faster, and safer adoption of AI in procurement and across the supply base, embedding both control and innovation in an explainable framework for transformation across the enterprise.

Remember that scaling is not just about repeating processes; it's about embedding organizational learning into daily operations. Quick wins only translate into durable transformation through continuous improvement. Capture lessons from test-and-learn projects and integrate them into supplier onboarding, sourcing practices, spot buying, and cross-functional workflows. Figure out how you can even remove steps from your fire drills and reactive cycles. This ensures that every new initiative starts from a higher baseline of knowledge on your team that compounds over time.

By standardizing, systematizing, and embedding learning into processes, the predictive enterprise becomes repeatable and scalable. Teams move from isolated quick wins to organization-wide transformation, ensuring that the CPO's initiatives deliver sustained, exponential impact across procurement and supply chain operations.

Step 7: Communicate and Show Results

By 90 Days your predictive initiatives as a CPO are running, projects are underway, and early wins are starting to materialize in your KPI dashboard. The next critical step is to ensure these results are visible, measurable, and communicated effectively, because transformation only gains momentum when the leadership, budget owners, and suppliers see that there is tangible impact. You have been updating key stakeholders along the way through your weekly standups, but it is just as important to trumpet your success to the broader enterprise. Your team has worked hard for this win. As the leader, you need to celebrate, appreciate, and recognize their efforts and give them opportunities to present the results that they own to your executive peers.

Every initiative, from quick wins to longer-term predictive projects, now has a clear and auditable metrics tracker. Where did we start? Where did we get after 90 days? Those are the most important questions. Track progress against these metrics consistently, whether it's cost savings, cycle-time reduction, supplier performance improvements, or risk mitigation. Showing measurable progress reinforces credibility and builds trust with stakeholders, both within procurement and across the enterprise.

Communicating results is not just about reporting numbers—it's about telling a story. What were the use cases? What were the challenges? What did we learn? How do our learnings impact how we are going to scale? How was the budget owner the real champion of the outcome? Use progress dashboards, project updates, and even meeting sentiment scores to make the transformation visible. Share how predictive initiatives and AI learnings are changing day-to-day work, resolving pain points, and enabling teams to act faster and smarter.

Visual storytelling helps stakeholders understand not only what has changed but why it matters to them. Remember the WIIFM from the beginning? Ask everyone whether they got the outcome that was not just beneficial to the enterprise as a whole, but satisfying to them personally.

Executives and frontline teams alike respond to concrete outcomes. Highlight both short-term wins and long-term impact. For example, demonstrate how predictive supply management located alternative sources for a scarce material, or how automated workflows and predictive data freed up team capacity for strategic initiatives. By connecting activities to business results, the CPO makes the transformation real and actionable across the enterprise. In the end it MUST support the overall strategy of the organization.

Looking Beyond 100 Days: Continuous Acceleration

As your first 100 days conclude, look back on a period of rapid learning, early wins, and foundational transformation. But the journey does not stop here. The real challenge and opportunity is sustaining escape velocity, maintaining momentum so that improvements continue to compound and the organization accelerates continuously. But sustaining velocity requires careful pacing.

Teams that move too fast without reinforcement risk burnout or disengagement. By celebrating early successes, capturing lessons, and balancing workloads, you can ensure that energy and focus are preserved. This approach allows teams to maintain continuous acceleration rather than stagnate after the initial burst of transformation.

Escape velocity is achieved and maintained through iteration. Every project and workflow is assessed using data, with insights feeding back into planning. Quick wins inform larger initiatives, and lessons learned are embedded into organizational routines. Each cycle compounds progress, creating a self-reinforcing engine where efficiency, agility, and predictive capability accelerate continuously. Over time, the enterprise moves faster and more effectively, achieving results that grow exponentially rather than linearly.

In this state, procurement stops reacting and starts predicting. AI highlights supplier risks before they surface, automation clears repetitive work, and real-time data drives smarter decisions. The organization gains momentum—anticipating challenges, optimizing resources on the go, and creating measurable impact at speed.

The CPO is at the center of this acceleration—supplier-focused, data-driven, and AI-enabled. By embedding insights, connecting cross-functionally, and leading with vision, they don't just manage procurement—they transform it into a system that continually enables and accelerates.

Continuous acceleration is how procurement moves beyond short-term wins into lasting impact. It's how organizations sustain escape velocity—and stay ahead.

Turning Naysayers into Allies: The 10 Most Common Objections and How to Answer Them

Every transformation effort encounters resistance. In procurement, especially, objections often stem from legitimate concerns—such as teams being stretched thin, legacy systems, or a fear of change. Rather than dismiss these objections, effective CPOs reframe them, acknowledging the problem while offering a constructive path forward. The table below outlines the most common objections and practical reframes that help sustain momentum.

The Top 10 Objections to Procurement Transformation

Objection	Helpful Response/Reframe
1. We don't have bandwidth	That's exactly why predictive tools and AI matter—they automate low-value tasks and free up capacity. Starting small reduces the load, rather than adding to it. Being too busy to reduce your workload guarantees that your workload will remain insurmountable. The only way out is through.
2. Our data sucks	Perfect data is not the goal—predictive systems get smarter with use. We will start with directional accuracy and refine as we go.

3. We have too many systems already	We're not adding noise; we're integrating and simplifying. The goal is fewer clicks and fewer silos, not more. When you clean a room, sometimes the room will get messier before it gets cleaner.
4. This will slow us down	The intention is to expedite our progress. Predictive workflows eliminate rework and surprises, resulting in a drop in cycle time. Predictive data reduces errors by pre-filling form fields with validated entries.
5. Suppliers won't adopt this	Suppliers win too—fewer manual asks, faster onboarding, and clearer expectations. We'll test-and-learn first with suppliers where the risks are lower and the potential rewards are higher.
6. Finance won't go for it	Finance is concerned with cost savings and risk management. Predictive AI approaches deliver both, with clearer business case visibility.
7. We tried this before, and it failed	That's why we're approaching it differently—smaller use cases, clearer outcomes, and AI tools tailored for today's environment.
8. AI is too risky	That's why we're applying a risk–reward matrix—AI where it adds value and ensuring human judgment where it's critical. We're aiming for a hybrid approach that reduces human execution of non-value add tasks, not fully delegating important decisions to AI.
9. We need more control, not less	Predictive procurement isn't about loosening control—it's about faster cycles, amplified savings, and removing steps.
10. It's too early or just not the right time	Transformation is never about the perfect moment. The cost of waiting is higher in the long term than the cost of starting small now. If we wait for the perfect moment, we risk never getting started.

Seen together, these objections reveal more than surface-level resistance—they expose the fears that sit underneath every transformation effort. These are the fears of losing time, losing control, repeating past failures, and adding complexity instead of removing it. Consider the anxiety about AI job loss—this is a real fear that people have. But probably more evident is the skepticism that AI will make their lives any easier. These fears are valid since procurement teams have lived through countless transformations that created more burden than benefit, and tech platforms that over-promised and under-delivered. For many, this is the story of System of Record technology—the benefit is for the manager and the enterprise, not to the end user.

However, when you reframe, those same fears can become a source of energy for change. A bandwidth concern becomes a case for automation. Messy data becomes a reason to start small and prove value. Resistance signals where the pain points—and therefore the opportunities—truly lie. As a leader, you don't need them to agree with you. But if they want to be part of your core transformation team, they need to be able to overcome objections, champion initiatives, and drive change with your stakeholders.

That's why the table above isn't just reference material but a practical coaching tool. CPOs can use it to prepare for pushback before it derails momentum. You can turn these reframes into an FAQ list that stakeholders can share, or role-play them with your team, so that you and your team are equipped with ready responses for daily conversations. Having your team be effective advocates is critical to your success. But the most effective advocacy is actually curiosity, deep listening, and empathy. Training your team to engage with stakeholders at a deep level is truly the key to unlocking the power of the Predictive Enterprise.

AI and The Techno-Industrial Revolution

by Packy McCormick, entrepreneur, investor, and creator of Not Boring

We're standing at the foot of a **Techno-Industrial Revolution.**

Progress shifted from atoms to bits and is now shifting to a combination of atoms and bits.

Cheaper energy, intelligence, and dexterity (i.e., robots), along with new materials and biotech will combine to increase tech's total addressable market to include large existing industries that have been relatively untouched by technology, including industrials and agriculture. Higher margins in large industries will make for very valuable companies.

These companies will look less like the tech giants of today and more like the giants of the Industrial Revolution.

Some, certainly, will be the incumbents that take advantage of cheaper, more capable inputs to improve their businesses.

There will be a crop of new companies that challenge incumbents head-on and win, capturing large markets at high margins in the process. I've started calling them Techno-Industrials.

Techno-Industrials use technology to build atoms-based products with structurally superior unit economics with the ultimate goal of winning on cost in large existing markets, or expanding or creating new markets where there is pent-up demand.

They can leverage their structurally superior unit economics in the form of lower prices to win market share, higher gross margins, or both.

Less fancily, they'll use new technology, processes, or approaches to make physical things that customers want more cheaply than existing companies can, in a way that existing companies can't match. Because they can manufacture more cheaply, they can either lower their prices to steal market share from incumbents or capture more gross margin. In some cases, they'll have enough room to do both.

Three examples might help explain what I mean.

Anduril

In a great conversation with Patrick O'Shaughnessey, Anduril cofounder Palmer Luckey captured the spirit of Techno-Industrials as well as I've ever heard:

> Our pitch deck page one says that Anduril will save western civilization by saving taxpayers hundreds of billions of dollars a year as we make tens of billions of dollars a year.

That's only possible if you figure out a fundamentally cheaper way to deliver capabilities.

In Anduril's case, that means using software to make hardware more capable. I described Anduril as a series of bets, one of which speaks to this point:

> Bet #4: By investing in software R&D upfront, it will be able to better deliver the capabilities the DoD needs to fight the new kind of war, more cheaply. Anduril's Lattice Operating System will enable Anduril to deliver more capable hardware products for less money, and its advantages will compound with each new product it plugs in.

The mega-bull case for Anduril is that it's able to capture more and more of the trillion-dollar defense market and do so at 40–50% margins instead of the 8–12% that incumbent Defense Primes lock in with cost-plus contracts. Lockheed Martin is worth $113 billion on $68 billion of revenue with 12% gross margins. If Anduril achieves a fraction of that revenue while maintaining much higher gross margins, it will be a very valuable company.

Solugen

Solugen is using biotech to attack the $4 trillion chemicals market. Instead of refining petrochemical feedstocks to produce chemicals, Solugen uses enzyme engineering to convert sugar and water (and eventually CO_2) into chemicals.

The takeaway is that by removing steps from the process and using software and biology in place of traditional chemical synthesis and energy-intensive physical processes, Solugen is able to produce chemicals at a higher yield, lower environmental footprint, lower cost, and higher margins than incumbents.

Solugen bills itself as a climate friendly company—its homepage announces "We decarbonize the physical world"—but the climate benefits are not the core of Solugen's commercial strategy. In fact, they are more competitive based on customer experience and price than based on the impact to climate.

What's illuminating is that by cutting steps out of the process and replacing expensive inputs with technology, which Solugen originally did for the climate benefits, it makes the chemicals cheaper to manufacture! It gets closer to the true **cost physics**—what it should cost to make given the technologies, materials, and processes intrinsically required to manufacture it—of chemical production. Higher yield, lower heat and energy requirements, no waste, cheaper product.

It's very early in Solugen's journey, but already, the company generates more than $100 million in annual revenue from its first bioforge at "software-like margins" of around 60%, founder Gaurav Chakrabarti told Bloomberg. It believes that it can build a library of enzymes and catalysts that could produce 90% of chemicals by 2030.

Monumental Labs

Monumental Labs' website pronounces: "Monumental Labs is building AI-enabled robotic stone carving factories. With them, we'll create cities with the splendor of Florence, Paris, or Beaux-Arts New York, at a fraction of the cost."

The company is much younger than Anduril and Solugen, but it's a Techno-Industrial: **using technology** ("AI-enabled robotic stone carving factories") to **build atoms-based products** ("cities with the splendor of Florence, Paris, or Beaux-Arts New York") with **structurally superior unit economics** ("at a fraction of the cost").

In my hunt for Techno-Industrials, I talked to Monumental Labs' founder Micah Springut to understand how he's thinking about the business. It sounded familiar.

In *I, Exponential*, I wrote about the use of modern technology like 3D models, CNC machines, Lidar scans, and 3D printers in the construction of Barcelona's unfinished *La Sagrada Família*.

Monumental wants to do something similar, at city-scale. The idea is that stone *should* be the cheapest material for construction, even cheaper than concrete. It has **cost physics** on its side: making concrete requires an energy-intensive process of heating limestone and other materials to very high temperatures (around 1,400–1,500 °C) in a kiln to make cement, which is then mixed with water, sand, gravel, and other materials. Concrete manufacturing is responsible for roughly 8% of global greenhouse gas emissions.

When you use stone, you just need to get it out of the ground. You can skip the heating and processing. The reason we don't use stone is that working stone is so labor intensive—70–80% of the cost is labor, not the stone itself. "Stone is a cheap material being sold like a Cadillac," Micah told me.

Monumental's bet is that by using AI-enabled robotic stone carvers, it can turn that OpEx into CapEx and dramatically reduce the cost of stone. The company is starting at the high-end of the market with its first robot—carving busts, sculptures, and architectural ornament at high margins—but Micah believes that they'll be able to build full buildings, structural elements and all, out of reinforced stone at scale.

If they succeed, they'll make buildings more beautiful, and cheaper. Micah pointed out that we add a lot of unnecessary material to buildings—like drywall—to cover ugly reinforced rebar, for example. He thinks working with stone can simplify buildings in the same way that an electric engine is so much simpler than a piston, and lower costs in the process.

Over time, if everything goes right, Monumental hopes to make a dent in the $1.5 trillion and growing building materials market, and capture margins by vertically integrating either backward into quarries or forward into delivering turnkey building solutions.

Obviously, getting everything to go just right is going to be insanely hard. It will require enormous warehouses staffed with fleets of robots, a tremendous amount of capital, an orchestra of flatbed trucks crisscrossing the country loaded with stone, selling into a fragmented and geographically far-flung market, and perhaps most dauntingly, changes to building code in the face of the concrete lobby and construction unions.

Building a Techno-Industrial won't be easy, but the prize—big margins in enormous markets—is worth the fight, and I think that cost physics is a powerful force.

Aggregators and Industrials

Anduril, Solugen, and Monumental Labs are just three examples, and all three are still relatively early in the journey. Most of the promise of Techno-Industrials as it stands lies in spreadsheets and techno-economic analyses.

A skeptic would argue that we've heard this story before. In the 2010s, companies that dealt in the physical world promised better margins through technology.

Companies like WeWork, Bird, and my company, Breather, failed to live up to that promise.

Ultimately, while they were *tech-enabled*, the technology wasn't infused into the product in such a way that they changed the cost physics of their industries.

From an economic perspective, it was like squeezing a money balloon: we just shifted dollars from one side to the other.

There are also a number of successes. DoorDash is worth $42 billion. Airbnb is worth $89 billion. Uber is worth $134 billion.

I would argue that these companies didn't change the cost physics of their industries, either. Food is not cheaper. Travel is not cheaper. Catching a ride is not cheaper.

These companies are examples of what Ben Thompson famously calls Aggregators.

Aggregators "aggregate modularized suppliers—which they often don't pay for—to consumers/users with whom they have an exclusive relationship at scale."

These companies *do* create value. There's value in convenience, and there's value in being able to monetize an underutilized resource, whether that's an empty house or an hour of time. But they don't structurally improve the gross margins on the products in their markets. They don't change the cost physics. Like the balloon squeezer, they just move them from one place to another.

One of the key ideas behind Aggregation Theory is Clayton Christensen's Law of Conservation of Attractive Profits. Note the word *conservation*. Aggregators didn't expand industries' profits as much as they moved them from one place to another.

Reasoning about Techno-Industrials requires us to go back further in time, all the way back to the Industrial Revolution in America. I'm calling this coming stage the Techno-Industrial Revolution, but the Industrial Revolution was a techno-industrial revolution too.

Companies like Alcoa and Carnegie Steel invented or leveraged new technology to atoms-based products with structurally superior unit economics with the ultimate goal of winning on cost in large existing markets, or expanding or creating new markets where there is pent-up demand.

Take Alcoa. In 1880, before Charles Martin Hall and Paul Héroult independently invented what became known as the Hall-Héroult Process for aluminum smelting, the metal sold for $17 per pound. In 1884, the United States only produced 125 pounds of aluminum, at least 100 ounces of which went to the capstone of the newly built Washington Monument, the tallest structure in the world at the time.

Charles Martin Hall / Wikimedia Commons

Charles Martin Hall with Illustration of Alcoa Steelman Street Facility

In 1903, the Wright Brothers built the engine for their historic plane using aluminum alloy. By 1930, aluminum sold for $0.20 per pound and Alcoa was responsible for over half of worldwide aluminum capacity. The United States alone produced 148,000 tons of the metal in 1939. When Sputnik launched in 1957, it brought its aluminum body into orbit. Today, it's impossible to imagine the world without the lightweight, flexible metal and its alloys.

Alcoa dominated the industry so handily that in 1938, FDR's Justice Department sued it for antitrust based not on rapacious practices, but on market share alone.

Hall invented a technology (and protected it with patents) to manufacture a product with structurally superior unit economics in order to bring down costs and both successfully compete in existing markets and create new ones.

Or take **Carnegie Steel**. In 1860, when Andrew Carnegie was dabbling in iron investments, the superior steel was so expensive to make that it was only made in small batches; the United States produced only 13,000 tons that year. But in 1872, Carnegie saw the Bessemer Process in action at a plant in England and introduced it to his

J. Edgar Thompson Steelworks in 1875. By the turn of the century, the United States produced over 11 million tons of steel, and Carnegie was its largest and most profitable producer.

The first ton of steel Carnegie produced cost about $56; by 1900, Carnegie was producing steel at $11.50 per ton, a 72% decline. At lower prices and increased manufacturing capacity, steel underpinned railroads, ships, and newly-possible-thanks-to-steel skyscrapers, which helped meet the growing demand for urban dwellings to house an influx of immigrants.

The 1901 sale of Carnegie Steel to JP Morgan's U.S. Steel for $480 million made Carnegie the richest man in the world and gave the newly created conglomerate two-thirds of the U.S. steel market.

Carnegie used a new technology, and vertically integrated around it, to manufacture a product with structurally superior unit economics in order to bring down costs and both successfully compete in existing markets and create new ones.

ALCOA and Carnegie Steel took two different approaches—innovation and integration, respectively—to achieve the same ends: driving down costs and increasing production.

By **structurally superior unit economics**, I mean that there is something in the way the product is manufactured or delivered that gives the Techno-Industrial a cost advantage that can't easily be replicated. For Alcoa, that was the patented Hall-Héroult Process. For Carnegie Steel, it was the application of the new Bessemer Process combined with vertical integration of the supply chain and a maniacal focus on cost across the whole thing.

In both cases, new technology was a necessary ingredient that the companies leveraged in their manufacturing processes in order to drive down costs, grow demand, and increase scale to drive costs down further. They didn't just change prices, they got closer to the true **cost physics** of their products.

Modern Techno-Industrials can take either the Alcoa inventor route or the Carnegie integrator route. I'd argue that Solugen is an example of an inventor and Anduril and Monumental Labs are integrators, although the line, in both the old examples and the new, is a little blurry. In either case, they will face enormous headwinds as they race to scale.

Techno-Industrial Challenges

Operating in the world of atoms is different than operating in the world of bits.

In the world of bits, you don't need to ask permission; in the world of atoms, you do.

In bits, you can pivot and iterate and ship updates and run experiments; in atoms, you need to have your strategy and roadmap dialed in early.

In bits, you can build early products with very little capital, and increasingly, you can scale with less capital; in atoms, you need large pools of capital, including venture capital, but also including debt, asset-based financing, and project financing.

As energy, intelligence, and dexterity get cheaper, the world of atoms will come to look *more* like the world of bits, but it will never be as fluid as the world of bits.

There are a few big categories of challenges that Techno-Industrials will need to face that software companies don't.

The first is that **manufacturing is hard**. Look at how painful Tesla's journey in making the Model 3 was. Getting something to work in the lab is famously very different than getting it to work at scale. Making one of something at whatever cost is very different than repeatedly making thousands of that thing at a cost that looks anything like the cost in a techno-economic analysis.

The incumbents that Techno-Industrials will be competing with are excellent at manufacturing. It's what they do. The chemical giants like BASF and Dow are manufacturing wonders operating at massive scale. The concrete industry produces billions of cubic meters of the product every year.

Second, **incumbents have scale and distribution**. They have long-standing supplier and customer relationships around the world. In many cases, these battles will be a race to see if incumbents can get technology before Techno-Industrials get scale and distribution.

Third, is Intellectual Property. Techno-Industrials (the inventors) might be protected by **patents**, but large companies might find it economically advantageous to ignore the patents and bleed poorer startups dry in court. And Chinese manufacturers will certainly aim to run roughshod over intellectual property and flood the market with cheaper versions of the same product. Competing in markets in which Chinese companies are unable to serve Western customers is a key consideration for Techno-Industrials, which is one reason we are seeing such strong investment activity in the defense sector.

Fourth, is Regulations. Regulations can either be helpful or harmful. **Regulatory capture** by incumbents is a real threat to Techno-Industrials. Lobbying efforts come up in every conversation with Techno-Industrial founders. Anduril famously hired more lobbyists than engineers in its first few months.

Fifth, as with all innovations, there's the matter of **timing**. These are such big and exciting opportunities that companies will attack them whether or not the economics make sense quite yet, in hopes that they will have gotten the tech right when the time is ripe. However, there's a graveyard full of companies that were too early for their market. I suspect we'll see many Techno-Industrials emerge in categories that have scarred investors but might now make sense.

Finally, building a Techno-Industrial is **capital intensive**. These companies will need to show consistent and rapid progress against their milestones in order to raise the funding they need to survive and grow. As Varda's Delian Asparouhov told me, "deep-tech companies should begin generating revenue within three years."

There are myriad ways to overcome these challenges, of course. Tesla and SpaceX are proof that it's possible. That might mean starting at the high-end of the market, where margins are higher and competition is less cutthroat. It might mean starting with a novel product with a smaller market that incumbents can't or won't build before scaling up into direct competition. It might mean positioning as a climate company in order to get customer buy-in and government subsidies before translating the efficiencies that come with climate-consciousness process reductions into efficiencies that then lock in higher margins. But have no doubt, it will be a battle. I think the prize is worth it.

Techno-Industrials as an Opportunity to Revitalize the Global Industrial Base

While software has been all about swamping upfront fixed costs with high gross margins as revenue grows, I think the defining characteristic of successful Techno-Industrials will be whether they have a structural cost advantage.

That might come from an in-house invention or the integration of a number of new capabilities in novel and defensible ways. In either case, if Techno-Industrials are to succeed, it will be because they leverage technology to do what technology is supposed to do: give people more and better for less.

We covered three examples—Anduril, Solugen, and Monumental Labs—taking three different approaches toward that end. Beautifully, there is no playbook written yet, and I suspect each Techno-Industrial will forge a different path.

For the first time in a long time, tech companies have the opportunity to rebuild the world's industrial base and tap into huge, existing pools of revenue at higher margins than incumbents can. Assuming the same revenue—a safe assumption, since revenue will likely grow with lower prices—structurally higher margins will create more valuable companies than the incumbent comps. This is also a wake-up call for incumbents that are large industrial enterprises today: there has never been a greater reason to re-think the cost physics of your business than when these challengers are still early, and before they have begun to build up steam, taking meaningful market share.

While conventional wisdom holds that large enterprises struggle to proactively introduce disruptive innovation, newer examples demonstrate that when faced with a challenger tech company, even the slowest of large enterprises can muster the will to adapt. In 2025, Volkswagen's ID.7 surpassed Tesla to become the best-selling electric vehicle in Germany. Launched in 2017, Domino's pizza delivery app with GPS tracking protected the pizza chain from similar margin erosion seen by other chains from food delivery app commissions during the ascendancy of UberEats, Grubhub, DoorDash, and Seamless. Wells Fargo's Zelle has been a hit with consumers in the area of payments, despite facing the social network effects from Venmo and CashApp's viral success. Perhaps we will begin to see similar dynamics arising out of Techno-Industrials, which through competitive pressure force legacy industrials to re-think their cost physics in order to protect market share and fortify their incumbent advantages. To be sure, the scale that many incumbents have in the industrial enterprise space will pose a significant barrier to entry for many Techno-Industrials. But as we saw with Tesla and SpaceX, the power that these newer players have in moving fast represents a disruptive advantage, especially by dramatically shortening cycles to launch new products, services, or even whole business operating models based on dramatically lower costs.

I suspect that in a decade or two, there will be dozens of trillion-dollar companies, and my bet is that many of them will be Techno-Industrials.

Packy McCormick, 2025 (essay originally appeared in Not Boring, January 23, 2024)

Postscript

We Asked 5 Leading Supply Chain and Manufacturing Futurists and 2 AI Models About How AI Will Change Supply Chain and Manufacturing over the Next 10 Years

ChatGPT5

In September 2025, ChatGPT5 took 17 seconds to generate the following response to the prompt: "How will AI impact manufacturing and supply chain at a global scale over the next 10 years?"

ChatGPT returned: "Here's the short, decision-useful view of what AI is likely to do to manufacturing & supply chains globally over the next decade—and what to prepare for.

What's coming (10-year horizon)

1. Planning becomes largely autonomous.
   Agentic AI ("virtual coworkers") will plan, simulate, and execute multistep workflows—think demand/supply planning that self-replans hourly, proposes mitigations, and triggers actions

with humans on the loop. Leading analysts now flag "agentic AI" as a top tech trend for operations at scale. McKinsey & Company+2McKinsey & Company+2

2. Better forecasts → leaner inventories, fewer stockouts.
   Peer-reviewed and field evidence point to double-digit forecast-accuracy gains from modern AI methods (often 10–20%+), with cascading benefits to inventory and service levels. Some studies report larger error reductions in specific contexts. Expect this to standardize as models mature and data quality improves. IACIS+2SSRN+2
3. Predictive maintenance goes mainstream.
   As sensor coverage and model quality improve, PdM will reduce unplanned downtime and maintenance costs across brownfield fleets. The business case is already strong because downtime routinely costs >$100k/hour in heavy industry; the PdM software market is scaling quickly. IoT Analytics
4. Quality, yield, and OEE lift on the line.
   Vision + foundation models will flag defects in real time, auto-tune process parameters, and close loops with MES/SCADA. Field reports and surveys show many manufacturers piloting AI on the shop floor, though only a minority are capturing full value—execution maturity is the bottleneck. Boston Consulting Group
5. Digital twins for end-to-end responsiveness.
   Plant and network twins—fed by AI summarization and scenario generation—will help planners trade off service, cost, and carbon in minutes, not days. (Think: "If this port halts for 72 h, which levers keep OTIF ≥ 95%?") McKinsey & Company+1
6. Labor shifts, not just reductions.
   Expect role reconfiguration (planners → exception managers; technicians → AI-enabled reliability engineers). The WEF's latest employer survey signals large workforce transitions (net job creation + significant reskilling) driven by AI across operations. World Economic Forum Reports+1
7. Cyber & model risk becomes a supply-chain risk.
   AI raises the attack surface: deepfake vendor fraud, prompt-injection against enterprise assistants, and model supply-chain

attacks are rising fast. CISOs are moving toward zero-trust and pre-emptive, AI-driven defenses. Make this part of your SCRM. IT Pro+1

8. Energy & compute constraints matter.
   AI's data-center demand will materially lift electricity growth (notably in the U.S.), which feeds into cost-to-serve and sustainability targets. Expect more edge inference, application-specific silicon, and scheduling AI around power/CO_2 constraints. The Times+1
9. Adoption gap persists—value concentrates in "operators."
   Multiple large surveys show many firms are stuck in pilots; leaders that redesign workflows, data foundations, and governance are the ones reporting bottom-line impact. Plan for operating-model change, not just tools. McKinsey & Company+2McKinsey & Company+2
10. Policy & assurance expectations rise.
    Auditable AI (explainability, data lineage, model lifecycle controls) will be required across regulated sectors and critical infrastructure. Build governance now to avoid later retrofit costs. McKinsey & Company

Practical Timeline

0–2 years (prove value & derisk):

- Target 3–5 "boring but big" use cases: demand planning copilot, MRO parts forecasting, PdM on a critical line, vision QC, automated claims/chargebacks.
- Stand up data & MLOps basics; add model risk controls; red-team gen-AI assistants. McKinsey & Company+1

3–5 years (scale & connect):

- Link plant twins with network twin; close the loop from plan → schedule → execution.
- Expand agentic planners to supplier collaboration (multi-tier PO confirmations, risk sensing).
- Embed AI security and supplier verification (voice/vid deepfake detection). McKinsey & Company+1

6–10 years (operate as AI-native):

- Majority of routine planning and tactical sourcing runs autonomously with KPI guardrails.
- Plants self-optimize toward cost, service, and carbon in real time; humans supervise and improve systems. McKinsey & Company

Targets & yardsticks to use:

- Forecast error: −10% to −20% (generalizable), higher in volatile SKUs with better data.
- Inventory: −5% to −15% while maintaining or lifting OTIF.
- Unplanned downtime: double-digit reduction on instrumented assets; PdM payback often <12–18 months in heavy industry.
- Planner productivity: 2–3× more scenarios per day; decision latency cut from days to hours.

  (These ranges synthesize evidence and analyst guidance; exact lift depends on data/OT cadence, asset mix, and change management.) IACIS+2IoT Analytics+2

What to do next (in order)

1. Name owners for five foundations: data products (SKU/site/supplier), event streaming, twin architecture, MLOps, and AI governance (policies, model registry, human-in-the-loop). McKinsey & Company
2. Prioritize use cases by "value × feasibility × data readiness." Start where you have sensor & transactional data and a ready process owner. McKinsey & Company
3. Design for security from day one. Put supplier/payment workflows behind deepfake-resilient checks; adopt zero-trust and prompt-safety patterns for assistants. IT Pro+1
4. Measure with business KPIs, not model metrics. OTIF, cash, CO_2 per unit, OEE, scrap, premium freight, COGS—review monthly. McKinsey & Company
5. Upskill & redeploy. Budget serious reskilling tied to new roles (AI planner, reliability data engineer, twin modeler). WEF expects material workforce transition; plan accordingly. World Economic Forum Reports

If you want, I can map these to your footprint (plants, suppliers, ERPs/MES) and propose a 12-month roadmap with quantified benefits."

Claude

In September 2025 we asked Claude Sonnet 4 to respond to the question: "How will AI impact manufacturing and supply chain at a global scale over the next 10 years?"

Claude returned: "AI is poised to fundamentally reshape global manufacturing and supply chains over the next decade. Here's how I see the transformation unfolding:

Manufacturing Transformation

Production Intelligence: AI will enable truly adaptive factories where systems predict equipment failures before they happen, automatically adjust production parameters in real-time, and optimize energy usage across entire facilities. We're moving from scheduled maintenance to predictive and prescriptive maintenance that could reduce downtime by 30–50%.

Quality at Scale: Computer vision and AI inspection systems will catch defects that human inspectors miss, potentially achieving near-zero defect rates in many industries. These systems will learn from every product inspected, continuously improving accuracy.

Workforce Evolution: Rather than wholesale job replacement, we'll see significant job transformation. Workers will increasingly collaborate with AI systems—think cobots (collaborative robots) that handle repetitive tasks while humans focus on problem-solving, oversight, and complex assembly. This will require massive reskilling initiatives.

Supply Chain Revolution

End-to-End Visibility: AI will finally deliver the "control tower" visibility companies have sought for decades, processing data from IoT sensors, satellites, port activities, and weather patterns to provide real-time supply chain transparency and predict disruptions weeks in advance.

Demand Forecasting: Machine learning models incorporating diverse data—social media trends, economic indicators, weather patterns, local events—will dramatically improve demand prediction accuracy, potentially reducing inventory costs by 20–30% while improving product availability.

Autonomous Logistics: We'll see increasing automation in warehouses (already accelerating), autonomous delivery vehicles in controlled environments, and AI-optimized routing that dynamically responds to traffic, weather, and delivery priority changes.

Global Implications

Reshoring Economics: AI and automation will change the calculus of offshoring. When labor costs matter less, proximity to customers and supply chain resilience matter more. We'll likely see some manufacturing return to developed markets, though this will be highly sector-dependent.

Sustainability Gains: AI optimization could significantly reduce waste, energy consumption, and emissions across supply chains. Companies will use AI to model carbon footprints in real-time and optimize for both cost and environmental impact.

Competitive Divide: A widening gap will emerge between companies that successfully implement AI and those that don't. Early adopters could gain 5–10 year advantages in efficiency, responsiveness, and innovation speed.

Geopolitical Shifts: Countries investing heavily in AI infrastructure, talent, and manufacturing technology will gain strategic advantages. We'll likely see increased competition around AI-enabled manufacturing capabilities, particularly in critical sectors like semiconductors, batteries, and pharmaceuticals.

Key Challenges

The transition won't be smooth. Major obstacles include:

- Massive infrastructure and technology investments required
- Data standardization across fragmented supply chains
- Cybersecurity vulnerabilities as systems become more connected

- Workforce displacement and the speed of reskilling programs
- Regulatory frameworks lagging behind technological capabilities

The companies and countries that navigate this transition most effectively—balancing automation with human capabilities, investing in both technology and people—will likely dominate global manufacturing by 2035.

Sasha Pailet Koff

Sasha Pailet Koff is a supply chain expert with 25+ years of experience in tech, pharma, and CPG. She advises C-suite leaders on digital transformation and was named one of the "Top 100 Women in Supply Chain." Her work spans Dell, Johnson & Johnson, and the Cyber Readiness Institute.

Imagine it's 2035. What looks different about manufacturing and supply chains? What are the biggest changes? What changes have the biggest impact? What processes or approaches have largely been left behind?

I see three major shifts that will define the next decade of global supply chains: their physical composition, their digital maturity, and their approach to cybersecurity.

The Physical Shift

In the years ahead, we will continue to see a repatriation of supply chain activity from global models built primarily on volume and cost to more regionally anchored networks designed for resilience. While cost will remain a critical consideration, leading organizations will increasingly recognize that sustained investment in reliability and availability is essential for long-term competitiveness.

Consumers, likewise, will evolve. They will be willing to spend more on differentiated products that enhance experience, lifestyle, and well-being. We will see deeper segmentation between commodity and premium products. Commodities will focus on functionality and price efficiency, while premium goods will command higher margins and loyalty. Across both categories, governments and consumers will insist on transparency from raw materials through final production, requiring far more rigorous tracking of bills of material and provenance.

We will also see new delivery and acquisition models emerge, particularly for high-value goods. These may include subscription, experience-based, or localized fulfillment approaches that redefine how products reach markets and how consumers perceive value.

The Digital Shift

Digitally, the coming decade will be marked by a more sophisticated understanding of how and where automation, intelligent agents, and generative artificial intelligence should be applied. The models supporting decision intelligence will evolve to reflect the complexity of the physical world, incorporating probability and context to refine recommendations and actions.

Organizations that have made deliberate investments in data products, analytics, and automation will continue to outperform their peers, achieving greater scalability and financial resilience. Those that have not will find it increasingly difficult to compete. As a result, we will see significant organizational restructuring and a growing emphasis on talent capable of integrating supply chain fundamentals with digital fluency.

The workforce will also evolve. While some predict a future dominated by lights-out factories, I believe a healthy population of skilled workers will remain essential to production. Office roles, however, will shift toward anticipatory problem-solving, systems design, and the governance of automated processes rather than ad hoc crisis response.

The Cyber Shift

The third and perhaps most urgent transformation will occur in cybersecurity. As organizations contend with the rapid expansion of artificial intelligence, a new frontier is emerging with the advent of quantum computing. The risks will be significant and far-reaching.

Supply chain organizations that proactively embed cyber resilience into their design and operations will be well-positioned to thrive.

Those that fail to do so will face increasingly frequent disruptions, prolonged recovery periods, and, in some cases, existential threats to their continuity. This environment will require a new generation of professionals who are not only digitally adept but also deeply aware of the intersection of cybersecurity, trust, and operational stability.

What are the top investments that large enterprises are making in transforming their supply chain and manufacturing tech stack? What short-term and long-term ROI are they delivering to owners? Why are you personally excited about predictive platforms that drive measurable ongoing P&L impact across the enterprise?

Across industries, large enterprises continue to invest in data and analytical capabilities, yet the pace and intensity of those investments remain uneven. Too often, organizations still look for short-term returns on data initiatives rather than treating them as long-term assets. Traditional financial models that justify capital investments in real estate or manufacturing infrastructure are rarely applied to data, even though data has become just as essential to sustainable value creation.

This short-term mindset is risky. Without adequate investment in data quality, governance, and accessibility, the full value of emerging automation and analytic technologies cannot be realized. The organizations that lead in this space understand that data is not a byproduct of their operations; it is a core asset that enables performance, innovation, and trust.

What sets these leaders apart is clarity of purpose. They are disciplined about the outcomes they aim to deliver and ensure those outcomes are tied directly to improving experiences for customers and employees. If the connection to value is unclear, they pause, refine, and persist until it is. Their approach mirrors the structured problem-solving rigor of earlier industrial frameworks such as DMAIC and DMADV, applied now to the digital and data-driven enterprise.

For those combining strong data foundations with thoughtful design thinking, the results are striking. They are moving from reactive problem-solving to proactive value generation. They identify where costs can be reduced without sacrificing quality, and they place more confident bets on new opportunities. They do so with a level of precision that comes only from high-quality, well-governed data.

Perhaps most importantly, these organizations are seeing measurable gains in engagement from both employees and customers, who recognize and appreciate the difference in experience. The financial impact follows naturally: improved profitability, stronger market positioning, and growing shareholder confidence.

Enterprises that continue to view data as a cost center rather than a value engine will find it increasingly difficult to compete. Those that embrace data as a strategic asset, that nurture, govern, and leverage thoughtfully will define the next decade of business performance.

In previous waves of disruptive innovation, manufacturing has often been a laggard—late to adopt, slow to invest, keeping costs low by prolonging legacy infrastructure. Is this dynamic changing with a new generation of leaders? What do you think is the most misunderstood aspect of tech transformation in manufacturing today?

I do not yet see a seismic shift in investment patterns across traditional manufacturing sectors over the next five to ten years, except where establishing in-country operations is required. Nor do I believe such a shift is universally necessary. The greatest value in the near-term will come not from new physical infrastructure but from the insights we generate, the automation we enable, and the enhanced decision-making our teams can achieve through well-targeted digital investments.

If I were prioritizing capital today, my focus would not be on large-scale brick-and-mortar expansions, except in cases driven by end-of-life assets, on-shoring requirements, or regulatory obligations. This is not to suggest that investments in automation, sensors, or digital retrofits are unnecessary. On the contrary, such enhancements to existing operations can deliver significant efficiency and visibility gains. However, for most organizations, greenfield projects are not the essential path forward.

When physical investments are made, organizations must insist that digital capabilities are designed into the build from the outset rather than added as an afterthought. Facilities should be conceived not only to support the processes occurring within their walls but also to feed the broader information ecosystem providing the data needed for downstream systems, cross-functional visibility, and end-to-end analytics.

Based on what you are seeing in the market, what is one piece of advice you have for executives in navigating the changes coming to manufacturing from AI in the next 1–5 years?

If there is one area that demands executive focus in the emerging digital landscape of supply chains, it is cybersecurity. The maturity with which cyber risk is understood, applied, and managed across the supply chain must advance substantially. For too long, cybersecurity has been treated as a secondary consideration, something addressed after the fact or delegated solely to information technology/cyber teams. This mindset is not only outdated but also irresponsible.

As organizations accelerate their digital transformations, they must recognize that every new connection, device, and data exchange introduces an additional surface for potential attack. The same technologies that create extraordinary opportunities for efficiency and innovation also expand the risk landscape.

Leaders must therefore invest in both education and capability-building around cyber resilience, much as they did five to ten years ago when building digital literacy across their organizations. Cyber readiness is the next frontier. It will only grow in complexity, and those who anticipate, design for, and respond effectively to evolving threats will secure not only their operations but also the continuity of their products, services, and customer trust.

David Warrick

David Warrick spent 23 years at Microsoft in supply chain leadership and technology roles and was most recently named the Executive Vice President of Enterprise at Overhaul, a supply chain visibility platform. During his time at Microsoft, David's efforts focused on implementing the latest in supply chain technologies, playing key roles in the release of every product since Windows 2000, including the rollout for the first Xbox gaming systems and the latest Surface laptops. Prior to this role, he held positions with Andersen Consulting and was a project engineer in the construction of the Hong Kong Airport.

Imagine it's 2035. What looks different about manufacturing and supply chains? What are the biggest changes? What changes

have the biggest impact? What processes or approaches have largely been left behind?

Finally end-to-end visibility and true digital twins, everything is virtual and constant simulations ensure optimization across all supply chain nodes. Manufacturing is now mostly evolving through dark facilities, highly automated with a robotic workforce. Autonomous trucks move cargo seamlessly and nonstop between automated facilities; customs processing, payment processing, all inventory related transactions will be digital and immediate. So, what looks different—highly visible layers of automation and robotics from manufacturing to shipping, the biggest changes are the seamless layers of transaction, all immediate, all correct, every time; there is no ERP, just multiple intelligent agents specializing in each aspect of supply chain, working together to ensure the right result. The removal of waste in the supply chain processes is by far the biggest impact; inventory is federated so availability is incredible while overall value on balance sheet has reduced—every truck is now a mobile inventory, and destinations are no longer relevant as inventory is always live and always available through the supply chain.

What has been left behind—the art of negotiation, the beauty of design, and the out-of-the-box thinking as to what happens next—this will remain the true innovation from the human mind.

What are the top investments that large enterprises are making in transforming their supply chain and manufacturing tech stack? What short-term and long-term ROI are they delivering to owners? Why are you personally excited about predictive platforms that drive measurable ongoing P&L impact across the enterprise?

This is a tough question; the top investments, to be honest, are continual fixes for legacy systems—trying to make the imperfect perfect and afraid to throw out years of investment even when the business needs are not met—it will suffice and be "good enough." The innovators are not getting caught up in this drama; instead they see Gen AI as a means of enhancing legacy systems and bringing the real value to the supply chain. The challenge here is not buying a "platform" or a "suite" of software; it is pushing the boundaries with creative minds that think about the problems through a different lens and ask about the art of the possible. Numerous spot solutions are now fixing age-old supply chain problems, from freight audit, through to forecasting and planning, even container utilization. The smart investments are leveraging these early stage technologies to enhance the current supply chain—short-term ROI and strategic long-term benefits—the beginning of the transition from fixed state reporting and processing to dynamic management and real-time accuracy.

I get excited because finally technology is widely available that can really transform, our ability to predict is key, we now have the data, building the smart models to enable the next iteration of supply chain intelligence is the goal. I consider supply chain as a thinking, living, breathing entity; it never slows and never stops, it should be self-optimizing and self-healing, and when it uncovers a problem it should think through the potential fixes and then act accordingly—the next 10 years will revolutionize supply chain and the businesses that we support.

In previous waves of disruptive innovation, manufacturing has often been a laggard—late to adopt, slow to invest, keeping costs low by prolonging legacy infrastructure. Is this dynamic changing with a new generation of leaders? What do you think is the most misunderstood aspect of tech transformation in manufacturing today?

I think it is a slow change. Is there more curiosity as the latest technology is so democratized? Absolutely. There are fewer excuses available to inhibit change, but I still see procrastination and slowness to invest—all of the old sayings—if it's not broken don't fix it, etc. etc., are still being rolled out. But this time will be different; this is not RFID or BlockChain, this is a completely democratized, freely available technology wave. You don't need specific training or advanced hardware to use it; the only barriers are individually created. There is a new level of curiosity breathing through the industry asking the right questions; I think the leaders are being forced to pay attention and hopefully that translates into action in the coming months and years.

I think the most misunderstood aspect is the velocity and scale of change—not everything has to be a rip and replace and not everything needs to have a big project title and price tag and timeline to match. Change can start anywhere, at any level and at any scale, it doesn't actually matter—as long as it starts somewhere, enabling a workforce to experiment, break things, and get excited about change. This offers a better chance of innovation and transformation than the biggest consulting project ever imagined.

Based on what you are seeing in the market, what is one piece of advice you have for executives in navigating the changes coming to manufacturing from AI in the next 1–5 years?

The one piece of advice—stop procrastinating. Done is better than perfect right now. Embracing the technology and being curious will pay dividends as the capabilities evolve rapidly in the next few years—don't be left behind ☺.

Charlotte de Brabandt

Dr. Charlotte de Brabandt is a world-renowned technology and negotiation keynote speaker with extensive global experience across automotive, technology, pharmaceutical, consumer goods, and medical device industries. A published author and TEDx speaker, she was recognized as an ISM 30 under 30 Megawatt Winner and serves on the ISM® Thought Leadership Council. Her latest books include: *Hyper-Leadership: How Great Leaders Attract, Inspire, and Develop Talents and Elevate Their Success* and *AI-Driven Business Transformation: Data Economy through Democratization and Monetization*. Dr. de Brabandt specializes in empowering professionals with negotiation strategies and techniques to achieve their goals with confidence.

Imagine it's 2035. What looks different about manufacturing and supply chains? What are the biggest changes? What changes have the biggest impact? What processes or approaches have largely been left behind?

Looking ahead to 2035, the most striking difference will be the truly collaborative nature of supply chains. The old procurement mindset of transactional, first-tier relationships will be a relic of the past. Instead, we'll see fully transparent, multi-tier networks where data flows seamlessly from raw material sources to end customers. AI won't just predict demand—it will orchestrate entire ecosystems of suppliers, manufacturers, and logistics partners in real-time, automatically adjusting to disruptions before humans even notice them.

The biggest impact will come from the convergence of predictive intelligence and deep supplier collaboration. We're already seeing companies move beyond simple automation to true cognitive procurement systems that learn from every transaction, negotiation, and market shift. By 2035, the rigid RFP processes and lengthy sourcing cycles that dominate today will largely be replaced by dynamic, continuous optimization models that balance cost, sustainability, risk, and innovation in real-time.

Perhaps most importantly, the siloed approach to supply chain security will be obsolete. After years of cyber attacks and geopolitical disruptions, organizations will finally treat supply chain resilience as a shared responsibility, with procurement professionals leading collaborative risk management across entire networks—not just with immediate suppliers.

What are the top investments that large enterprises are making in transforming their supply chain and manufacturing tech stack? What short-term and long-term ROI are they delivering to owners? Why are you personally excited about predictive platforms that drive measurable ongoing P&L impact across the enterprise?

The most strategic investments I'm seeing are in integrated procurement platforms that combine spend analytics, supplier intelligence, and predictive capabilities in one ecosystem. Companies are also investing heavily in digital procurement infrastructure—moving away from fragmented legacy systems toward unified platforms that provide visibility across categories, geographies, and business units.

In the short term, these investments deliver immediate wins: faster cycle times, better pricing through data-driven negotiations, and reduced maverick spending. But the long-term ROI is where things get truly exciting. These platforms fundamentally change how procurement creates value—transforming the function from a cost center to a strategic driver of innovation, sustainability, and competitive advantage.

What excites me about predictive platforms is their ability to democratize procurement excellence. In my work across automotive, pharma, consumer goods, and technology sectors, I've seen how the best procurement professionals combine deep market knowledge with sharp negotiation skills and strategic thinking. Predictive platforms don't replace that expertise—they amplify it. They enable every procurement professional to make decisions backed by comprehensive data, market intelligence, and scenario modeling. When you can show stakeholders not just savings but also risk mitigation, supplier innovation, and sustainability impact, procurement earns its seat at the strategic table.

In previous waves of disruptive innovation, manufacturing has often been a laggard—late to adopt, slow to invest, keeping costs low by prolonging legacy infrastructure. Is this dynamic changing with a new generation of leaders? What do you think is the most misunderstood aspect of tech transformation in manufacturing today?

The dynamic is absolutely changing, and it's not just about generational shifts—it's about survival. The disruptions of the past five years—pandemic supply shocks, cybersecurity threats, geopolitical instability, and climate pressures—have made it painfully clear that clinging to legacy approaches is no longer just inefficient; it's existential. I'm seeing procurement and supply chain leaders who understand that digital transformation isn't a "nice to have" IT project; it's fundamental to organizational resilience.

The most misunderstood aspect is that technology transformation isn't primarily about the technology—it's about the people and culture. You can implement the most sophisticated AI-powered platform, but if your procurement team doesn't trust the data, doesn't understand how to interpret the insights, or isn't empowered to act on recommendations, you've simply automated inefficiency. Successful transformation requires investing in talent development, creating cross-functional collaboration models, and building a culture where procurement professionals are comfortable with experimentation and continuous learning.

I've also observed that many organizations underestimate the importance of change management when it comes to supplier relationships. Your suppliers need to evolve with you. If you're implementing predictive sourcing but your suppliers are still operating with manual processes and limited visibility, you're only transforming half the equation.

Based on what you are seeing in the market, what is one piece of advice you have for executives in navigating the changes coming to manufacturing from AI in the next 1–5 years?

Start with your data foundation, but don't wait for perfection to begin. Too many organizations delay AI initiatives because they believe their data isn't "clean enough" or comprehensive enough. The reality is that AI systems today are remarkably good at working with imperfect data, and they actually help you improve data quality through use.

My advice is to identify a specific, high-impact procurement challenge—whether it's strategic sourcing for a critical category, supplier risk management, or demand forecasting—and pilot an AI solution with a clear success metric. Learn from that pilot, scale what works, and iterate on what doesn't. Build your organization's AI literacy through doing, not just through training.

Most critically, involve your procurement professionals from day one. They understand the nuances that technology alone might miss—the supplier relationship factors, the market dynamics, the organizational constraints. The most successful AI implementations I've seen are those where human expertise and machine intelligence work in partnership, each amplifying the other's strengths. That partnership model will define which organizations thrive in the AI-enabled future of procurement and manufacturing.

Saeed Amidi

Saeed Amidi is the founder and CEO of Plug and Play Tech Center, with over 30 years of experience spanning real estate, bottled water, packaging, and technology investing. His journey began when The Amidi Group purchased a Palo Alto building that became home to early startups like Google, PayPal, and Logitech—earning the nickname the "Lucky Building." Since founding Plug and Play in 2006, Saeed has helped scale it into the world's leading innovation platform, supporting 90,000+ startups, making 2,000+ investments, and nurturing over 30 unicorns, including Dropbox, PayPal, and Honey. A strong believer in family and relationships, he's built a company culture rooted in collaboration and care.

Imagine it's 2035. What looks different about manufacturing and supply chains? What are the biggest changes? What changes have the biggest impact? What processes or approaches have largely been left behind?

By 2035, supply chains and manufacturing will operate more like living systems, powered by technologies like Physical AI, Agentic AI, and Data Intelligence. Routine work will increasingly run autonomously, allowing people to focus on strategy and long-term value. The real challenge for leadership will be adapting quickly enough to help their organizations, which are constantly evolving.

What are the top investments that large enterprises are making in transforming their supply chain and manufacturing tech stack? What short-term and long-term ROI are they delivering to owners? Why are you personally excited about predictive platforms that drive measurable ongoing P&L impact across the enterprise?

Large companies are investing in technologies that are making their operations stronger and more ready for the future. They can no longer depend on just a few suppliers, which limits flexibility and increases risk. Startup companies like Arkestro, DYNA Robotics, and GenLogs are helping large companies address challenges such as improving supplier management, enhancing warehouse flexibility with humanoid robotics, and improving real-time freight tracking to prevent theft.

In previous waves of disruptive innovation, manufacturing has often been a laggard—late to adopt, slow to invest, keeping costs low by prolonging legacy infrastructure. Is this dynamic changing with a new generation of leaders? What do you think is the most misunderstood aspect of tech transformation in manufacturing today?

We're about to see a new generation of manufacturing leaders emerge who embrace AI-enabled manufacturing—a generation that treats data as an asset and sees transformation as both cultural and technological. The biggest misunderstanding is that progress comes from buying tools. In reality, it comes from reimagining processes so innovation can scale, creating connected ecosystems where every machine, supplier, and decision learns and adapts together. This new generation of leaders has to embrace change because it is happening faster than ever.

Based on what you are seeing in the market, what is one piece of advice you have for executives in navigating the changes coming to manufacturing from AI in the next 1–5 years?

Focus on real results, impact, and not just hype. AI is becoming core to every modern business and adopting it is no longer optional. Build your data foundation early and invest in use cases that drive clear ROI across operations. Prove value fast, scale what works, and keep learning as much as you can. The winners will be those who treat knowledge like money—investing it where it multiplies over time.

Chase Koch

Charles Chase Koch is an American businessman, philanthropist, and investor. Chase directs the venture capital company Koch Disruptive Technologies, which is an investor in Arkestro.

Imagine it's 2035. What looks different about manufacturing and supply chains? What are the biggest changes? What changes have the biggest impact? What processes or approaches have largely been left behind?

While it's hard to predict the future, it's clear that manufacturing and supply chains will keep digitizing, decentralizing, and adapting. Compared to 10 years ago, the old, siloed ways of operating are giving way to integrated, intelligent networks built for speed and flexibility. In a decade's time, real-time data powered by AI will drive even faster, more accurate decision-making. Take Koch's Georgia-Pacific business, for example, which a few years ago began using AI and sensor technologies to connect tens of thousands of assets across facilities to work more efficiently and safely while delivering more value to our customers. That kind of real-time, AI-powered data will continue to help companies improve.

What are the top investments that large enterprises are making in transforming their supply chain and manufacturing tech stack? What short-term and long-term ROI are they delivering to owners? Why are you personally excited about predictive platforms like Arkestro that drive measurable ongoing P&L impact across the enterprise?

Transformation is never a one-size-fits-all proposition at Koch or elsewhere—each business is different. That said, there are some commonalities: integrated data platforms, AI-driven tools, and automation to optimize every link in the value chain. In the short term, we see these investments improving efficiency and reducing costs; in the long term, we look at how they're enabling us to create superior value for customers. Predictive platforms like Arkestro empower teams to make better, faster decisions.

Koch Engineered Solutions (KES), the Koch business that specializes in process and pollution equipment and technologies for refineries and other plants, buys a lot of bulk materials for multiple manufacturing sites globally. As you can imagine, it's hard to continually scrutinize each purchase for the best mutually beneficial outcome for both KES and the material suppliers. Arkestro has been helping KES teams hit or exceed savings targets ahead of schedule while scaling the predictive procurement solution across sites. The platform adds a layer of intelligence, which makes strategic sourcing faster and strengthens relationships with KES suppliers.

In previous waves of disruptive innovation, manufacturing has often been a laggard—late to adopt, slow to invest, keeping costs low by prolonging legacy infrastructure. Is this dynamic changing with a new generation of leaders? What do you think is the most misunderstood aspect of tech transformation in manufacturing today?

There's been a history in traditional manufacturing of relying on rule-based approaches and incremental improvements, but there's no question now that more people, regardless of where they are in their careers, are waking up to the idea that clinging to legacy systems is riskier than investing in innovative technologies. However, it's not just about the tools; it's about changing mindsets, building knowledge networks, and fostering a culture of challenge and experimentation. One of the most misunderstood aspects of transformation is that failure, when approached with openness and a desire to learn, is not a setback but a catalyst for progress. Incorporating lessons from failure accelerates our ability to adapt, innovate, and unlock new opportunities.

Based on what you are seeing in the market, what is one piece of advice you have for executives in navigating the changes coming to manufacturing from AI in the next 1–5 years?

Strengthen your organization's ability to learn and adapt by intentionally designing experiments, capturing insights, and making principled, knowledge-driven decisions. Organizations that treat knowledge as a strategic asset—and empower the people closest to the problems to test, learn, and share—create a bottom-up culture that fuels both continuous improvement and transformation.

Notes

Introduction

1. Deloitte Insights, Tech Trends 2026, Kelly Raskovich, December 10, 2025.

Chapter 2

1. Sharon Moar (Interview), "From Buying for the Business, to Building the Business," Procurescape, March 17, 2026, https://procurescape.com/from-buying-for-the-business-to-building-the-business/

Chapter 3

1. Paul Oyer, "Fiscal Year Ends and Non-Linear Incentive Contracts: The Effect on Business Seasonality," The Quarterly Journal of Economics 113, no. 1 (1998): 149–185, https://doi.org/10.1162/003355398555514
2. Access Partnership, *Rethinking Taxi Pricing and Reforms: Spurring Innovation and Choice in the Taxi Industry* (July 2023), https://accesspartnership.com/wp-content/uploads/2023/07/Rethinking-taxi-pricing-Web-spread.pdf
3. Daniel Kahneman, "Thinking, Fast and Slow," interview by Big Think, YouTube video, 5:03, posted by Big Think, 2013, https://www.youtube.com/watch?v=tyDQFmA1SpU

Chapter 4

1. Rhiannon Williams, "What is Vibe Coding, Exactly?" *MIT Review*, April 16, 2025, https://www.technologyreview.com/2025/04/16/1115135/what-is-vibe-coding-exactly/.
2. Matt Li, "Top Vibe Coding Statistics and Trends [2026]", Secondtalent, October 27, 2025, https://www.secondtalent.com/resources/vibe-coding-statistics/.
3. Buckminster Fuller, as cited in "The Techno-Optimist Manifesto," October 16, 2023, https://a16z.com/the-techno-optimist-manifesto/.
4. Shalabh Kumar Mishra, Satyvir Singh, Ashu Soni, Nishi Deepa Palo, Saurabh Singh, and Charu Arora, "Development and Deployment of a Biometric Lock System," *Journal of Information & Optimization Sciences*, 46, no. 1 (2025), 253-262.
5. Paul Graham, "Tablets," December 2010, accessed November 9, 2025, https://paulgraham.com/tablets.html.
6. Marc Andreessen, "Why Software Is Eating the World," August 20, 2011, accessed November 9, 2025, https://a16z.com/why-software-is-eating-the-world/.
7. Tao Huang, "Content Moderation by LLM: From Accuracy to Legitimacy. *Artificial Intelligence Review*, 58, no. 320 (2025), https://link.springer.com/article/10.1007/s10462-025-11328-1
8. Fernando Brugge. "Predictive Maintenance Market: The Evolution from Niche Topic to High ROI Application, (2021), https://iot-analytics.com/predictive-maintenance-market-evolution-from-niche-topic-to-high-roi-application/

Chapter 6

1. Cameron Nakashima, "Why BBB Says You Should Get at Least 3 Quotes," *Argus Observer*, July 27, 2024, https://www.argusobserver.com/free_access/why-bbb-says-you-should-get-at-least-3-quotes/article_2538cb9c-4536-11ef-9d4c-33bfeab601f8.html.
2. Jason Dowlatabadi, Meng Liu, and Erik Brynjolfsson, "How Digital Platforms Reduce Moral Hazard: Uber vs. Taxis", Centre for Economic Policy Research, October 12, 2018, https://cepr.org/voxeu/columns/how-digital-platforms-reduce-moral-hazard-uber-vs-taxis/.
3. Richard Thaler, *The Winner's Curse* (Free Press, 1991).

4. Adam D. Galinsky and Thomas Mussweiler, "First Offers As Anchors: The Role of Perspective Taking and Negotiator Focus," *Journal of Personality and Social Psychology* 81, no 4. (2001), 657–669.
5. Ashleigh Shelby Rosette, Shirli Kopelman, JeAnna Lanza Abbott, "Good Grief! Anxiety Sours the Economic Benefits of First Offers," *Group Decision and Negotiation* 23, no. 33 (2014), 629–647.
6. https://www.oneusefulthing.org/p/the-bitter-lesson-versus-the-garbage

Chapter 8

1. CAPS Research. Metrics of Supply Management Dashboard, accessed November 9, 2025 from https://capsresearch.org/benchmarking/metrics-dashboard/.
2. Remko Van Hoek and Mary Lacity, "How Global Companies Use AI to Prevent Supply Chain Disruptions," *Harvard Business Review*, November 21, 2023, accessed November 9, 2025 from https://hbr.org/2023/11/how-global-companies-use-ai-to-prevent-supply-chain-disruptions.
3. Dave Dotson, "Engineering a Transformation," *Discovery* 25, no. 4, 2019, accessed November 9, 2025 from https://discovery.kochinc.com/discovery/issues/2019/november/engineering-a-transformation.

Chapter 9

1. Peter Bendor Samuel, "Why Digital Transformations Fail: 3 Exhausting Reasons," Everest Group, accessed November 9, 2025, https://www.everestgrp.com/2019-08-why-digital-transformations-fail-3-exhausting-reasons-blog-51164.html.

Chapter 10

1. Tien Tzuo, *Subscribed: Why the Subscription Model Will be Your Company's Future – and What to do about It* (Penguin, 2018).
2. GE Aerospace. "TrueChoice Flight Hour." https://www.geaerospace.com/commercial/services/true-choice/flight-hour.
3. Ashu Garg & Jaya Gupta, "The $4.6T services as software opportunity: Lessons from year one," Foundation Capital (July 3, 2025), https://foundationcapital.com/the-4-6t-service-as-software-opportunity-lessons-from-year-one/

4. David Malitz, "How Many Photos?", Talking About Data, February 26, 2024, accessed November 9, 2025 from https://dmalitz.substack.com/p/how-many-photos.
5. Charles Magee, "The Age of Imagination: Coming Soon to a Civilization Near You," accessed on November 9, 2025 from https://web.archive.org/web/20110727132753/http://www.oss.net/dynamaster/file_archive/040320/4a32a59dcdc168eced6517b5e6041cda/OSS1993-01-21.pdf.
6. Ibid.
7. Christian Brose, *The Kill Chain: Defending America in the Future of High-tech Warfare* (Hachette Books, 2020).
8. Matthew P. Funaiole and Brian Hart, "China's Military in 10 Charts," Center for Strategic and International Studies, September 2, 2025, accessed November 9, 2025 from https://www.csis.org/analysis/chinas-military-10-charts.
9. United States Senate Committee on Armed Services, "Summary of the Fiscal Year 2024 National Defense Authorization Act," accessed November 9, 2025 from https://www.armed-services.senate.gov/imo/media/doc/fy24_ndaa_conference_executive_summary1.pdf.
10. Clayton Christensen, *The Innovator's Dilemma: When New Technologies Cause Great Firms to Fail* (Harvard Business Review Press, 2013).
11. Fidji Simo, "AI as the Greatest Source of Empowerment for All," July 21, 2025, accessed November 9, 2025 from https://openai.com/index/ai-as-the-greatest-source-of-empowerment-for-all/.
12. McKinsey Global Institute, "A New Look at How Corporations Impact the Economy and Households," May 31, 2021, accessed November 9, 2025 from https://www.mckinsey.com/capabilities/strategy-and-corporate-finance/our-insights/a-new-look-at-how-corporations-impact-the-economy-and-households.
13. Sam Altman, "The Merge," December 7, 2017, accessed November 9, 2025 from https://blog.samaltman.com/the-merge.

Chapter 11

1. Klaus Leopold and Seigfried Kaltenecker, *Kanban Change Leadership: Creating a Culture of Continuous Improvement* (Wiley, 2015).
2. Thomas Hout, "The Secrets of Extraordinary Low-Cost Operators," *Harvard Business Review* (March-April 2025), https://hbr.org/2025/03/the-secrets-of-extraordinary-low-cost-operators.

Chapter 12

1. Rimini Street "C-Suite Imperatives: Evolving IT and Enterprise Investments" June 202, 2024.
2. Steve Sanghi, *Up and to the Right: My Personal and Business Journey Building the Microchip Technology Juggernaut* (Steve Sanghi, 2023), 64.

Chapter 13

1. Austin Weber, "Lights-out Automation: Fact or Fiction? *Assembly Magazine*, May 9, 2019, accessed November 9, 2025 from https://www.assemblymag.com/articles/94982-lights-out-automation-fact-or-fiction.
2. Ibid.
3. "RedPajama-Data-v2-An Open Dataset with 30 Trillion Tokens for Training Large Language Models," GitHub, accessed November 9, 2025 from https://github.com/togethercomputer/RedPajama-Data.
4. Sergey Levine "Sporks of AGI" Substack, July 21, 2025
5. Bandaru, Rohit (2025, September 28), "Foundation Models for Robotics: Vision-Language-Action (VLA)." Rohit's Blog, https://rohitbandaru.github.io/blog/Foundation-Models-for-Robotics-VLA/.
6. Rodney Brooks "Why Today's Humanoids Won't Learn Dexterity" September 26, 2025 available via rodneybrooks.com
7. Raquel Brandao "Surreal humanoid robots are set to begin border patrol duties between China and Vietnam" December 26, 2025 https://www.earth.com/news/surreal-video-reveals-humanoid-robots-for-border-patrol-pr25/
8. Golod, Vita & Burtsev, Dmytro (2026, January 24). "China's Drone War in Ukraine," The Diplomat, https://thediplomat.com/2026/01/chinas-drone-war-in-ukraine/.
9. Business Insider (2026, January 27) "Over 80% of Every Battlefield Hit Against Russia Is Now Being Carried Out by a Drone, Zelenskyy Says," https://www.businessinsider.com/drones-80-percent-battlefield-hits-russia-ukraine-war-zelenskyy-2026-1.
10. Baskaran, Gracelin (2025, October 9) "China's New Rare Earth and Magnet Restrictions Threaten U.S. Defense Supply Chains," Center for Strategic and International Studies https://www.csis.org/analysis/chinas-new-rare-earth-and-magnet-restrictions-threaten-us-defense-supply-chains.

Chapter 14

1. Wharton School of Business, "2025 Report: Accountable Acceleration: Gen AI Fast-Tracks into the Enterprise," (October 28, 2025), https://knowledge.wharton.upenn.edu/special-report/2025-ai-adoption-report/.
2. Eric Geller, "Shadow AI is widespread — and executives use it the most," *Cybersecurity Dive*, (November 12, 2025), https://www.cybersecuritydive.com/news/shadow-ai-employee-trust-upguard/805280/.
3. Rui Dai, Hao Liang, and Lilian Ng, "Do US companies outsource their carbon footprints to overseas suppliers to maintain competitiveness?" Principles for Responsible Investment, (January 20, 2022), https://public.unpri.org/pri-blog/do-us-companies-outsource-their-carbon-footprints-to-overseas-suppliers-to-maintain-competitiveness/9363.article.
4. Department of Justice, "Justice Department Sues RealPage for Algorithmic Pricing Scheme that Harms Millions of American Renters," (August 23, 2024), https://www.justice.gov/archives/opa/pr/justice-department-sues-realpage-algorithmic-pricing-scheme-harms-millions-american-renters.
5. Rogé Karma, "We Are Entering an AI Price-fixing Dystopia," *The Atlantic*, (August 10, 2024), https://www.theatlantic.com/ideas/archive/2024/08/ai-price-algorithms-realpage/679405/.
6. Erik Sherman, "Pricing Algorithms Cost Renters $3.8 Billion In 2023 Says White House," *Forbes*, (December 25, 2024), https://www.forbes.com/sites/eriksherman/2024/12/25/pricing-algorithms-cost-renters-38-billion-in-2023-says-white-house/
7. Federal Trade Commission, "Price Fixing," https://www.ftc.gov/advice-guidance/competition-guidance/guide-antitrust-laws/dealings-competitors/price-fixing
8. Erik Sherman, "Pricing Algorithms Cost Renters $3.8 Billion In 2023 Says White House," *Forbes*, (December 25, 2024), https://www.forbes.com/sites/eriksherman/2024/12/25/pricing-algorithms-cost-renters-38-billion-in-2023-says-white-house/
9. Maureen Olhausen, "Should We Fear The Things That Go Beep In the Night? Some Initial Thoughts on the Intersection of Antitrust Law and Algorithmic Pricing," (May 23, 2017), https://www.ftc.gov/system/files/documents/public_statements/1220893/ohlhausen_-_concurrences_5-23-17.pdf
10. Priyanshi Joshi, "Regulating Tacit Algorithmic Collusion: Meaning, Scope and its Challenges," *The Contemporary Law Forum*, (n.d.), https://

tclf.in/2020/07/24/regulating-tacit-algorithmic-collusion-meaning-scope-and-its-challenges/
11. Katrina Krämer, "AI & robotics briefing: There's a 5% risk that AI will wipe out humanity," *Nature*, January 16, 2024, https://www.nature.com/articles/d41586-024-00147-z.
12. Falyn Stempler and Michael D. Carroll, "AI expert calculates 99.9% risk of human extinction within," *Express*, December 9, 2025, https://www.express.co.uk/news/science/2143931/ai-expert-calculates-99-9-risk-human-extinction-within-next-century
13. Joshua Gans, "AI and the Paperclip Problem," *CEPR*, (June 10, 2018), https://cepr.org/voxeu/columns/ai-and-paperclip-problem.
14. Shakeel Hashim, "OpenAI's new model tried to avoid being shut down," *Transformer*, (December 5, 2024), https://www.transformernews.ai/p/openais-new-model-tried-to-avoid.
15. Mary L. Cummings, "What Self-driving Cars Tell Us about AI Risks," *IEEE Spectrum*, (July 30, 2023), https://spectrum.ieee.org/self-driving-cars-2662494269
16. CMS Law. "Autonomous vehicles law and regulation in California, United States," (September 10, 2025), https://cms.law/en/int/expert-guides/cms-expert-guide-to-autonomous-vehicles-avs/california-united-states
17. Skadden, "Landmark California AI Safety Legislation May Serve as a Model for Other States in the Absence of Federal Standards," (October 2, 2025), https://www.skadden.com/insights/publications/2025/10/landmark-california-ai-safety-legislation.
18. SAE International. "SAE J3016 Levels of Driving Automation," https://brx-content.fullsight.org/site/binaries/content/assets/sae-org/content/news/blog/sae-j3016-visual-chart_5.3.21.pdf.
19. The Decision Lab. "The OODA Loop," https://thedecisionlab.com/reference-guide/computer-science/the-ooda-loop
20. Stanford Report, "AI-Driven Insurance Decisions Raise Concerns About Human Oversight," (January 6, 2026), https://news.stanford.edu/stories/2026/01/ai-algorithms-health-insurance-care-risks-research
21. Richard Blumental, "CT Senior Shares Experience Being Denied Care by Medicare Advantage at Blumenthal-Led Senate Hearing," (May 18, 2023), https://www.blumenthal.senate.gov/newsroom/press/release/ct-senior-shares-experience-being-denied-care-by-medicare-advantage-at-blumenthal-led-senate-hearing.

22. American Medical Association, "Augmented Intelligence Development, Deployment, and Use in Health Care," (November 2024), https://www.ama-assn.org/system/files/ama-ai-principles.pdf
23. Lexology, "The Dangers of Employee Recruitment on Autopilot: AI and Discriminatory Hiring Decisions," https://www.lexology.com/library/detail.aspx?g=60570bba-285f-40a1-88bd-5ad8613c78bd
24. NYC Consumer and Worker Protection, "Automated Employment Decision Tools (AEDT)," https://www.nyc.gov/site/dca/about/automated-employment-decision-tools.page

Chapter 15

1. Noah Smith, "Make-Work Is Not the Future of Work," Noahopinion (blog), October 2, 2024, accessed November 9, 2025 from https://www.noahpinion.blog/p/make-work-is-not-the-future-of-work?utm_source=publication-search.
2. Aurelia Glass, "Unions Give Workers a Voice Over How AI Affects Their Jobs," Center for American Progress, (May 16, 2024), https://www.americanprogress.org/article/unions-give-workers-a-voice-over-how-ai-affects-their-jobs/.
3. Marguerita Lane, Morgan Williams, and Stijn Broecke, "The Impact of AI on the Workplace: Main Findings from the OECD AI Surveys of Employers and Workers, "OECD Working Papers No. 28, (March 22, 2023), https://www.oecd.org/content/dam/oecd/en/publications/reports/2023/03/the-impact-of-ai-on-the-workplace-main-findings-from-the-oecd-ai-surveys-of-employers-and-workers_ad686e91/ea0a0fe1-en.pdf.
4. Will Oremus, "What Everyone's Getting Wrong about the Toilet Paper Shortage," Marker (blog), April 2, 2020, accessed November 9, 2025 from https://marker.medium.com/what-everyones-getting-wrong-about-the-toilet-paper-shortage-c812e1358fe0.
5. Ralf W. Seifert and Richard Markoff, "How COVID-19 Exposed the Fault Lines of Product Complexity," International Institute for Management Development, July 2020, accessed November 9, 2025 from https://www.imd.org/research-knowledge/supply-chain/articles/how-covid-19-exposed-the-fault-lines-of-product-complexity/.
6. Susan Helper and Evan Soltas, "Why the Pandemic Has Disrupted Supply Chains," The White House, June 17, 2021, accessed November 9, 2025 from https://bidenwhitehouse.archives.gov/cea/written-materials/2021/06/17/why-the-pandemic-has-disrupted-supply-chains/.

Acknowledgments

THIS BOOK IS the culmination of hundreds of interviews, informal conversations, and shared projects with individuals and organizations too numerous to list by name. Indeed, many of these discussions occurred explicitly off the record to enable candid deep dives into AI within the inner workings of private enterprise supply chains and operations management. To anyone who spoke with me about the role of AI in supply chain, procurement, and manufacturing: thank you.

However, there are also quite a few people whom I would like to specifically acknowledge. The team at Wiley of Alison Bohn, Zachary Schisgal, Deborah Schindlar, Julie Kerr, Pradesh Kumar Chandran and Deborah Williams who have been extraordinary to work with and who helped bring the stories in this book to life for a general business audience.

The leadership team at Arkestro and especially my co-founder Rob DeSantis and the Arkestro executives who supported our growth throughout the three year period we focus on in this book (2022–2025), including Ben Leiken, Greg Cruz, Bill Seagrave, Anna O'Leary, and the inimitable Stuart Gold: thank you for the time and collaboration to make this book happen. Thanks also to external members on our Board of Directors, including Cindy Padnos, JP Bauman, and especially Jeffrey Immelt for contributing the Foreword.

I would also specifically like to thank Clark Bernier, Vasuki Subbarao, and Philip Golucci for visionary technical leadership in laying the foundation for the Predictive Enterprise approach, and the early team of Kait Ries, Aziel Ferguson, Sam Griffiths, Corey Turoff, Eric Buras, Lisa Bernhardt, Alexzander Manning, Tyrone Crosswell, Pedro Meyer, Flávio Miyaji, Holland White, Chad Evans, Lateisha Thomas, Chase Williams, Tom Pallack, and John Magner.

This book would not exist without the Predictive Enterprise approach implemented at global scale within Arkestro customers with powerful executive champions and articulate internal storytellers who have been willing to elevate the role of operations, and especially the role of procurement and supply chain. Those individuals include Mike Novello at KES, Joshua Flowers at Chevron, Magnus Lundgren at Solventum, Michael Raphael at JLL, Jim Cuff at Crown Cork & Seal, Dirk Meuzelaar at Provisur, and Mike Shin at Trinity Industries, although the full list is much longer.

A special thank you to Matteo Stefani, Linda Chuan, Susan Clapham, and Sean Park who have been incredible thought partners along this journey, and to Martin Beck and Sven Theysohn whose deep conversations and experiments early on inspired so much of our journey.

I am also quite appreciative for the perspectives from the AI and robotics communities, especially those individuals who support commercial AI applications in manufacturing and logistics, including Dr. Jana Boerger, Ben Levin, Charlie Haley, Gabrielle Gantus, Lior Susan, and Anna Walling.

Contents of this book were previewed in a session at the 2025 Roots of Progress Conference where Jason Crawford, Heike Larson, and Ben Thomas created space for an engaging discussion of superhuman supply chains and Techno Industrials with Packy McCormick. I'd also specifically like to thank Noah Smith and Brian Potter, whose work on the history of automation and efficiency in supply chains has been illuminating and thought-provoking. There are also a few manufacturing, supply chain, and procurement executives and thought leaders to thank by name who offered valuable perspectives including John Haley, Steve Sanghi, Katherine Dei Cas, Jason Busch, Shaz Khan,

Jason Kra, David Schultz, Dr. Elouise Epstein, Tom Maher, and Kate Denissova. I'd also like to recognize the academic supply chain community including Remko Van Hoek, Mary Lacity, and Damian Beil whose writing on auctions inspired a lot of our early experiments around mechanism design, as well as the analyst team at Gartner, especially Micky Keck and Leonard Ammerer whose writing on supply chain decision automation and maturity models has been quite inspirational. The chapter on Responsible AI Governance for Suppliers was developed through a program of the Artificial Intelligence Objectives Institute (AOI) called the AI Supply Chain Observatory, and included the contributions of two AI ethicists at Ethical Resolve, Dr. Ben Roome and Dr. Jake Metcalf. Thanks to AOI's leadership and especially Colleen McKenzie and Julia Jerome for supporting this program's launch and growth. The Responsible AI Governance for Suppliers material was further developed via a partnership series with the Sustainable Procurement Pledge at the suggestion of Thomas Udesen, and supported by SPP's Emerging Technology chapter led by Mat Langley. Elements of this original series also inspired the development of a certificate program at the Sourcing Industry Group University on the topic of Responsible AI for Suppliers, with a focus on the development of supplier due diligence, supplier lifecycle management, and supplier codes of conduct. Thanks to Dawn Tiura, Liz Mantovani, Geoff Talbot, Brittany Cayless, and Loren Neely for patient rounds of feedback in championing and launching this Responsible AI certificate program focused on procurement and sourcing practitioners.

During the writing of this book I was able to join several executive sharing and learning circles among Chief Procurement Officers and Chief Supply Chain Officers, and am especially grateful for the conversations within Florian Selch's Masters of Supply Chain community, as well as the Institute for Supply Management's Data & Analytics Thought Leadership Committee, where I have long been an enthusiastic participant. A special thanks to ISM's leadership team, especially Susan Marty, Jim Fleming, and Angie Miller, who supported our first workshop on this topic back in 2024, a session that was so oversubscribed that we ended up hosting it a second time later in the same day. Thanks to our futurists: Dr. Charlotte De Brabandt, David Warrick, Sasha Pailet Koff, Saeed Amidi, and Chase Koch for daring to imagine the long future of predictive AI in industrial operations. I'd also like to thank CSCMP's Art Mesher, whose 3V Framework (Visibility, Variability, Velocity) provides a foundational core for understanding the role of innovation within supply chain and operations and whose group hosted us for an early presentation of the Predictive Enterprise approach, and Matthias Gutzmann, whose Digital Procurement World (DPW) CPO audience voted Arkestro as "Best Startup" back in 2019 when we were still very early and still called Bid Ops.

Finally, I would like to express profound gratitude for my research and editorial team, including Logan Gramzinski, Avi Shah, Riya Pahuja, Julie Schwietert Collazo, and Josh Raab who assisted mightily with background, editing, and fact-checking, and Tien Tzuo, who encouraged me to write this book in the first place.

About the Authors

Edmund Zagorin is an entrepreneur and inventor specializing in applications of artificial intelligence within supply chains. Edmund holds several patents for artificial intelligence inventions and was recognized by the Institute for Supply Management as "Supply Chain Management Executive of the Year" in 2024 for his work on price simulations. He is the founder of Arkestro, the world's leading predictive procurement platform, and has been a featured speaker on the evolving role of enterprise AI at Reuters Supply Chain USA, Sourcing Industry Group Summit, Chief Procurement Officer Summit, Institute for Supply Management World, and Digital Procurement World. Edmund lives in San Francisco.

Len DeCandia is the former Chief Procurement Officer at Johnson & Johnson, where he was directly responsible for $40B in spend. Prior to Johnson & Johnson, Len was the Chief Procurement Officer at Estée Lauder, and the former Chief Supply Officer, Roche NA. Len is a founding advisor to Rutgers School of Business Supply Chain program, including an undergraduate major, MA, and MBA. Len's widely read 2020 article, “Building a Future-Ready Procurement Organization,” is an inspiration for key themes within this book.

Jeffrey Immelt is the former CEO of General Electric and current venture investor at NEA. Named “America’s Best CEO” three times by Barron’s, Jeff is the best-selling author of *The Hot Seat*, which provides an overview of Jeff’s career journey and leadership at GE.

Index